WITHDRAWN

Animal Ethics in Context

D1056495

WITHDRAWN

Animal
Ethics
in
Context

Clare Palmer

COLUMBIA

UNIVERSITY

PRESS

New York

Columbia University Press

Publishers Since 1893

New York   Chichester, West Sussex

Copyright © 2010 Columbia University Press

All rights reserved

Library of Congress Cataloging-in-Publication Data

Palmer, Clare, 1967–

Animal ethics in context : a relational approach / Clare Palmer

p. cm.

Includes bibliographical references and index.

ISBN 978-0-231-12904-6 (cloth : alk. paper) — ISBN 978-0-231-12905-3 (pbk. : alk. paper) —

978-0-231-50302-0 (e-book)

1. Animal welfare—Moral and ethical aspects. 2. Animal rights. I. Title.

HV4708. P34 2010

179'.3—dc22

Columbia University Press books are printed on permanent and durable acid-free paper.

This book is printed on paper with recycled content.

Printed in the United States of America

c 10 9 8 7 6 5 4 3 2 1

p 10 9 8 7 6 5 4 3 2 1

References to Internet Web sites (URLs) were accurate at the time of writing.
Neither the author nor Columbia University Press is responsible for URLs that may
have expired or changed since the manuscript was prepared.

Contents

ACKNOWLEDGMENTS

Papers that later contributed to this book were given at the University of Missouri, Kansas City (2005); California State University, Long Beach (2006); the University of Minnesota, Morris (2008); the University of Washington, Seattle (2008); the Animal Humanities Conference, Austin, Texas (2006); the Royal Geographical Society annual conference, London (2007), and the Twelfth Annual Inland Northwest Philosophy Conference, Moscow, Idaho (2009). On all these occasions I was asked sharp and useful questions that helped to shape this project; I am grateful to all those concerned.

A number of individuals have been helpful in talking through ideas in this book or in reading earlier versions of papers and chapters. In particular, I would like to thank Emily Brady, J. Baird Callicott, Peter Sandoe, and José Luis Bermúdez.

During the course of writing this book, discussions with several groups of people assisted me in thinking through the problems discussed here. The UK Animal Studies Group was always a source of up-to-date information, critical comment, and astute reflection on animal issues. The meetings and discussions on animal experimentation organized by the Physicians Committee on Responsible Medicine during 2008 and 2009 made me think much more carefully about issues concerning created vulnerability. I am very appreciative of the assistance given to me by members of both groups.

Columbia University Press was very supportive and patient during the extended process of writing this book. Wendy Lochner, my editor at Columbia University Press, in particular was unfailingly helpful and responsive. I would like to thank the two anonymous readers for Columbia University Press, whose thoughtful and critical comments helped to improve the manuscript considerably. I am particularly grateful, in addition, to a third reader for Columbia University Press, Alice Crary, whose comments were extremely important in revising the manuscript into its current form. Finally, I would like to thank my copy editor, Robert Fellman, for his care and patience with my endless corrections.

Animal Ethics in Context

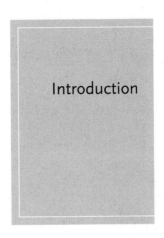

Introduction

Every year, more than a million wildebeest migrate from the Serengeti Plain in Tanzania to Kenya in search of better grazing. To do so, they need to cross Kenya's Mara River. The crossing is always dangerous, as the river has steep embankments, strong currents, and many predators, especially crocodiles. Wildebeest are frequently drowned, injured, or killed by predators while crossing. In 2007, migrating wildebeest tried to cross the river at a particularly treacherous location. Once in the water, the river embankments proved too steep. Some wildebeest were unable to climb out, and many were swept away. At least ten thousand wildebeest died; as many as two thousand deaths occurred in a single afternoon. Camera crews and tourists on safari watched and photographed the mass drowning, and the story made headlines worldwide.[1]

In May 2009, five members of a British family in Amersham, Buckinghamshire, were convicted of—among other charges—failing to meet the welfare needs of 114 horses. Officers of the Royal Society for the Prevention of Cruelty to Animals had found the horses on the family's farm suffering from dehydration, starvation, and various infections; all were infested with worms. A further thirty-two horses and ponies were found dead. Although the horses had previously been destined for slaughter, the RSPCA spent nearly a million pounds nursing them back to health, launching an "Amersham Horses Appeal" in an attempt to cover the costs and find homes for the horses in places where they would be cared for. This has been described as Britain's "worst ever" case of animal neglect.[2]

As these news stories were propagated online, viewers and readers commented on and blogged their responses. Many were awed by the size of the wildebeest migration and by the scale of the mass drowning, though they were unsurprised that the lives of wildebeest are hazardous and, frequently, short. And, while there was little shock expressed about the existence of farms that served as holding places for horses destined for slaughter, widespread horror and disgust were expressed about the neglect and suffering of the Amersham horses.

Yet, on reflection, these stories and such responses to them, when considered together, raise puzzling questions. They are both stories about animals that, most people agree, can feel pain and undergo suffering. In both stories, many animals do undergo just such pain and suffering. But the pain and suffering are regarded quite differently in these two stories; they are told in very different ways and invite—and generate—different responses from their audiences. There was no suggestion in any of the extensive media coverage of the wildebeest mass drowning that the tourists, photographers, or members of conservation organizations who watched the wildebeest suffer and die should have attempted to rescue any of them or tried to drive the herds toward safer crossing places. There were no indignant accusations that those who were present were guilty of animal neglect, a lack of care, or cruelly allowing avoidable suffering. But the Amersham horse case, in contrast—although involving far fewer individual animals—provoked widespread moral condemnation. It was *wrong* not to have provided food, water, shelter, and medical attention to these horses. Their suffering should have been prevented, the animals had been wrongfully neglected, and not to provide for these animals according to the British Horse Society constituted "inexcusable cruelty."[3]

Of course, the legal situation in these two cases is different. The owners of the Amersham horses, under the UK Animal Welfare Act of 2006, had a legal responsibility to care for them. In contrast, no legal responsibility exists to do anything for the wildebeest. But this *legal* difference is not what is at the heart of the puzzle. What is curious and interesting is an apparently widely (though not universally) held intuition that we have different *moral* responsibilities toward domesticated horses and wild wildebeest. Following this intuition, while there is a moral obligation to feed, protect, and provide medical care for domesticated horses, it is morally permissible—and perhaps even morally required—to leave the wildebeest to their fate.

The intuition that while we should care for and assist domesticated animals (such as the Amersham horses) we should just leave wild animals alone, I will call the *laissez-faire intuition*. (By "wild animals," I mean wild animals *living in the wild* and not, for instance, zoo animals; these distinctions will shortly become clearer.) Although I believe the laissez-faire intuition to be widely held, it has not been systematically explored by those interested in the ethics of our treatment of animals. There is a good reason for this. The laissez-faire intuition seems to conflict with another highly plausible and widely held view about how we should treat animals: that where animals have similar capacities, they should be similarly treated. This message has been fundamental to various popular campaigns for animal liberation. The UK Vegetarian Society, for example, ran a campaign in 2009 called "Butcher's Cat," leading with the slogan: "Why do we make pets out of some animals and mincemeat out of others?"[4] The campaign rested on the premise that since there are no morally relevant differences (in terms of, say, intelligence or the capacity to feel pain) between cats and dogs, on the one hand, and pigs and cows on the other, this similarity should be reflected in our moral attitudes and behavior. If we would not butcher Kitty the cat for Sunday lunch, we should not butcher Daisy the cow either; their similar capacities should lead to similar treatment. On this view, the laissez-faire intuition appears mistaken. If something is owed to one animal, it is owed to all animals that are relevantly similar. So, if we should assist one animal on the basis of particular capacities that it possesses, then we should also assist others that are relevantly like it, whether they are wild or not.

I was led to write this book because I felt the pull of both these positions while at the same time seeing that they would be hard to reconcile. Simple reconciliations—such as that human intervention is always ineffective in assisting wild animals or that the obligation to assist is always outweighed by other, more pressing, moral concerns—seemed unsatisfactory. These resolutions did not seem to touch what I take to be the heart of the laissez-faire intuition: that we *just do not have* duties to assist wild animals such as the drowning wildebeest. Of course, although intuitions have played an important role in ethics, they may be a poor guide as to what it is right to do, especially when they conflict with other principles for which we can adduce good reasons. And the principle of same treatment for those that are relevantly alike does seem to be supported by good reasons. But rather than abandon the laissez-faire intuition, I wanted to see whether it was possible to construct arguments that would support it or at least render it plausible. This turned out to be a messy task, extending beyond just a laissez-faire approach to wild-animal assistance and forming a complex of ideas about the ways in which human relations to animals may be relevant to what is morally owed to them. In part, this complexity arises because, as I will suggest later in this introduction, it is impossible to make a neat dichotomy between wild and domesticated animals and because humans affect animal lives in a variety of importantly different ways. And even the laissez-faire intuition itself, on closer inspection, turns out to have different possible forms. For instance, it might be taken to mean that we are not morally *required* to assist wild animals but that it is morally acceptable or even desirable to do so. On this view, though no one did wrong in leaving the wildebeest alone, it would have been acceptable and perhaps a very good thing to have tried to divert them or to have attempted to rescue some of them from drowning. But alternatively, the laissez-faire intuition could be taken to mean that we should not assist wild animals and that had anyone tried to help the wildebeest, the person would actually have been acting *wrongly*. This is rather a different claim.

Untangling all these issues would be, to say the least, an ambitious undertaking. In an attempt to make the focus more modest and to concentrate on questions that have been less widely explored, my central concern in this book is on the ethics of *assisting* animals, rather than on the ethics of harming (or not harming) them. However, harm and assistance cannot and should not be completely separated. Although I have taken the case of the Amersham horses as an instance of culpable failure to assist and to care for animals' well-being when assistance is morally required, from some perspectives, failing to assist when one could have done so *just is* to harm. Additionally, in the human case, we often accept that earlier harms can generate subsequent special obligations to assist or "make good"—as when reparations are agreed to; I will argue that such backward-looking concerns may also be relevant in the case of animals. And reflections about human-animal relations inevitably raise questions about what we might call "relational" harms—for instance, whether there is something morally problematic about deliberately creating beings to be vulnerable to a harm one intends to inflict later, a question that is rarely explicitly considered in the ethical literature on harming animals.

4

But rather than centering my attention on paradigm controversies about harm—such as hunting or meat eating—I will instead explore less well-trodden territory: coyotes displaced by housing developments, elk with fatal diseases, polar bears affected by climate change, dumped pedigree kittens, and garden birds. By focusing on these cases, I do not intend to sideline the extremely serious ethical issues raised by the slaughter of billions of animals for food each year. But there are many existing—and excellent—ethical discussions of these kinds of animal harms. As discussion about animal ethics matures, there is also room for ethical consideration of other kinds of human-animal relations. Indeed, the contextual, relational approach to animal assistance I will be developing is not intended, in itself, to be a comprehensive account of animal ethics. My more modest aim is to explore and develop some aspects of animal ethics that have been passed over or not well thought through in existing accounts. This approach is at least compatible with some existing prominent accounts of animal ethics, in particular with some forms of rights theory.

THE STRUCTURE OF THIS BOOK

Given the controversial nature of debates about what animals are like and the bearing that this has on why animals matter, I begin by asking why we should take animals into account ethically at all. I suggest that there are good grounds, based on the nature of animal minds as far as we can currently understand them, for accepting that mammals and birds, at least, can feel pain; that other aversive feelings (such as fear and frustration) can also plausibly be attributed to them; and that these capacities can form the basis for an experiential account of animal well-being. I argue that because animals have experiential well-being, they can be harmed and assisted in ways that matter morally. This account of animal capacities and why they matter provide the basic starting point for my arguments—as, indeed, for almost all accounts of animal ethics.

The emphasis in chapter 1 is on animals' capacities leads naturally to thinking about the role animals' capacities have played and should play in animal ethics. In chapter 2, I consider three leading approaches to animal ethics that rest almost exclusively on animals' capacities: utilitarian, rights, and capabilities approaches. These three distinct approaches—which I will call *capacity oriented*—in principle subscribe to something like the view that if something is owed to one animal, it is owed to all animals that are relevantly similar. Though each approach is rich and interesting, they do not, I will argue, deal well with questions about assistance; in their existing forms, they either imply (or actively argue for) substantial intervention in the wild or have little or nothing to say about assistance at all. They certainly do not, in their current forms, provide any secure underpinning for the laissez-faire intuition.

So while animals' capacities are indisputably important for animal ethics, what emerges here is that—in thinking about assistance at least—another approach is also needed. This other approach, I suggest, must focus on the different relations humans have with animals, not just on what capacities animals possess. To develop this approach, in chapter 3 I look more closely both at what a capacity is (and the ways in which even capacities can be affected by relations) and at what a relation might be taken to be. The idea that both relations and capacities should play a role in animal ethics is not, of course, an original one. So I also use this chapter as a way of teasing out—and sometimes plundering—useful ideas that already exist about morally significant human-animal relations. Drawing on this existing work, I suggest that relational states such as dependence and vulnerability and certain kinds of causal relations (when human actions have been important in shaping both animals' natures and situations) are of moral significance.

These ideas are developed much further in the rest of the book. In chapter 4, I outline a range of different human-animal relations, complicating ideas of "wild" and "domesticated" and analyzing different possible accounts of the laissez-faire intuition. I suggest that the most plausible arguments can be made to support what I will call the "No-contact" LFI where (a) we have *prima facie* duties not to harm any animals (though these duties can be outweighed in certain circumstances); (b) there are normally no requirements to assist wild-living wild animals, though we are usually *permitted* to do so; and (c) we are often *required* to assist domesticated animals and (on occasions) other animals that fall into what I will call the human/ animal "contact zone," where human actions have affected animals' lives negatively. The adoption of this view raises some tricky philosophical questions—because in not requiring us to assist when we could, it suggests that we do not always have a moral responsibility to try to bring about the best state of affairs in the world. Some ethical theories—such as utilitarianism—that emphasize bringing about best consequences cannot easily accommodate this aspect of a relational approach (and this in part explains why this relational approach may be more compatible with rights theory than with utilitarianism).

Chapter 5 develops a two-pronged argument to support the kind of relational approach to animal ethics that is manifested in the "No-contact" LFI. One part of the argument picks up on the suggestion that humans just do not have the kind of relationship with wild-living wild animals that generates duties of assistance. The second part of the argument maintains that we do, in contrast, have just this kind of assistance-generating relationship with (most) domesticated animals and also, at least on occasion, with animals (such as zoo animals or feral animals) in the "contact zone." I suggest that when humans create sentient animals that are vulnerable and dependent or put animals into situations where they become vulnerable or dependent, special obligations to care for or to assist these animals are generated. These kinds of special obligations just do not get a foothold in the case of wild animals living lives without human contact, and (I will argue) they do not generally apply to human contramensals (animals that live alongside humans to the detriment of humans, such as rats). This argument is developed further in chapter 6. Taking the idea of reparations to humans as a very rough model, and using the case of coyotes displaced by a housing development as an example, I develop the argument that harming sentient animals, for instance by displacing them from their habitats, can generate special obligations to assist. But these kinds of claims raise a variety of questions, particularly concerning *who* has *what* moral obligations toward *whom*. In particular, in this chapter, I explore what connection to a past harm or created vulnerability someone must have in order for such special obligations to be created.

Five more key problems and questions about this relational approach to animal assistance are investigated in chapter 7: worries about a nature/culture dualism, concerns about the possible implications of this view for assisting distant *people*, questions about whether either domestication or painless killing should be thought of as in themselves harmful and whether there are some relations it is just wrong to create, and whether the position for which I am arguing requires an excessive amount of contextual knowledge. Some of these problems, I should note, would apply to any relational account that makes contextual distinctions between cases where assistance is and is not required; others are contingent on specific aspects of the account I have given—in particular, on my experiential account of animal well-being.

Since the arguments in chapters 5, 6, and 7 are somewhat theoretical, I use the final chapter, chapter 8, to return to everyday problems about assisting animals in a variety of contexts, from the global scale of climate change to the small-scale, local conflicts of the suburban backyard. The *Polar Bears* section asks whether we should assist sentient animals in the context of climate change, *Wild-elk Disease* concerns policy making about disease control among wild-living wild animals, *Squirrel* and *Squirrel 2* pose questions about individual encounters with injured wild animals, and *Blue Tit* concerns assistance in situations where garden birds and predatory pets are in the mix.

My aim throughout is to think through questions about assistance in animal cases and to take some first steps toward giving reasoned answers to these questions. In particular, by the conclusion, I hope to have provided some explanation, at least, as to why there is (at present, anyway) no moral obligation to prevent the migrating wild wildebeest from drowning in the Mara River, even if that would bring about a better state of affairs in the world, but that those who allowed the Amersham horses to suffer and starve were indeed behaving in a way that was morally reprehensible.

A NOTE ON KEY TERMS

Although most key terms will be explained when they first appear, there are some additional comments I should make. The first concerns the term "animal." I have been using "animal" in this introduction to mean "nonhuman animal"—and this is often thought to be problematic. It is sometimes argued that "animal" used in this way rests on an implicit denial that humans are themselves animals and that it functions to elide differences between individuals and species of nonhuman animals by grouping them all into one class. For instance, MacIntyre (1999, 45) maintains that this use of "animal" implies "that the differences between nonhuman species are of no importance, or almost no importance in any relevant respect."[5] While I recognize these difficulties, "animal"—used in a human-exclusive sense—still seems the only practical one to adopt. It is cumbersome to insert "nonhuman" before every use of the term. I hope the implication—that the term fails to allow differentiation between different species, let alone different individuals—is explicitly countered by some of the arguments in this book. But ultimately—as Henry Salt maintained as long ago as 1895—"my only excuse for using it [the term animal] . . . is that there is absolutely no other brief term available."

The other terms I want to say something about here are "wild" and "domesticated." I will give a fuller account of how I understand these terms, and the relationship between them, in chapter 4. But I want to note here that both "wild" and "domesticated" are problematic when applied to animals and that a straightforward opposition between the terms is too simplistic. "Wild" when applied to an animal can mean rather different things: we might mean that the animal's habitat is relatively untouched by human activity, that it is not a tame animal, or that the animal has not been domesticated. And domestication, too, has different senses: it can (for example) be taken to mean animals whose breeding is controlled by humans or more loosely used for animals that are accustomed to living around people. And on any of these interpretations, there are animals that are neither clearly wild nor domesticated or that are wild or domesticated on one interpretation but not on another. For the purposes of the early chapters of this book, though, a rough distinction between wild and domesticated animals will do. I will take a wild animal to be one that is both outside human control in terms of breeding and that is living in a fairly wild place—like the wildebeest.[6] I will take a domesticated animal, in contrast, to be one over which humans do have control in terms of breeding, like the Amersham horses. There are, of course, plenty of animals in situations that raise serious questions over this distinction (feral dogs, barn cats, or members of endangered species enrolled in zoo breeding programs), but exploration of these more finely grained distinctions will be pursued in chapter 4.

1

Animals' Capacities and Moral Status

This book depends, most basically, on the claim that we have some moral responsibilities toward animals. Although I will go on to argue that what is owed to different animals flows, in part, from their context and relations to us, that anything is owed to them at all depends on this basic claim. Since this claim is so fundamental, it needs some support. This chapter provides grounding for the view that we have moral responsibilities toward at least some animals. Drawing on recent research, I will argue that animals have the ability to feel pain and to undergo other positive and aversive experiences; this means that they have an experiential well-being. I will maintain that—in contrast to some theoretical positions—having an experiential well-being is sufficient for moral status. Finally, I will outline what—given this account of experiential well-being—I take "harming" and "assisting" to mean.

THE IDEA OF MORAL STATUS

The idea that there might be moral responsibilities toward animals—that, for instance, there are some constraints on what it is permissible to do to them for their own sakes—is often captured by saying that they have "moral status" or "moral considerability." Mary Anne Warren (1997, 3) defines moral status as follows:

> To have moral status is to be an entity towards which moral agents have, or can have, moral obligations. If an entity has moral status, then we may not treat it just in any way we please; we are morally obliged to give weight in our deliberations to its needs, interests or wellbeing. Furthermore, we are obliged to do this not merely because protecting it may benefit ourselves or other persons, but because its needs have moral importance in their own right.[1]

If it were impossible to argue that animals are beings to whom moral status or con-siderability can be attributed in this sense, then there would be little to discuss in animal ethics. Of course, the treatment of animals might affect *people*. And animals might also be seen as important contributors to (or detractors from) ecosystems or ecosystemic processes significant to human well-being. But in these cases, ani-mals would be of only indirect moral concern; even though the *object* of the con-cern would be the animal, the *ground* of the concern would be human beings (see Narveson 1987, 35).[2] Animals would be considered only inasmuch as their treatment affected other entities that did have direct moral status.

However, the main thrust of work in animal ethics has been to argue that animals themselves have moral status or considerability. To be clearer about what is meant by this, it is useful to use two key distinctions, both made by Goodpaster (1978). First, to say that a being has moral considerability, or status, need not mean that it has *rights*. Although "rights" is sometimes used just to mean moral considerability (what DeGrazia [2002, 15] calls the "moral status" sense of rights), the narrower, philosophical sense I will be using takes rights possession to refer to a particular, usually high-level, form of ethical and/or political status. To argue, then, that animals are morally considerable is not the same as to argue that they have rights. Even if one accepts rights language, it is not necessary to think that everything with moral status must have rights.[3] Second, Goodpaster distinguishes between moral *considerability* and moral *significance*. Moral considerability concerns whether a being counts at all in moral decision making. If it does—to return to Warren's definition—we have, or may have, moral obligations toward it. But that an entity counts for something does not tell us how much it counts for, that is to say, its comparative weight along-side other considerations or entities. Goodpaster calls this comparative weighting "moral significance." So, whereas *moral considerability* concerns whether an entity should be taken into account at all, *moral significance* concerns how much an en-tity should be taken into account. In this chapter, I will primarily be concerned with moral considerability.

Many accounts of animal ethics proceed something like this. A single (or several) "keystone" capacities, capabilities, or attributes that bestow moral considerability are identified.[4] It is then argued that (some or all) animals possess the keystone ca-pacity (or capacities), attribute (or attributes), or capability (or capabilities) and are therefore morally considerable. Certain duties (their exact nature varies in differ-ent accounts) are thus owed to all animals that possess the relevant capacities. In some accounts, while moral considerability creates certain baseline duties, further duties may be generated if a being has more than minimal moral significance. That is, there may be some additional capacities, attributes, or capabilities that lead to addi-tional, or more weighty, moral responsibilities. Central here is a universalizing move of the kind I identified in the introduction: if something is owed to one being on the grounds of its capacities, then it is owed to all beings that possess similar capacities.

Although this book ultimately qualifies this move (with respect to assisting animals, at least), for the purposes of this chapter, I will adopt a similar approach. First I will identify particular capacities that at least some animals may be thought to have, and then I will consider the moral relevance (or otherwise) of these capacities. I have adopted a fairly modest account of animal capacities, in two ways. While some animals (such as chimpanzees and cetaceans) may have very highly developed mental abilities, I will not draw on such sophisticated capacities to underpin this account. And while it is plausible that fish and reptiles (for example) are able to feel pain, I will not explicitly discuss them here, since their possession of relevant capacities is significantly more uncertain than in mammals and birds.[5]

ANIMAL CAPACITIES

What capacities might underpin moral status? Many possibilities have been canvassed: being alive, being sentient, being self-conscious (interpreted in various different ways) being rational (again, variously interpreted), being part of a contract in which moral considerability is stipulated, and so on. My (unoriginal) proposal here is that some animals can feel pain and have other kinds of aversive and positive mental states, that these animals have a well-being, and that having a well-being is sufficient for moral considerability.[6]

Animal Pain

Animal pain has been central both to moral and legal debate about human treatment of animals. What's meant by "pain," however, is not straightforward. Very simplistically: it is possible to distinguish between pain understood as a sensation, and affective-cognitive-behavioral states, sometimes called *attitudinal* states, of pain. One might, therefore, have pain sensations without the negative attitudinal state of "hurting" (as, apparently, is reported by some lobotomized patients), or, alternatively, be in the negative attitudinal state of pain without having pain sensations (Nelkin 1986, 129). So, a question about whether animals feel pain might be a question about whether animals have pain sensations, whether they can be in affective and cognitive states of pain, or both.

Arguments about animal pain have primarily drawn on material from two sources: our ordinary practices of relating to, observing, and responding to animals; and scientific research on animals, along with philosophical reflection on that research.

First, our everyday interactions with animals are fundamental in shaping our general intuitions about what animals are like, including their capacity to feel pain.

Jamieson (2002, 54–70) argues that drawing on our "ordinary practices" to ascribe particular states to animals, including the ascription of being in pain, is quite defensible, and he proceeds to defend it (see also Searle 1998, 49). Some philosophers go further than this, maintaining that there are circumstances where to question animal pain is to ask one question too many. Suppose that your car has just hit a dog and crushed one of its back legs. The dog is lying in the road, writhing and yelping, its eyes dilated and its breath labored and quick. To stop and question whether the dog is feeling pain might suggest that one lacks a proper grasp of what pain *is*.[7] As Gaita (2002, 44) suggests, one just cannot doubt it; in such circumstances one is *absolutely certain* that the dog is in pain.

However, it is not unreasonable to argue that this "everyday-response" view is at least reflectively inadequate, even if it is appropriate as an immediate response to a bleeding, writhing dog in the road. For—a skeptic might respond—our everyday responses can, after all, be mistaken. A being could yelp and writhe but not feel pain, or be still and silent while experiencing it. Many organisms, including some plants and amoeba, move away from noxious stimuli, but on other grounds it seems extremely unlikely that they feel pain. Research on human fetuses indicates withdrawal reflexes before the development of the thalamocortical circuits associated with pain perception.[8] Equally, there might be animals (or perhaps alien beings) that can feel pain but that have quite different kinds of behavioral manifestation of pain from humans.[9] It seems wise, such a skeptic might argue, to be wary of our immediate reactions to painlike animal behavior and at least also to consider other kinds of evidence.

Scientific investigation of pain has tended to focus on behavior patterns that might reflect pain (such as protecting injured parts, the reduction of activity when sick, and self-administering of opiates),[10] studies of brain and neurological "wiring," and physiological indicators (such as levels of particular hormones and the effects of analgesics). Behaviorally, for instance, the phenomenon of "pain guarding"—where a damaged area is protected from touch, weight bearing, and so on—may provide evidence of pain. It is possible that pain guarding is a reflex, but conscious pain is certainly the most plausible explanation; some organisms—insects, for instance— that lack sophisticated neurological systems continue to use damaged parts of their bodies and do not pain guard (Rowan, Loew, and Weer 1994, 74). The demonstration of *adaptive responses* with respect to renewed encounters with a negative stimulus—avoiding contact with it, for instance—is sometimes also argued to be further evidence that an animal feels pain (DeGrazia 1996, 108). Learning behavior is not conclusive, however; rats that have had their spinal cords severed cervically, and so would not be able to feel pain in their hind legs, not only have hind-leg responses to noxious stimuli but also demonstrate the ability for associative learning with respect to the noxious stimuli (Allen 2004). However, while it is problematic to *assume* from an animal's behavior that it feels pain, behavioral evidence points strongly in the direction that it is *very likely* that mammals and birds feel pain consciously.

Physiological arguments focus on the similarities shared by the brains and nervous systems of animals, in particular mammals and humans. Many animals have nociceptors (the free nerve endings of neurons), the stimulation of which is central to the process that leads to pain in humans. In all mammals, nociceptors are connected to a central nervous system, endogenous opioids (which have analgesic effects) are present, and what seem to be pain responses can be modified by analgesics.[11] (For birds, all these criteria are also met, with the exception of the connection of nociceptors to the nervous system.)[12] Colpaert et al. (2001, 33), for instance, discovered that rats with arthritis self-administered analgesic fentanyl solution, a solution that was avoided by healthy rats, and concluded that this behavior was a response to pain. This kind of neurological evidence has led many scientists and philosophers to accept that animals do feel pain.

However, some skepticism remains. Nelkin (1986), for instance, emphasizes the role that the neocortex plays in human pain sensations. Nonhuman mammals—with the exception of some primates—have little neocortex. Thus, he argues, their pain sensations are likely to be rather different from those in humans, if indeed there are such sensations at all. Others maintain that the existence of similarity between humans and other mammals in aspects of the "wiring of pain" does not provide firm evidence that such mammals feel pain in any conscious sense.[13] That is to say, although nociception may be *necessary* for an organism to feel pain, it is not clear that it is *sufficient*.[14] We know that nociception continues in humans who have severed spines, and they can self-report on their own lack of pain (MacPhail 1998). More broadly, it seems to be the case that, even among humans, there can be a disassociation between "feeling a pain" and "minding a pain." Patients taking morphine, for instance, may say that they still feel pain but that they no longer mind it. Research suggests that different pathways are involved in processing feelings of pain and negative responses to pain in humans (Price 2000). Experimental results indicate that the feeling of "minding pain" in humans may be related to excitement in the anterior cingulated cortex (ACC); when the ACC is damaged or removed in humans, similar pain responses to those in patients who have taken morphine is observed. This argument, however, does not count against *mammals* feeling pain, at least. Mammals, although not birds or reptiles, all have an ACC, and research suggests that it operates similarly to a human ACC (Johansen and Fields 2004). Experimental evidence from rats after electrolytic lesion of the ACC, for instance, indicated similar responses to those of humans with damaged ACCs: electric shocks seemed to produce reflex paw withdrawals but not aversive behavior (LaGraize et al. 2004; Shriver 2006).

Neither the presence of nociceptors, their attachment to a nervous system, the success of analgesics in altering behavior, nor experimental work on the ACC provide *conclusive* evidence that mammals and birds feel pain. Nociceptors form part of an extremely complex neurological system in humans, from which pain experiences emerge. No other species has exactly that system, so it is impossible to be certain exactly what members of other species feel and whether pain is among the sensations available to them. However, even the most skeptical of philosophers maintain that pain, understood in *some* sense, is aversive to animals. Nelkin (1986) argues that animals have attitudinal pain states that function in their lives just as attitudinal pain states function in human lives (and that these states are of moral importance); Carruthers (2004) argues for the "awfulness" of animal pain and maintains that it is an appropriate state for which to feel sympathy and moral concern.

Additional arguments that animals feel pain consciously call on evolutionary theory. Conscious pain may be evolutionarily adaptive, providing organisms that have a capacity for it with an advantage. Dawkins (1998), for instance, maintains: "Pain evolved because, by being unpleasant, it keeps us away from the larger evolutionary disaster of death. Pain is part of a mechanism for helping us to avoid immediate sources of injury, and also to refrain from repeating actions that have resulted in damage."[5] So, if pain is useful, humans feel pain, other animals have similar behavior and physiology to humans, and all emerged within the same evolutionary process from (at some point) common ancestors, is not it likely that pain evolved in other animals?

Yet, as experiments on rats with cervically severed spines indicate, both painlike behavior and learning responses to noxious stimuli may occur when no consciously felt pain can be present. This might suggest that benefits can accrue from unconscious responses to pain, without the need for the conscious sensation of pain, in many organisms at least. And even if humans alone—or perhaps humans, some primates, and cetaceans alone—have evolved felt pain, this need not (it might be argued) mean a huge evolutionary gulf between humans and other species, where humans alone operate in a world of conscious experience. Carruthers (2004) and, independently, Bermond (1997) argue that much more human behavior and learning than is generally thought operates at an unconscious level—that is, humans are closer to other mammals and operate far more often on the basis of unconscious cues than we tend to think. This suggests, they maintain, that the evolutionary gap between humans and other mammals, even if humans consciously feel pain and other mammals do not, is less than might at first appear.

Nonetheless, the evolutionary argument in favor of mammalian pain, at least, is powerful. As Jamieson (2002, 67) argues (of mental states, rather than pain specifically): "Given these facts about biological continuity and similarity, it would be quite surprising if human psychology in all its depth and richness were completely unique. Indeed, it would be the biological equivalent of the immaculate conception." Of course, that something would be surprising does not mean that it is not the case. However, evolutionary arguments do provide some further supporting evidence that mammals and birds are likely to be able to feel pain consciously.

The balance of evidence, then, strongly indicates that pain—however one inter-prets it—*matters* to mammals and birds. This is the view taken by the overwhelm-ing majority of biologists and philosophers.[16] Further, most agree that animals expe-rience pain sensations aversively, if unreflectively; that is, when an animal is in pain, it is in an unpleasant experiential state that it will, if it can, make strenuous attempts to escape (see Dawkins 1995, 144).[17] This book works on the premise that mammals and birds experience pain, although what causes pain, and pain sensitivity, is spe-cies specific: for instance, underwater sonar may not affect humans but may cause pain to, and even kill, cetaceans (see Simmonds et al. 2003). As Allen (2004, 19) com-ments, "at this stage of our understanding of behavior and neuropsychology, to cir-cumscribe phenomenal consciousness ... would be far more scandalous than taking seriously the prima facie evidence that animals feel pain consciously."

A *very* modest account of animal capacities would probably stop here. However, there is also substantial evidence for a view that accepts that animals can undergo fear and frustration and some intentional states such as simple desires.[18] Although these may not be directly relevant to establishing moral status, they do raise issues relevant to animal well-being and may add to moral significance. For instance, if it makes sense to say that animals in some sense have desires, then the possibility of desire frustration, a potentially aversive state, follows. In order to judge what kinds of human actions might harm or assist animals, we need to know something about what might benefit or set back their well-being.

Aversive States

To understand aversive states such as desire frustration or fear in animals, it's useful to have some basic information about different animal behaviors. Reflexive behaviors, or "releasers," are simple stimulus-response behaviors. The sight of the red spot on the bill of a parent herring gull, for instance, causes herring-gull chicks to peck at it. But they will peck at any red spot on any bill-like object. They do not respond to the parent or a bird as such; red spots invariably and inflexibly lead to chick pecking behavior. Similarly, the parent gull regurgitates food when the red spot is pecked at; the pecking is a stimulus, the regurgitation of food the response. A second group of behaviors are usually called fixed-action-pattern responses. These are an "innate and stereotypical" (Gould 1982) unfolding of behaviors that, when stimulated, continue to completion without alteration or the need for further input. A nesting goose rolls an egg that has moved away from the nest back into the nest in a fixed-action pattern. If the object is not an egg, or if the egg is removed part of the way through the action, the goose continues with the action until the behavior pattern is complete. More complex strings of behavior may be characterized as *preprogrammed sequences*

(Ristau 1995, 81); these are, again, behaviors that are rigid, invariant, inflexible, and unresponsive to changing circumstances. Such reflexive, fixed, or programmed behaviors are not goal directed. However, it is widely (though not uncontroversially) thought that other kinds of animal actions—especially some of the behaviors of birds and mammals—are best explained by imputing goal directedness and may be difficult to account for satisfactorily without doing so. That is, as Dreckmann (1999, 98) suggests, even though there may be a complete mechanistic explanation for a behavior undertaken by an animal, "teleological explanations possess explanatory power which mechanistic explanations do not possess."

Ristau (1995), for instance, investigated the behavior of piping plovers, who feign injuries in order to keep potential predators away from their nests. After studying this aspect of plover behavior, she entertained a variety of different hypotheses as to what explanation might be appropriate, including reflexive behavior, fixed-action-pattern responses, and preprogrammed sequences of behavior. But the plovers' behavior made these interpretations seem awkward. The birds almost always displayed in such a way as to move intruders away from the nest, and they displayed in front of rather than behind the intruder, seeming to recognize at least the direction of intruder movement, if not the direction of gaze. The birds moved closer to the intruder before beginning their displays, and seemed to monitor the intruder's response by looking back over their shoulders. Further, the birds modified their display in response to the behavior of the intruder. The best explanation of this kind of flexible and responsive behavior, Ristau suggests, seems to be something like: the birds desire to keep intruders away from their nests, and they act in ways that aim to achieve the goal of leading the intruders away. What exactly this means is somewhat opaque. But what is plausible, at least, is that some kind of purposive explanation is appropriate. As Ristau (1995, 85) points out, this need not be interpreted as suggesting that the birds have the "fully flexible, fully cognitive, fully conscious, purposeful behavior we humans sometimes have."

If mammals and birds can have desires or goals, they can be in what are called "intentional states." That is, their minds can be directed to objects or states of affairs; they can be in states of "aboutness" with respect to the world.[19] That it makes sense (not just heuristically) to attribute intentional states, or at least "protointentional states," to animals is widely—although far from universally—thought to be the case, among both philosophers and cognitive ethologists.[20] Hurley (2003, 235), for instance, argued that animals can be seen as occupying "a normative middle ground between a mere stimulus-response system and full, context-free abilities." Drawing on the work of the comparative psychologists Tomasello and Call, Hurley described an intentional agent as a being that "distinguishes ends from means, recognizes that there can be different means to the same end, that the same behavior can be means to different ends, and that the same behavior can be an end or a means." Animals understood in this way can be seen as having practical, context-oriented beliefs, desires, and goals that they act to bring about. This practical, action-oriented intentional agency need not require language or conceptual ability.[21] Of course, this view is not universally accepted; there are both biologists (such as Rosenberg 1999) and philosophers who reject it. Nonetheless, such a view is at least plausible and appears to provide the best explanation for some animal behaviors.

What is important here is how both hard-wired and more flexible behavior might be relevant to welfare. Evidence suggests that preventing animals from carrying out particular kinds of behaviors and satisfying desires is experienced aversively. (DeGrazia 1996, 130, maintains that being disposed to have "unpleasant feelings at a prolonged failure to attain X" is a necessary condition of a desire for X.) Experimental research on captive or confined animals, for instance, suggests—using a variety of indicators—that when animals are frustrated in their desire to carry out particular behaviors important to their species—such as moving around, suckling, swimming, nesting—they become stressed. This stress can be measured in terms of mortality and morbidity, reproduction, changes in body weight, immunological functions, levels of particular hormones believed to indicate stress, and abnormal behavior patterns. Animals undergo measurable physiological changes when they cannot enact these behaviors. In humans, such physiological changes would be associated with mental states of stress and frustration.[22]

The idea that animals are strongly motivated to carry out particular kinds of behavior and may experience aversive states of frustration if unable to do so underpins a considerable body of current research on animal behavior. Mason and Warburton (2003), for instance, investigated what costs (in terms of pushing a door that became increasingly heavy) captive mink were prepared to pay in order to access food, a ball, water for swimming, and other mink. Built into the premise of their study was the view that mink were motivated to access some resources more than others because some resources were particularly important in securing pleasurable experience and in avoiding frustration. The results of their experiments suggested that mink desired water in which to swim and would work very hard to access it. Likewise, Dawkins' work on free-range chickens concluded that future studies could give "an objective measure of what parts of the [bird]house the birds like or dislike and the extent to which environmental 'enrichments' constitute an improvement from the animal's point of view" (Dawkins et al. 2003, 158).[23]

Desire frustration is likely to be only one of the aversive experiences animals can undergo. It is also very likely that they can experience fear. Again, behavioral evidence (such as vocalization and trembling) and physiological evidence (such as sweating, frequent urination, diarrhea, and raised heart rate) are manifest in animals in strange or threatening situations, and as with pain, it is not difficult to see why fear might be evolutionarily adaptive.[24]

17

Given this kind of evidence, I will take the view here that mammals and birds can consciously feel pain and that they can be in aversive states such as desire frustration and fear. This is a relatively conservative view of animals' capacities; much more expansive claims for the capacities of at least some animals and birds can be and have been made, in terms both of their cognitive abilities and their mental states. It is sometimes argued, for instance, that some or all adult mammals have *self*-awareness or *self*-consciousness and/or a sense of themselves as beings that persist over time (a claim made by Regan 1984).[25] Others argue that some or all adult mammals can attribute beliefs and desires to *others* (involving behavior such as deception) and that they possess a "theory of mind" (the ability to "explain and predict the actions, both of oneself and of other intelligent agents" [Carruthers 1996]). Support for these claims, even in primate research, is unclear. Experiments by Povinelli (1996), for instance, raise doubts as to whether even chimpanzees have a theory of mind (although the conclusions to be drawn from these experiments are contested). It may be that some individuals of some mammalian species—or even all individuals of some mammalian species—have some or all of these capacities, or, at least, that they can "minimally mind read"; that is, their behavior can be "systematically dependent on changes in the psychological states of other participants in the interaction" (see Bermúdez 2007, 2009). I am not going to rely on animals' possession of such capacities here. However, if some animals do possess such sophisticated capacities, these capacities are likely to be relevant to thinking about their well-being and perhaps their moral significance. I will consider some issues about complex cognitive capacities—in particular, in the context of painless killing—later.

ANIMAL WELL-BEING AND INTERESTS

The ability to feel pain and to undergo other positive and aversive experiences provides a basis for an account of animal well-being. To use Bernstein's (1998, 13) definition: "to have a welfare or well-being is to have the capacity to be benefited or harmed, to be capable of being made both better and worse off." I will take it that if an animal X has a well-being, things can go better or worse for X.

What is meant here by "going better or worse"? Drawing on what I have outlined above, I will adopt a subjective, experiential account of animal well-being. (This does not, I think, necessarily commit me to an experiential account of *human* well-being.)[26] On this view, persistent or intense pain, or extreme fear, reduce experiential well-being; the frustration of animal desires is *experientially* aversive and therefore harmful to well-being. (Desire frustration is not *independently* harmful to well-being.) When animals undergo prolonged negative experiences such as frustration and fear, we can say that they *suffer*; the avoidance and reduction of experiential suffering is critical to animal well-being.

There are, of course, other possible accounts of well-being. Some argue that well-being concerns the satisfaction of preferences or desires understood in ways that do not collapse into experiences (in an animal as well as in a human context). Others maintain an "objective-list" understanding of well-being: there are some qualities of life—such as a state of good health—that contribute to well-being, whether or not such states are experienced or desired; on these accounts, beings can be harmed without the harm being experienced. Objective accounts of well-being are appealing: for instance, they allow us to make sense of not obviously implausible claims that things can be good or bad for a tree (in terms of, say, flourishing), even though the tree does not experience anything. There are, however, a number of difficulties with the descriptive aspect of objective-list approaches (see Bernstein 1998). But even if these descriptive difficulties could be overcome, there is still a question about how unexperienced goods relate to moral considerability, which is why we are interested in well-being in this context. As O'Neill (1993, 23) argues: "That Y is a good of X does not entail that Y should be realized unless we have some prior reason for believing that X is the sort of thing whose good ought to be promoted." That something is "good for greenfly" in the sense that it encourages greenfly to flourish (non-experientially) does not in itself mean that humans should defend or promote that good. There needs to be some *further* reason for thinking that such goods should be defended or promoted. Subjective experience more obviously provides grounds for moral considerability than objective-list approaches. However, as I will note at various points in the book, the approach to animal ethics I am developing *does not depend* on an experiential account of well-being; one could endorse an alternative account of well-being but still accept something like this relational approach.

The ability to experience pain and other positive and aversive feelings provides not only a basis for an account of well-being but also for an account of *interests*. The term "interests" can be understood in several ways: one might, for instance, distinguish between "having an interest" and "taking an interest." The former is generally taken to concern well-being, while the latter suggests some *active engagement* on the part of the being concerned, not necessarily relating to well-being. After all, it is possible to *take* an interest in something that is irrelevant to well-being (watching a particular television program each week) or even something potentially harmful to well-being (speeding along a particular narrow street). It seems plausible to say this of animals, too: that a dog *takes* an interest in a cat might be irrelevant to, or even detrimental to, the dog's well-being. But this sense of "taking an interest" is different from "having an interest." A being has an interest, on this account, in what contributes to its well-being and in avoiding what detracts from it. I have given an experiential account of animal well-being; interests should also be interpreted experientially. On this account, for an animal P to have an interest in the occurrence of X, X must contribute to P's experiential well-being.[27]

One further point should be made here. It might seem that one implication of an experiential view of well-being would be that *all* pain constitutes either a misfortune or a wrongful harm. But there are many cases where it would be odd to say this—for instance, when an animal is giving birth or being painfully treated to relieve a medical condition. In this sense, well-being, even understood experientially, should be seen as experiential well-being *over time*, not solely in terms of the instant experiential responses of the moment.

ANIMALS AND MORAL CONSIDERABILITY
Why Pain Matters

For some positions in ethical theory—such as classical utilitarianism—painful and pleasurable experience just is what matters morally. And it is not difficult to make sense of this, even though it is notoriously difficult to provide a detailed justification for it. Singer (1975, 154) argues that if a being feels pain, things matter to it in a particular kind of way. This kind of mattering, he suggests, should be the basis of moral considerability. Feinberg (1978, 58) maintains that "the claim that all pain is evil in itself is a plausible candidate for a self-evident moral proposition, if only because no one can sincerely bring himself to doubt it in his own case." Perhaps these kinds of arguments are inadequate: they fail to provide a sound enough reason as to why we should think that the kind of experience that pain is should generate a moral concern either to avoid inflicting it or to relieve it. But it is very difficult to provide any further argument in this case. As Nagel maintains, pain is just awful, in normal circumstances everyone is immediately and unreflectively averse to it, and that this is of moral importance seems to Nagel "self-evident," even though he can find "nothing more certain with which to back it up" (Nagel 1986, 160). And in the end, although this may be unsatisfactory, there seems to be no further justification than this.[28]

Most extant views in moral philosophy accept the capacity to feel pain as sufficient—or even both necessary and sufficient—for moral considerability. Nonetheless, there are some moral theories where pain does not provide grounds for moral considerability: where, for instance, *rationality* understood in ways only possible for (some) humans is required. Most prominent among current positions of this kind are some contractarian moral theories.[29]

Contractarian Moral Views and Animals: A Very Brief Sketch

Contractarian moral theories claim that "moral norms derive their normative force from the idea of contract or mutual agreement" (Cudd 2002, 1). This requirement for consent or agreement is usually taken to mean that the parties are free, rational, and able to understand to what they are consenting. In standard versions of moral contractarianism, those who *make* the contract (moral agents) are those that are *taken into account* by it (moral patients). That is, to paraphrase Nussbaum (2006, 21), those who frame the moral contract are those for whom the principles are framed.[30] One can be a moral patient if and only if one is a moral agent. On such an account, animals are not morally considerable, because they are not rational in the sense that they can understand and agree to a moral contract.

It is worth noting that only some forms of moral contractarianism take this view. Not all moral contractarians understand the *whole* of morality to be governed by moral contract; some maintain that while a substantial part of morality is governed by contract, this is not exhaustive of the moral sphere. Carl Cohen for instance—well known as a robust opponent of the idea of animal rights—argues that while *rights* are contractual, and that all humans but no animals possess them, animals capable of feeling pain are *morally considerable* and that "we should refrain from imposing pain on them as far as we can" (Cohen 1986, 865–70; see also McCloskey 1979). In this case, the sphere of *rights* is human exclusive, but the sphere of moral considerability, more broadly construed, includes animals. Thomas Scanlon (1998, 178) comments of his own contractarian view that "it is not meant to characterize everything that can be called 'moral' but only that part of the moral sphere that is marked out by certain specific ideas of right and wrong, or 'what we owe to others.'" Inflicting pain on animals, or failing to relieve it, can be morally wrong in a broad sense, even though it does not fall within the narrower scope of the moral contract. Equally, *animal-inclusive* versions of moral contractarianism have also been suggested: here animals are either directly included in the moral contract as moral patients, or trustees who represent the interests of animals are proposed.[31] So only some versions of moral contractarianism, then, maintain both that the entire moral sphere is constituted by contractual agreement *and* that animals are entirely excluded from, and unrepresented in, such a moral contract.

The problems with such animal-exclusive moral-contractarian accounts have spawned a substantial literature that I will mention only in passing here. The question that has generated the most debate concerns what this means for those *human beings* who are not currently moral agents (fetuses, infants, those in comas, future generations, and so on). One standard objection runs: if moral agency is required in order to join a moral contract and to have moral status, then some humans and all animals must be excluded from moral status. But no human should be denied moral status. So some other capacity must establish the boundary of moral status. But any criterion that "lets in" all humans will let in some animals also.

Versions of this argument have (unfortunately) become known as the Argument from Marginal Cases (AMC).[32] Of course, if one is not concerned by the exclusion of some humans from direct moral considerability, then the AMC is not problematic.[33] (And certainly, a strong *indirect* account could probably be given in most cases, since infants, for instance, will often have other human beings who are extremely attached to them. Such an indirect argument would, though, apply to some animals too.) However, a number of critics—including recently Nussbaum (2006)—have argued that such moral contractarianism must be fundamentally revised or abandoned, owing to its failure to take into account these so-called marginal groups of humans.

Responses to these objections are possible. Some humans that are not moral agents could be included in a moral contract while all animals are excluded by introducing a *potentiality condition* (in the case of infants) or by arguing that being *of the same kind* as actual contractors is sufficient for a being to count as if though it were itself a contractor (Frey 1977; Cohen 1986). But both these suggestions are problematic. Potentiality arguments are hard to justify, because we do not generally accept that individuals who have the potential to obtain a particular status already have the rights that go with that status: "a potential president of the United States is not on that account Commander-in-Chief [of the U.S. Army and Navy]" (Benn 1973, 102).[34] And potentiality arguments, of course, only work for *some* of those humans who are not moral agents, *viz.* some fetuses and infants.[35] What we might call "of-the-same-kind" arguments also attempt to include all humans. Cohen (1986), for instance, maintains that even though some individual humans are not themselves able to exercise free moral judgment, they nonetheless belong to a *kind* that can. Membership of such a kind is sufficient for possession of moral rights. But, as Nobis (2004) and Norcross (2007) effectively argue, "of-the-same-kind" arguments are at least as problematic as potentiality arguments (and share some similarities with them). Such arguments again involve attributing to individual beings that do not have certain capacities the status of those individuals who do have those capacities. If kind is taken in this case to imply "statistical normalcy," the claim, as Nobis (2004, 48) puts it, runs: "If normal human beings are of some kind K then marginal human beings are of some kind K as well." But one could hardly say, for instance, that since statistically normal human beings are of the kind that talk, "marginal" human beings are of the kind that talk as well, or that they should be considered as talking beings. Arguments that it is *natural* for humans to have such properties seem to fail in the same way.[36] It is (at least) extremely difficult to find any criterion that will successfully include all humans and exclude all animals in a moral contract.

I will not pursue these issues further here; I have merely gestured in the direction of difficulties generated by arguments that all and only humans have moral status. Many philosophers have taken the position that—given, in their view, the undeniable moral significance of pain, or suffering more broadly understood—if a theory cannot give an account of the direct wrongness of inflicting suffering on animals, so much the worse for the theory. I have tried to go just a little further than this, by pointing out other difficulties with such arguments.[37]

THE MEANING OF HARM AND ASSISTANCE

So far in this chapter, I have maintained that mammals and birds can feel pain and that they have the capacity for other aversive and positive experiences. On the basis that they possess these capacities, I have argued that they are morally considerable. This discussion of what animals are like also provides the basis for what constitutes harming or assisting (or benefiting) them. These are important terms here—and their use is much debated—so I want to conclude this chapter with an explanation of how I'll be using them. I understand harm, then, as follows:

A. A harm is an action (or sustained series of actions) carried out by a moral agent or agents. That is, to use Feinberg's (1992b, 4) terms, for an act to harm in this sense, it must wrong; it can be distinguished from a hurt or a misfortune.[38] A tree that blows down in the wind onto a sleeping animal, for instance, hurts it, and that may be a misfortune, but it is not a harm in this sense. Difficult questions are raised here, however, about intention. Must harms be intended? What about negligence? Or cases where interest setbacks (see below) were foreseeable, though unintended? What about, for instance, the negative effects of human-induced climate change on individual animals' well-being—do these constitute harms? I will touch on issues regarding intention, negligence, and foreseeability in connection with particular harms in chapters 6 and 8.

B. A harm sets back the interests of an animal, where interests are understood in an experiential sense. Here, I need to make a number of qualifications. First—as I noted earlier—understanding animals' well-being and interests as purely experiential need not necessarily extend to the human case. Second, the use of the term "interests" is supposed to convey the sense that a harm must be something of experiential significance in intensity, over time, or both. So an animal's fleeting moment of fear while bounding away from a stalking photographer would normally be insufficient to be called a harm. Nor would medical treatment that causes short-term pain but long-term experiential benefit be a harm, because it does not set back experiential interests over time. An extended journey to a slaughterhouse in cramped and hot conditions with insufficient water would be sufficiently substantial to be called a harm.

C. A counterfactual condition: the animal must made be worse off (in terms of its experiential interests and given a foreseeably normal course of subsequent events) on account of the action than it would have been had the agent or agents not acted in the way they did (see Feinberg 1992b, 7).[39]

I take assistance in a similar way: as an action (or series of actions) carried out by a moral agent (or agents) that promotes an animal's (experiential) interests over time and that makes the animal (experientially) better off than it would have been had the agent(s) not acted the way he, she, or they did.

One question that immediately arises: this account of both harm and assistance seems to have implications for a view on painless/fearless killing (which I have not discussed in this chapter). On at least one interpretation of this view, painless killing may not be seen as harmful. After all, it might be argued that painless killing does not set back experiential interests; it just means that there are no further experiences (thus, the counterfactual condition is not met, since an animal is not experientially worse off by dying). Euthanasia understood as assistance might also be rendered problematic on this account.[40] This is obviously a difficulty for experiential accounts of well-being and is a particularly problematic question in animal ethics, although this is not the only possible interpretation of painless killing on an experiential view of harm and well-being. I will discuss this "painless/fearless killing problem" further in chapter 7.

To conclude: this chapter has endorsed a widely accepted, fairly conservative position on animal capacities and the moral status of animals. Some readers will reject this account on empirical grounds (they may have less or more expansive accounts of animal capacities) or on grounds of moral theory (primarily, those who take the view that direct moral obligations can only hold between moral agents). Those who hold either (or both) of these views will not find the remainder of this book persuasive, since they will regard its starting point as fundamentally flawed. As Nozick (1974) pointed out, it is difficult to prove that animals count for anything (a problem that, he suggests, applies to humans as well). The remainder of the book is aimed at those who descriptively accept that some or all mammals and birds feel pain and undergo other aversive and positive experiences and that on this basis, mammals and birds have a well-being and some kind of moral status.

2

Capacity-Oriented Accounts of Animal Ethics

In chapter 1, I outlined a basic account of key capacities mammals and birds may reasonably be thought to possess, how these capacities might both underpin moral status and be relevant to their well-being, and what it might mean to harm and assist animals. However, the central claim in this book is that, important though coming to a view about animal capacities, moral status, and well-being is, we need *more than this* in order to work out our moral responsibilities toward animals in different contexts, in particular with respect to assisting them. What was outlined in chapter 1, I will suggest, is more like a starting point than an endpoint in terms of the factors that should play into developing a richer and fuller account of animal ethics.

One way of providing support for this claim is to consider how existing leading theoretical accounts of animal ethics respond to questions about context and to look at the difficulties that are generated by focusing, virtually exclusively, on animals' capacities. To illustrate this, I will consider a utilitarian account, a rights account, and a (more recently developed) capabilities account here. Rather than giving a general overview of these positions, I will focus on more specific questions, in particular: What gives a being moral status on this account? Is it the being's capacities (such as sentience) alone? Do we have different responsibilities to animals in different contexts or relations to us, such as wild in contrast to domesticated animals? More specifically, is assisting animals morally required, permitted, or impermissible, and in which circumstances?

I will suggest that these three theoretical approaches—while each having considerable merit—are problematic, or at least incomplete, when we start to think about what is owed to animals with different relations to us. These difficulties, I will argue, both in this chapter and in chapter 3, flow from the same underlying cause: a virtually exclusive focus on capacities. It is this "capacity orientation" (as I call it) that can generate otherwise implausible prescriptions in some contexts and that makes it difficult to accommodate some important moral considerations. These considerations can be better accommodated, I will argue in the rest of the book, by thinking about certain morally relevant *relations* alongside morally relevant *capacities*.

UTILITARIANISM, CONTEXT, AND ANIMAL ETHICS

Utilitarianism is best understood as a family of theories with different ideas about what states of affairs are intrinsically valuable and what decision-making procedure best brings about such states of affairs.[1] All utilitarian theories, though, share a *consequentialist* form: we should aim to bring about the best consequences—the best balance of good over bad—and the best consequences are all that we should take into account.[2]

Most utilitarian theories from the work of Jeremy Bentham (1789) onward have included animals within their scope. The goods (or bads) that utilitarian theories argue should be maximized (or minimized) are goods that animals are widely thought to be able to experience or to participate in creating (such as pleasure/pain or preference satisfaction/frustration). It is unnecessary here to give an exhaustive account of *how* different forms of utilitarianism incorporate animals.[3] Instead, I will focus on just one very well-known account—Peter Singer's—since what is of particular interest here is sufficiently constant across different forms of utilitarianism to allow for some generalization. I will consider two factors of Singer's account in particular: what gives a being moral status and the significance of aiming at best consequences in moral decision making. It is these two factors that help explain how utilitarian animal ethics responds to context.

Moral Status

In his early work (such as *Animal Liberation*), Singer's account of moral status is similar to the one I outlined in chapter 1. It is the capacity for suffering that qualifies a being for moral consideration, and that means that the being has *interests*; suffering is a "prerequisite for having interests at all" (Singer 1983, 9).[4] Singer takes suffering to mean not only pain but also aversive states generated by overcrowding and "small, cramped cages" (Singer 1983, 10), feelings of fear and terror (Singer 1983, 18, 106), frustration of natural instincts (Singer 1983, 114), boredom, and inappropriate or absent social arrangements (Singer 1983, 118–119). A being that can suffer has an interest in avoiding suffering; a being that can feel enjoyment has an interest in sustaining or increasing enjoyment. If "a being is not capable of suffering, or of enjoyment, there is nothing to be taken into account" (Singer 1983, 9).

In the second edition of *Practical Ethics*, Singer adds a further dimension to this pleasure/pain based account by distinguishing between "persons"—understood as "rational and self-conscious" (Singer 1993, 87)—and beings that are conscious, sentient, and have interests but that are not self-conscious. Persons, he argues, have conceptions of themselves as beings that persist over time, with a past and a projected future; sentient beings that are not persons have no such sense. Persons have long-term preferences, most fundamentally the preference to go on living and to carry out plans for the future. A person's interests, then, are "on balance and after reflection on all the relevant facts, what the person prefers" (Singer 1993, 94). Frustrating or failing to fulfill these fundamental preferences sets back the interests of the being that has them; fulfilling such preferences promotes their interests.[5] "Person" or "self-conscious being" does not coincide for Singer with "human being"; some nonhuman animals (such as apes and cetaceans) are self-conscious in this sense, while human infants are not persons; they do not have a sense of their own future nor desires to go on living (Singer 1993, 111).

Beings that are sentient and those who have preferences (and of course, those who have both) have moral status on Singer's argument. Critically, Singer argues that the interests of all beings should be taken equally into account when making moral decisions. "The interests of every being affected by an action are to be taken into account, and given the same weight as the like interests of any other being" (Singer 1983, 7). To be sure, some beings have interests that other beings lack, some actions or events will have much larger effects on one being's interests than on another being's interests, and some interests are more basic than others. But moral decision making should be based on interests, which in turn are based on capacities.

Singer's claims here capture something common across utilitarian theories that deal directly with the moral status of animals. Certainly, utilitarians do draw on different empirical evidence about animals' capacities. Some (such as R.G. Frey) maintain that animal capacities are in general less sophisticated than Singer does, and others make more detailed discriminations among proposed capacities for purposes of ranking.[6] But in all utilitarian accounts, psychological capacities, and in particular psychological complexities, are crucial. Differentiation of moral significance between beings hinges on their possession of more interests, or of more complex interests, based on these psychological capacities.

One implication is that distinctions elsewhere argued to be of moral relevance are morally irrelevant on this view. Singer is well known for maintaining that species membership should not factor (directly, in any case) into moral decision making. Being a member of the human species, he insists, does not entitle one to privileged moral significance nor to unique moral status. What matters are one's *interests*, not one's *species*. But equally—of particular relevance here—there is no obvious way in which any distinction between wild and domesticated animals could be of any moral relevance in itself. Inasmuch as a domesticated housecat and a wild bobcat could both have negative experiences of suffering or have preferences satisfied or frustrated, both call on our moral attention in similar ways. Of course, the actual preferences that a bobcat is likely to have will be rather different from those of a housecat; different behaviors on my part might be required equally to satisfy the interests of the two different animals. But even though I might need to *treat* them differently to achieve the same degree of preference satisfaction, I nonetheless must take them into account equally and owe them the same amount of moral concern—in terms of both harm and assistance. On Singer's view, it is capacities and related interests *alone* that stand out for moral attention.

Consequentialism

Singer combines this capacity-and-interest-oriented view with a form of consequentialism: we should aim to produce the best outcome (in terms of minimizing pain and maximizing satisfied preferences).[7] What is immediately striking about this is that the *source* of the pain we should minimize, or the preferences whose fulfillment we should maximize, is—as with species membership—not directly relevant. What we need to know is: "How could I best relieve suffering?" There are no types of suffering that—because of the way they came about, for instance—are more or less morally salient than others. Indeed, this is a general feature of utilitarian views: "In judging an action there is no need to know who is doing what to whom so long as the impact of these actions, direct and indirect, on the impersonal sum of utilities is known" (Sen and Williams 1977, 5).[8] Utilitarianism is not backward looking: sources and causes are only relevant inasmuch as knowing them can help create a better *future*. And so on this basis, wild-animal pain in the wilderness calls for moral attention just as much as domestic-animal pain in an industrial farm; the responsibility to relieve pain (other things being equal), however caused, is equally strong in both cases. Of course, practical issues are relevant here: it might in practice be easier to relieve pain in the context of the industrial farm. In a world of limited resources, the farm may thus be prioritized over the forest. But still, since pain minimization is a central moral aim, wild pain and domestic pain are equally bad. From a utilitarian perspective, of course, this need not mean that all pain should be relieved and no pain caused, for causing or failing to relieve some pains might be the only way of preventing greater pains in others or at another time or may lead to greater pleasures. (As we will see, versions of this argument can be used by utilitarians to argue that utilitarian commitments to action in the wild are not as strong as they might initially seem.)

Let us think, then, about wild animals, since that is a key concern of this book. At first sight, on this view, humans look to have just the same duties toward wild animals as they do to all animals. This implies that humans should not inflict pain on wild animals unless one might expect this to reduce pain (or increase pleasure) overall. Hunting, for instance, except for vital subsistence or possibly "therapeutic hunting" (to reduce overall animal pain) would be morally unacceptable.[9] But it is not only human-produced suffering that should be minimized: as I have pointed out, the origin of the suffering is not relevant, since utilitarianism is not backward looking. Thus, utilitarianism might appear to mandate the relief of wild-caused suffering. After all, animals suffer pain in the wild from a variety of causes: disease, storm, accident, floods and drought, predation. Pain from any source is bad and should be minimized; this suggests that, where possible, and where more suffering would not be caused by doing so, humans should intervene in wild processes to this end.

Wenz (1988, 198–199) outlines a particularly graphic (and, he acknowledges, somewhat unsympathetic) account of the implications of a utilitarian animal ethic in the wild. He maintains that wilderness preservation would not be favored, for life in the wild can be "nasty and brutish"; a product of human engineering is likely to produce less suffering overall; that animals are likely to fare best with benevolent human care and management; that predator species and carnivores should be eradicated and prey species kept in check by sterilization; and that new species of small, tranquil herbivorous animals should be bred in large numbers, replacing the current predator-prey system.

This may be a *reductio* of a utilitarian view, but still, some weaker version of wild intervention does look as though it must follow, and certainly is not ruled out, by utilitarian views. Yet Singer is uncomfortable with the idea of managing the wild for animal welfare. "Once we give up our right to claims to 'dominion' over other species we have no right to interfere with them at all. We should leave them alone as much as we possibly can. Having given up the role of tyrant, we should not try to play Big Brother either" (1983, 251). But it is not obvious how these claims about noninterference and not playing Big Brother would follow from a utilitarian position; they certainly do not appear to be ruled out in principle. There are no "zones"—such as the wild—where humans are relieved of trying to bring about best consequences. As Jeremy Bentham (1843) maintains, when discussing the cultivation of benevolence in an animal context, "The time will come, when humanity will extend its mantle over every thing which breathes."

Singer subsequently maintains either that we do not know enough about wild ecosystems to predict the outcomes of our actions or that any action we take would inevitably have negative consequences that we cannot appreciate: "any attempt to change ecological systems on a large scale is going to do far more harm than good" (1983, 252). We can remove the lion from the ecosystem—perhaps by painless sterilization—to prevent pain to the gazelle, but we do not know what role the lion plays in the ecosystem and thus we do not know what kind of suffering down the line might be generated were we to do so (Singer 1973). Similar practical answers, I suppose, could be given to other questions, such as feeding animals in winter, replacing pred-atory species with herbivores, treating wild-animal diseases—all these might have consequences that we cannot foresee and that might cause more suffering in the long term.

But these arguments are not entirely convincing. First, such responses are dif-ficult to accept if we really take seriously the scale and intensity of wild animal suf-fering. As Schmidtz (2008, 147) notes, Singer maintains that similar human and animal suffering are of comparable moral importance. And Singer also argues that we must take distant *human* suffering extremely seriously—so seriously that we should make enormous sacrifices to relieve some distant human hunger and thirst, for instance. But then, as Schmidtz (2008, 147) argues, "animals everywhere are dy-ing from easily preventable thirst and hunger and from easily preventable diseases"; the plight of these animals may be *even worse* than that of most needy humans. If we take this suffering as seriously as we take human suffering, and if we should aim to bring about best consequences, it *must* be critically morally important that we develop strategies to relieve such animal suffering, even at considerable cost to our-selves.

Second, Singer's case is essentially a provisional argument from ignorance: we do not know the consequences, the consequences could be very bad, so we had better do nothing. But in an increasing number of cases, perhaps on a smaller scale than the gazelle/lion case, the consequences of human actions in the wild are reasonably predictable and, in terms of pain reduction at least, intervention is likely to be better than nonintervention. The rapid development of management techniques such as vaccination, radio tracking, and wildlife contraception or sterilization make manage-ment of the wild for animal welfare increasingly possible, with reasonably predict-able outcomes.[10] Ignorance of the consequences is not likely to be a resilient argu-ment that management of the wild is ethically undesirable in principle; it will apply to a diminishing number of cases in practice, at least on relatively small scales. And ultimately Singer (1973) accepts that if reducing suffering were *really to result*, then management of the wild would be the best strategy: "If, in some way, we could be reasonably certain that interfering with wildlife in a particular way would, in the long run, greatly reduce the amount of killing and suffering in the animal world, it would, I think, be right to interfere."

One possible response here is just to bite the bullet and advocate pursuit of the best outcome, including attempts to reduce suffering, whatever its source. This could mandate a high level of interference in the wild, possibly including intervention in predation, assistance to relieve pain, and perhaps in the longer term a remodeling of natural ecosystems. After all, we are not talking here only about the responses of *individuals* to wild-animal pain, where it is possible that there are frequently more urgent or immediately feasible actions that can bring about good outcomes. We are also thinking about the principles that should govern the management of wild areas in a more proactive, policy-focused sense. But even if we did focus only on individuals, and on every occasion each individual had more pressing claims than to respond to wild-animal pain, this utilitarian view is still starkly different in principle from the laissez-faire intuition outlined in the introduction. The part of the LFI concerning assistance—in rough form—runs something like this: "Humans should relieve suffering in, and provide for, individual domesticated animals. However, they have no such responsibilities to wild animals. Wild animals should be left alone." The LFI is not the view that ethical responsibilities to assist wild animals are outweighed by other priorities or by worries about our competence; such ethical responsibilities to assist are just *not there at all*. What goes on in the wild, as it were, is *not our moral business*. What is more, the LFI plainly makes a contextual distinction—one that is just not available to a utilitarian position.

There is another, related, potentially troubling aspect of a utilitarian view such as Singer's. Utilitarianism, I have maintained above, is not backward looking; the *source* of pain or aversive experience is irrelevant. But (in the human case) we often think that backward-looking claims *do* command special moral attention. So, for instance, much of the debate about reparations has focused on what is morally owed to those who have been unjustly treated in the past. Utilitarians, however, can only make a place for reparations by arguing that (in some particular case) reparations would have forward-looking benefits and that these provide the necessary moral justification. This does not satisfy the claim that some past wrong should be "made good"; what is at stake is rectifying an injustice, not bringing about the best consequences in the future. These kinds of backward-looking arguments (I will suggest) are also relevant in the animal case. There may be reasons for assisting particular animals that relate to past unethical treatment of them; reasons of justice (or something similar in form to justice) matter in these cases, not the goal of minimizing pain or frustrated preferences in the world. But this introduces a kind of contextual concern—a special relationship—to which utilitarians cannot be directly sensitive.

It *may* be possible to generate a utilitarian view that is responsive to these worries; I'll consider this possibility later. But this is likely to be this difficult, because of the central role that both capacities and consequentialism play in utilitarianism.

RIGHTS, CONTEXT, AND ANIMAL ETHICS

Arguments that animals have moral rights have a long history; animals' rights can be traced at least as far back as Salt's *Animals' Rights* (1892). Most arguments, from Salt's work onward, take something like this form: (a) it makes philosophical sense to talk about "rights"; (b) it is appropriate to attribute rights to some or all humans;

(c) *if* rights can be attributed to some or all humans, *then* there is no secure way to deny rights to at least some animals. Such arguments have been widely attacked, primarily at points (a) and (c). However, I will not discuss rights theory in a general sense here. Rather, I will consider how two leading formulations of animal rights— those of Tom Regan and Gary Francione—account for moral status (in this case, for being a rightsholder), and, as with utilitarianism, I will explore questions about *context* and *assistance* in these accounts.

Regan and Francione on Moral Considerability

Regan argues that mentally normal adult mammals over the age of roughly one year are "subjects-of-a-life." They have "beliefs and desires; perception, memory and a sense of the future, including their own future; an emotional life together with feelings of pleasure and pain; preference and welfare interests; a psychophysical unity over time and an individual welfare in the sense that their experiential life fares well or ill for them" (Regan 1984, 244). He suggests that we should also give the benefit of the doubt to animals that do not fall into this category (infant mammals, birds, amphibians, reptiles, and fish). We "do not know with anything approaching certainty" that these beings are *not* subjects-of-a-life, and allowing "their recreational or economic exploitation is to encourage the formation of habits that lead to the violation of animals who are subjects-of-a-life" (Regan 1984, 336–337, 416–417).[11]

On the basis of this account, Regan develops an idea of welfare. Beings that are subjects-of-a-life can have preference autonomy—that is, they can initiate actions with a view to satisfying their preferences (1984, 85); they are capable of living well, and they live well when they have a life "that is characterized by the harmonious satisfaction of . . . desires, purposes and the like, taking account of . . . biological, social and psychological interests." Animals have both preference and welfare interests (things in which they take an interest and things that are in their interests), and they can be harmed by infliction or deprivation. They need not be aware of a deprivation to have been deprived; indeed, Regan argues that death harms by deprivation. Thus, even when animals are not aware of what they are missing and have not been pained, they may still be harmed.[12]

Beings that are subjects-of-a-life in this sense "have a distinctive kind of value— inherent value." This inherent value accrues just in virtue of being subject-of-a-life, and as such it does not come in degrees. Either a being has it or lacks it (Regan 1984, 243). Inherent value is nonexperiential, and while experiences and preference satisfactions are also valuable, they are "distinct from, not reducible to and incommensurate with what constitutes a being's inherent value" (1984, 277). Beings with inherent value should be treated in ways that respect their inherent value (1984, 265); they are neither merely means for others' ends nor receptacles for their own experiences.

32

Thus their lives may not be traded off in consequentialist calculations.

The principle of respect is, for Regan, the link between inherent value and the possession of rights. For Regan, "to have a moral right to something is to have a valid claim against others to be treated in a particular kind of way with respect to something one has a right to" (Taylor 1987, 21).[13] The validity of the claim must rest on a valid moral principle; for Regan, this is the principle of respect for inherent value.[14] All subjects-of-a-life have inherent value and (particular specified) rights, even if they are not able actively to claim such rights. These rights, Regan insists, are not acquired rights, ones that arise out of "voluntary acts or one's place in an institutional arrangement" (1984, 37). They are unacquired rights of justice and apply universally to all beings that are subject-of-a-life. "If any individual (A) has a right then any other individual like A in relevant respects has a right" (1984, 267). The primary rights all subjects-of-a-life possess are the right to respectful treatment (1984, 327), meaning that they should not be treated as instruments nor solely as receptacles of experiences, and the right not to be harmed (which includes not to be killed). Not only are moral agents required not to harm those who have inherent value, but they are also required to come to the defense of those who have inherent value when they are threatened by other moral agents. Although these rights can be overridden, such instances are rare and must be justified, Regan argues, by valid moral principles.

Regan's account of mammals' psychological abilities is high level (and contrasts with my outline in chapter 1). But accounts of animal rights do not necessarily draw on such high-level views and need not be as complex in form as Regan's. On some recent accounts—such as those of Steiner (2008) and Francione (2000)—it is argued that sentience alone is sufficient to underpin animal rights. Francione argues that if any being is sentient, it has interests both in not suffering and in continuing to live. Where different beings have the same interests, their interests should be taken equally into account. So, if it is wrong to inflict suffering on, or kill, humans, it is also—and equally—wrong to kill or inflict suffering on animals. Yet although most people accept that inflicting suffering on animals is wrong in principle, still they tolerate or perpetrate it in ways that they would find unacceptable if it was inflicted on humans. The basic reason for this tolerant inconsistency toward animal suffering, Francione argues, is that animals still have the status of property; they are available to be treated merely as resources—as "things." The most basic right animals should have, therefore—the one that would protect their fundamental interests in living and not suffering—is the right not to be property (Francione 2000, xxxiv). This right— which should be a legal one—Francione argues to be absolute. Like Regan, he maintains that animals' basic interests should not be traded off even for greater benefits, just as we do not, on principle, accept trade-offs of the most basic human rights for overall benefits to others.

Regan and Francione, then, provide different accounts of what capacities are

33

required for a being to have rights. Both are controversial. Regan proposes a very high-level view of mammals' capacities, one that is more complex than can be supported by most accounts of mammalian cognition. Francione's account is much less controversial in this regard, since it is widely accepted that many animals are sentient. However, it is this very quality that makes Francione's account more problematic than Regan's from the point of view of most rights theorists. For those who argue that rights can only hold between moral agents, Regan's argument that being subject-of-a-life is sufficient for having rights is troubling enough; the idea that sentience alone could qualify a being for rights—whether moral or legal rights—looks even more difficult to justify.[15]

This opens up a large and important debate about the capacities required for rights and the relationship between moral and legal rights. Indeed, the very idea of unacquired moral rights is famously troublesome—for humans as well as for non-humans (see, for instance, Frey 1983, 45). But I do not need to get further into this dispute here. Although I will not specifically be arguing here for a rights view, the position I will adopt is certainly compatible with both these rights views. What I want to suggest here—by thinking through some concerns about context and assistance—is that a number of important questions are not answered or are answered inadequately by existing animal rights views. Someone who adopts such a view could, therefore, accept much of what I am proposing as an "add-on" to their existing rights position.

Negative/Positive Rights in Context

Understanding what is entailed by any particular rights approach means knowing what rights are taken to mean in it—for instance, whether there are any positive rights and, if there are only negative rights, whether one has a duty to protect others' negative rights or just not to infringe on them oneself.[16] First, I need to clarify what is meant by negative and positive rights. Narveson's definition is as follows: To say that A has a negative right that p means that B must not intentionally make it the case that not-p (or bring it about that not p), whereas to say that A has a positive right that p means that B must help, to some relevant degree, to *bring it about that* p (Narveson 1983, 46).

A few animal-rights theorists attribute both positive and negative rights to animals. How might this work? Suppose one argued that animals have both positive and negative liberty rights. What would one be claiming? First—to respect the negative right—would be the claim that no moral agent should intentionally make it the case that an animal's liberty is impeded, curtailed, or interfered with. Second is the claim that moral agents should protect the animal's liberty from infringements or interference by other moral agents (at least), and third—to respect the positive right—

that moral agents should help to some relevant degree to bring it about that an animal gains or maintains its liberty. And every animal that meets the requirements to be a rightsholder (whatever these might be) would have these positive and negative liberty rights.

The attribution of positive rights, then, concerns duties of assistance, benefit, protection, or provision, alongside negative duties not to harm. However, a position that attributes both positive and negative rights to animals, coupled with the trumping strength usually attributed to rights claims, would appear to be very demanding. Suppose, for instance, we took a very basic right—the right to life—as a positive right and thought about what this would mean in the wild. If wild animals have a positive right to life, not only should we not kill them, but we should protect them from being killed (by other animals or harsh weather, for instance) and provide for them, for instance, if a winter storm prevents them from accessing their normal food supply. But this would require very extensive intervention in the wild, especially given the "trumping" strength usually attributed to rights claims. In an attempt to soften such demands, one recent rights view (Franklin 2005) weakens the degree of importance attributed to rights, reducing their "trumping" quality, and suggesting that on many occasions it would just be too impractical to fulfill such basic rights. (It is worth noting that this would be generally regarded as a very problematic view were basic *human* rights at stake.)

Such wide-ranging animal rights approaches as Franklin's are, however, in a minority. Both Regan and Francione have more restricted rights accounts, ones that mainly defend *negative* rights. I will concentrate particularly on Regan's account here; his view does not diverge substantially on this point, at least, from Francione's.

Two principles follow from Regan's argument that all subjects-of-a-life have inherent value: a principle of respect and a harm principle. The unacquired *right to respectful treatment* and the *right not to be harmed* can be claimed by or on behalf of all subjects-of-a-life. Regan is not completely clear about what claims animals have on the basis of these rights, but moral agents certainly have negative duties not to harm or kill animals. Regan also claims that there is a duty to assist when *others* treat animals in ways that violate their rights (Regan 1984, 283). But this duty can only arise when the threat to an animal is from a moral agent, for only moral agents *can* threaten rights. "Nature has no duties; only moral agents do. . . . Nature no more violates our rights than it respects them" (Regan 1984, 272). Only (some) humans are moral agents. Consequently, there are no duties to intervene when animals are threatened by beings and things that are *not* moral agents. This means, for example, that there is no responsibility to intervene in predation (since predators are not moral agents and so cannot threaten anyone's rights nor commit any injustice). So, Regan (1984, 285) maintains: "In claiming that we have a prima facie duty to assist those animals whose rights are violated, therefore, we are not claiming that we have a duty to assist the sheep against the attack of the wolf, since the wolf neither can, nor does, violate anyone's rights."

Regan does not explicitly comment on (for instance) whether the right to respectful treatment generates duties of provision in the case of need. A straightforward reading of his work suggests that this would depend on how a being came to be in need. If a child were hungry because a hurricane had destroyed his home, the need is not caused by a moral agent, so it looks as though the right to respectful treatment does not entail assistance. (This is not to say that some other principle of assistance could not be introduced here, but any assistance would not be on the basis of a right.) If the child were hungry because an iniquitous landlord had made it impossible for his parents to earn enough to buy food, then the child is hungry due to the actions of a moral agent, and assistance would be required on the basis of a right to respectful treatment; the iniquitous landlord would have already infringed on the child's rights. This would then be a case of assisting because rights have been breached, though this raises complicated questions about *who* should do the assisting. (These kinds of cases—of prior harm by moral agents—are important for this book, but they are not much discussed in existing animal rights literature).

Regan's view, then, does not seem to support a general duty of provision derived from a right to respectful treatment. If an animal is hungry, and the hunger is not caused by a moral agent, then there is no duty to assist. As Jamieson says: "although we are required to assist those who are victims of injustice, we are not required to help those in need who are not victims of injustice" (Jamieson 1990, 351). This does not mean that it would be *impermissible* to assist, nor that one would not be doing something superogatorily good by doing so, but assistance is not *required*. This certainly seems to be the outcome that Regan wants, for in as much as he discusses wild animals, he maintains that they should be left alone. "Wildlife managers should be principally concerned with letting animals be, keeping human predators out of their affairs, allowing these 'other nations' to carve out their own destiny" (Regan 1984, 357).[17] This is very close to the position Francione (2008, 13) also takes on assistance in the wild; of nondomesticated animals, he suggests that "we should simply leave them alone."

However, Regan's position generates two possible (alternative) difficulties. One difficulty concerns his account of rights: perhaps rights do, in fact, generate duties to assist that Regan does not consider. The alternative difficulty accepts that there is no problem with Regan's (and Francione's) account of rights but maintains that the ethical position that results from it is too restricted, in terms of assistance, both in the human and in the animal case. I will take these in turn.

Regan's rights view cannot be straightforwardly mapped onto a distinction between positive and negative rights. But it has been widely taken to advocate only negative (noninterference) rights; duties to assist only follow from or are generated to prevent rights infringements. However, some have argued that the very idea of what it means to *have* a right creates positive duties for which Regan's account does not allow. Henry Shue (1996), for example, in a discussion about what is owed by affluent nations and individuals to the distant poor, argues that the distinction between positive and negative rights is itself a problematic one. It is not any right in itself that is positive or negative but rather the duties for others generated by someone having a right (Shue 1996, 54). More strictly, Shue argues, a right generates threefold correlative duties.[18] So, for instance, a right to life generates a duty not to deprive rightsholders of life nor to prevent their access to the means for living, a duty to protect others against those who would deprive of life or the means to life, and a duty to aid in what's needed for life, for example, in providing sustenance if necessary.[19] If Shue is right—and his argument is at least plausible—then in affirming a right to life one is affirming a range of correlative duties, calling on different kinds and degrees of action and restraint, more and less positive in nature, that may include assistance. He argues that this threefold correlative structure applies to *all* rights.

On this account of rights, if a starving deer has a right to respectful treatment, then positive as well as negative duties will flow from this right. A right to respect, on Shue's account, would very likely include a positive duty to provide food for a starving deer. And although Regan does not himself accept this, such positive duties do fit well with other aspects of Regan's view. For the death of an animal that is a subject-of-a-life means the loss of the inherent value its life carries, even if no moral agent is involved in causing the death.[20] And it is the inherent value, on Regan's account of rights, that grounds the right to respect. One way of interpreting a right to respectful treatment that is in at least some sense coherent with Regan's view would be that a moral agent has a duty to protect the inherent value that would be lost by death, even where the threat is not from a moral agent.[21]

However, as has already become clear, Regan himself does not formulate his view in this way. Adopting Shue's rights account would certainly entail revising Regan's laissez-faire view of duties to assist in the wild. Indeed, as with utilitarianism, such a revised rights view would be highly demanding. So it is understandable that Regan prefers to construct his view of rights in terms of negative duties. This prevents him from being committed to too much in the wild. However, the view that he defends leaves him open to the alternative difficulty: the accusation that he is, instead, committed to too *little*.

Jamieson (1990) probes at this problem in a series of fictional "boulder-rolling" cases. In each of these cases, I see a falling boulder that will kill a man walking below, and I am in a position to warn the man at little cost to myself. In one case, the boulder is intentionally loosened by a woman; in another case, it is accidentally loosened by the woman; in another, the rockfall is initiated by a hunting wolf; in another, it is a natural rock fall. On Regan's account, one only seems to have a duty to assist (by warning) when the boulder has been loosened by a moral agent (and as Jamieson points out, it is also unclear whether the woman needs to *intend* to kill the man with the boulder for the duty to be generated). There is no duty of justice to warn in the case of the wolf or the natural rock fall, since neither of these are moral agents and no rights would be infringed. Yet, Jamieson argues, to suggest that one only has duties to warn when the threat comes from a moral agent produces all kinds of strange outcomes. And this seems right. On a view like this, I would seem not have a duty to set off a tsunami alarm to alert thousands of coastal settlements about their imminent inundation, since a tsunami is not a moral agent and hence threatens no one's rights. This looks like a problem for Regan's account as it is currently constituted. Either Regan must accept the view that we have no duties in these cases, or an alternative explanation for the existence of nondiscretionary duties, one not generated by rights infringements, is needed.

What is notable here is that Regan's concern that wild animals should be allowed to "let be," to "carve out their own destiny," does not, in fact, apply only to *wild* animals. There are no rights-generated duties, at least, to assist any subjects-of-a-life, in cases where a threat or some past harm is not from a moral agent. Francione (2000, 185) accepts something like this position too: on his account, the basic rights view does not necessarily mean that "we have moral or legal obligations to render them [animals or humans] aid or to intervene to prevent harm from coming to them." This distinguishes Regan's and Francione's view from the laissez-faire intuition I have outlined, since the LFI differentiates between situations where assistance is required and situations where it is not. While there are no duties to assist *wild* animals, there may be duties to assist humans and domesticated animals, even in situations where threats do not originate from moral agents.

Of course, it is reasonable to respond to concerns of this kind—as Regan indeed does—by maintaining that duties of justice in defending against rights infringements do not constitute *all* the nondiscretionary duties there might be: "the rights view is not a complete theory in its present form" (Regan 2001, 51, quoting Regan 1984). It is plausible, Regan maintains, that there are additional nondiscretionary duties that require one to warn the threatened man in all the boulder-rolling cases, though these would not arise out of rights violations; they might instead be acquired duties of beneficence (2001, 51). Indeed, the possible existence of such acquired duties is mentioned several times in *The Case for Animal Rights*; these kinds of duties arise "from our voluntary acts and institutional arrangements." Regan does not, however, give an account of such duties.

One way of thinking about this book is that it is an attempt to understand and account for these "acquired duties" in the case of animals. What is clear about such duties, though, if they are to differentiate between assistance in different contexts (such as between wild and domesticated animals), is that they would have to have a rather different foundation than the one on which Regan and Francione base their existing accounts. That is, the foundation of our acquired duties to assist animals must be *something other than individual beings' morally relevant capacities*. In terms of morally relevant capacities—such as sentience or being subject-of-a-life—alone, as pointed out earlier in the chapter, a wild bobcat and a domesticated cat cannot be distinguished. So, if we should owe assistance or provision to one and not to the other, this must be based on something other than the animals' psychological capacities; something about the animals' context or its relationship to us must be what is of moral relevance. I will be developing an account of this kind here, and such an account could be seen, as I have suggested, as an "add-on" to an animal-rights view, though it need not be understood in this way.

CAPABILITIES, CONTEXT, AND ANIMAL ETHICS

The capabilities approach is a recent and, so far, less developed way of thinking about animal ethics. Even in its currently undeveloped form, however, it is characterized by interesting and relevant ideas with respect to the project I am undertaking here. The capabilities approach is by no means unified, but only Martha Nussbaum has, in any sustained way, so far applied it to thinking about moral responsibilities toward animals. I will therefore concentrate on her most comprehensive account, in *Frontiers of Justice* (2006). Again, I will primarily focus on questions of moral status, context, and assistance here.

First, I need to say something about what a capabilities approach *is*, since this view is generally less well known than either a utilitarian or a rights approach. Nussbaum understands capabilities, in the human case, as "what people are actually able to do and to be" (2006, 70). There are, she suggests, a number of basic capabilities that humans need to realize, at least to a certain minimal threshold, in order to reach "truly human functioning as citizens." The social goal, then, "should be understood in terms of getting citizens above this capability threshold" (2006, 71). Realization of these capabilities forms a central part of living a life of human *dignity*; having dignity is, at least in part, constituted by fulfilling one's basic capabilities.

Nussbaum (2006, 182) points out that this idea of capabilities is "evaluative and ethical." That is, it is not the mere possession of some capability that makes its fulfillment desirable; it must be judged desirable for other reasons—reasons that concern what it is to live a good human life (since humans have capabilities that it is better not to realize, such as the capability of being racist). Part of the capabilities view is the evaluative judgment that there are some capabilities (Nussbaum identifies a negotiable list of ten) essential to living a flourishing human life, and, she claims, these capabilities can be widely accepted cross-culturally. Even where individuals of some cultures do not want to actualize particular capabilities—such as the capability to engage in political decision making—it is important that the capability is respected.

This capabilities approach, Nussbaum maintains, is superior to a preference-utilitarian view (such as Singer's) on several counts. The aggregative nature of utilitarianism both means that the good of some may be sacrificed for the good of all, thus permitting large inequalities between individuals, and it fails to identify a range of specific human goods that must be met, potentially permitting some vital goods to be traded off to promote others. Further, the utilitarian emphasis on a subjective understanding of well-being in terms of preferences does not recognize ways in which preferences (unlike capabilities) may themselves be socially shaped and thus fail to reflect "what people are actually able to do and to be."[22] The capabilities approach, Nussbaum suggests, avoids these pitfalls. It is, in some central ways, not dissimilar to a *rights* view, with an emphasis on the inviolability and dignity of each human life.

How does Nussbaum apply this capabilities approach to animals? First, she maintains that (broadly speaking) the capacity to feel pain is the boundary of moral considerability.[23] If a creature can feel pain, it matters morally. But sentience alone cannot give sufficient guidance as to human duties to animals, since it is not only the absence of pain that is important to animals. It is also, as with humans, the fulfillment of their capabilities.[24] Every species, she maintains, has its characteristic way of flourishing, its own species-specific capabilities, its own particular dignity. Individuals of a species do well when they flourish in that species-specific way or, at least, when a "group of core capabilities" are secured, up to "some minimum threshold" (2006, 381). What constitutes a species' core capabilities can only be worked out by close observation of members of the species; it cannot be known a priori. But once these core capabilities have been identified, sentient animals are *entitled* to have them secured by humans; this is, on Nussbaum's account, a matter of *justice*. Humans are responsible to "bring each creature up above a capability threshold specific to each species" (2006, 383).

One implication of a capabilities account—rather as in Regan's rights account—is that animals may be harmed by being prevented from fulfilling their core capabilities, even if this does not cause them suffering and even if they are unaware of the deprivation. Among these harms in cases where animals have quite sophisticated capacities (and Nussbaum 2006, 385, argues that some do—she suggests for instance that some may feel shame and embarrassment) is the harm of killing, even painless killing. Indeed, life is the first entitlement of sentient animals, although this entitlement is not absolute. The capabilities approach, according to Nussbaum, entitles animals to a healthy life, to bodily integrity, to pleasurable experience and the avoidance of nonbeneficial pain, to appropriate attachments to other members of their species, and to respect for their habitats. Humans should not interfere with animals' own abilities to realize their species-specific capabilities and to get what they are entitled to, and, where necessary, they should assist animals in this realization.

This capabilities approach to animals claims to be more sensitive to species difference than either the utilitarian or rights views. In both the utilitarian and rights views, Nussbaum points out, species membership is irrelevant: what matters are the few morally relevant characteristics that are valuable in whatever species they are manifested. Beyond the level of feeling pain, where beings start to matter in themselves, what is important for Nussbaum is the fulfillment of species-specific capabilities, where each living being flourishes in the characteristic way of the sort of being it is. There is even room to take into account not just what is species specific but even what might be individually specific, since what matters is the flourishing and fulfillment of individuals. This points to a complex prescription for human moral responsibilities to animals, since animals both should be permitted to flourish and assisted in flourishing to the best of their species-specific capabilities.

This (somewhat truncated) account already raises questions about assisting animals, especially in the wild context. At least at first sight, it potentially suggests more extensive, or at least more complex, human responsibilities toward all animals than either a rights or a utilitarian approach.

Capabilities, Context, and Assistance

Fundamental here is the claim that fulfilling the capabilities basic to the flourishing of any morally considerable being should be promoted, whether this is best achieved through noninterference or through assistance. This is certainly the position that Nussbaum takes in the human context, explicitly rejecting a distinction, however drawn, between negative duties without accompanying positive duties (2006, 372). We would expect this argument to extend to animals, wild and domestic alike. However, this is not what Nussbaum at first suggests in the case of animals:

> In the case of animals, however, there might appear to be room for a positive/negative distinction that makes some sense. It seems at least coherent to say that the human community has the obligation to refrain from certain egregious harms towards animals, but that it is not obliged to support the welfare of all animals, in the sense of ensuring them adequate food, shelter and health care.
>
> (Nussbaum 2006, 373)

This suggestion is tentative, but Nussbaum (2006, 373) offers it some support by proposing the following "imagined argument," which—although imagined—contains "much truth." Central elements of this "imagined argument" are as follows: first, species might themselves have the task of ensuring their own flourishing, providing that humans refrain from harming them; second, we would just "mess up the lives of animals" if we tried to be benevolent despots of the world; third, the idea of a benevolent despotism of humans over animals, where humans supply animals' needs is morally repugnant (the sovereignty of species, like the sovereignty of nations, has moral weight); and finally, "part of what it is to flourish, for a creature, is to settle certain very important matters on its own, without human intervention, even of a benevolent sort."

Initially, Nussbaum presents this "imagined" argument as applying to all animals. But (and I suppose this is the point of it being only an "imagined" argument!) she then suggests that actually it applies to no animals. First, many animals—domesticated ones and wild animals in captivity—are "under humans' direct control" and consequently dependent on humans for provision. These animals cannot be held entirely responsible for their own flourishing, even if humans do not harm them. But then, looking more closely at wild animals, she maintains, owing to our "pervasive involvement" with them, we have positive responsibilities toward them too. Drawing on Botkin (1990), she argues that humans maintain ecosystems in many cases, and we may not be able to tell which those are. So (it seems) humans have much greater moral responsibility to assist wild animals' flourishing than may at first appear, as we may be causally responsible for the situation in which the animals find themselves.

This argument seems plausible; indeed, I will defend a view a little like it in this book. But Nussbaum almost immediately retreats, ultimately abandoning the "imagined" argument altogether, along with the insight that human prior actions may generate special obligations that would not otherwise exist. For she suggests: "We have the power to save animals who might otherwise die of disease or the after effects of a natural disaster. It seems implausible to think that we have no duties of material aid in such cases" (2006, 374). Duties to assist in promoting flourishing in these cases are not generated by prior human intervention. Certainly, such aid should "preserve and enhance autonomy"; it would be "a bad result if all animals ended up in zoos, completely dependent on human arrangements." But in the case of animals in general, she suggests "paternalism is usually appropriate," although this should be pursued along with "species autonomy." For domesticated animals, this entails human guardianship, which includes training, discipline, and attention to species norms and the needs of particular individuals. And this guardianship extends in some sense into the wild. For "the capabilities approach, as [for] utilitarianism, what happens to the victim is the key issue, not who does the bad thing. The death of a gazelle after painful torture is just as bad for the gazelle when torture is inflicted by a tiger as when it is inflicted by a human being" (2006, 379).

Nussbaum suggests, then, that if painful predation can be prevented without causing worse harms, it should be. This brings Nussbaum's view much closer to a utilitarian view than to Regan's rights view. For Regan, what goes on between the wolf and the sheep or between the lion and the gazelle is none of our moral business, however torturous it might be. But whereas Regan looks at who is doing the torturing—and whether the torturer is a moral agent—in order to decide whether what is happening is a breach of rights and therefore triggers some moral response, both Nussbaum and Singer (one concerned with capabilities, the other with suffering and desires) look at the one being tortured. Although there are ways in which the state of the tiger must be taken into account on these views (a utilitarian must include the desires or pleasures of the tiger, and a capabilities theorist must consider the fulfillment of the tiger's predatory capabilities), nonetheless, if intervention can be carried out without worse consequences, it should be. Rather than reintroducing predators, for instance, in cases where the population of prey species is a problem, Nussbaum suggests sterilization is to be preferred.

Indeed, by the end of her account, Nussbaum has moved very far away from the "imagined argument." Not only should sick wild animals be aided, but she expresses discomfort with wild animals' habits of "humiliation of the weak" (2006, 399) and suggests that where wild animals commit "egregious harms" to weaker species members, humans should intervene, although perhaps humans should tolerate (though not promote) hierarchies within species. For in the end, Nussbaum maintains, Nature is no model to follow, including with regard to the treatment of wild animals. Nature is never going to provide all species with "co-operative and mutually supportive relations." So, Nussbaum suggests, there should be a "gradual supplanting of the natural by the just."

Ultimately, then, Nussbaum gives short shrift to her "imagined argument" in which moral agents should not harm but do not need to assist animals (or some animals). And, given what is entailed by the capabilities approach, her retreat from the imagined argument seems right. For the basic claims of the imagined argument sit uncomfortably with a capabilities approach. After all, Nussbaum does not (for instance) think that the sovereignty of nations should prevent the affluent in one country from assisting the impoverished in another country to fulfill their capabilities. Nor does she accept the idea in the human case that people should "settle very important matters on their own"—at least, not if this means that they fail to realize their basic capabilities. The *very form* of capabilities arguments press toward the view that the capabilities of all morally considerable beings should be fulfilled up to a certain minimum threshold, and this applies whether human or animal, and, among animals, whether wild or domesticated. That is because—in an argument I will develop in chapter 3—the capabilities approach, like utilitarianism and (unmodified) rights views, is essentially capacity oriented. What matters ethically depends entirely on *what a being is like*, even though this is construed in a more complex way than in either the utilitarian or rights views. On this basis alone, there are no grounds for the kind of distinction that underpins the "imagined argument"—or something like the laissez-faire intuition. In chapter 3, I will look more closely at the role that capacities—and, in contrast, relations and contexts—might play in animal ethics.

43

3

Capacities,
Contexts,
and Relations

In the last chapter, I sketched the relevant aspects of three approaches to animal ethics: utilitarian, rights, and capabilities approaches. I maintained that all three were "capacity oriented" and that this committed them—in their current forms at least—to problematic positions with respect to assisting animals. Here, I will push this discussion a step further, discussing what I take "capacities" to be, acknowledging the important role that they should play in animal ethics, but suggesting that capacity orientation alone gives an incomplete picture of our ethical responsibilities toward animals. I will argue that, alongside capacities, we also need to pay attention to *relational* features of our contact with animals. I will explain what I take "relation" to mean in this context and begin to outline some ways in which human relations with animals can be of ethical significance. To do this, I will draw on leading existing "relational" approaches—approaches that focus on what I will call affective relations, causal relations, and contractual relations. I will pick out from these relational approaches some proposed grounds for distinguishing between our duties to animals in different contexts. Although (for reasons I will explain where necessary) I will not adopt any of these views as currently formulated, these existing relational approaches provide important starting points and raise fundamental questions for developing an account of animal ethics in context.

CAPACITIES IN ANIMAL ETHICS
Capacities and Capacity Orientation

The term "capacity" in the context of animal ethics is usually taken in a general sense just to mean having an ability to do, produce, or experience something. However, capacities are significant to animal ethics in several different ways. First, they can function as markers of moral thresholds—that is, the possession of certain capacities, it can be argued, either gives a being moral status or additional moral significance. Second, capacities can function as markers of morally significant interests. That is, it is in the interests of beings with certain capacities to express or use (or not to express or use) some of their capacities; this is important for their well-being. Third (and least significantly), a capacity may just be something a being can do, use, or express, but it might not be of any particular importance either as a moral-threshold marker or as an interest marker. Some capacities—such as the capacity to experience pain—are widely understood to function *both* as a moral-threshold marker and as an interest marker. So, as I argued in chapter 1, if a being can feel pain, it has crossed a threshold of moral considerability (pain as a *moral-threshold* marker), but it is also in the interests of a being not to feel pain, so pain also operates as an *interest* marker. Of course, it is necessary to have crossed some basic moral threshold in order to have any morally relevant interest-marking capacities at all.

It is also worth noting here how these different senses of *capacities* relate to Nussbaum's idea of *capabilities*. Certainly, a "capability"—in terms of the capabilities approach to ethics—is a kind of capacity. But not all capacities are capabilities. Suppose mink can stand on one leg but rarely do so and do not take opportunities to do so even when encouraged with food and so on. The capacity to stand on one leg does not seem to be important to a mink's flourishing and therefore is not a capability, in Nussbaum's sense. But if—as suggested in chapter 1—swimming is of central importance for mink to live a flourishing life, then swimming *is* a capability for mink. A capability, therefore, is similar to an interest-marking capacity. However, there is one key difference between my account of interest-marking capacities and Nussbaum's interpretation of capabilities: I take interest-marking capacities to be *experiential*, while on Nussbaum's account there might be a capability that contributes to flourishing even though it is not experienced.

Capacities are central to virtually all accounts of moral status and welfare (including the account I am developing here). The possession of certain capacities is widely used to distinguish those beings that are directly morally considerable from those that are not; there are few accounts of what we owe morally to rocks, sticks, or automobiles, because these objects are not generally thought to possess the kinds of capacities that pull them over the threshold into direct moral considerability. However, many ethical positions *stop* at capacities, maintaining that capacities and their exercise are *all or virtually all that is relevant* to establishing both a being's moral considerability and everything that might be owed to it.

In the case of utilitarianism and rights theory, this capacity orientation takes the form of a kind of "class system." Animals are grouped on the basis of their membership in a particular class, and the class is defined by the possession of a particular innate keystone capacity or cluster of keystone capacities (such as those required to be a subject-of-a-life). These selected characteristics not only group animals and provide the basis for moral considerability, but they also solely and equally determine moral obligations to all animals in the relevant class.[1] The implication of this approach is that humans should take equally into account all animals in any class that has members thought to have similar capacities (so on Singer's terms, for instance, all sentient beings or all self-conscious beings; on Regan's terms, all beings that are subject-of-a-life).

The capabilities approach to animals is somewhat different in structure. The capacity for sentience (primarily) is what makes a being morally considerable. Beyond this, morally considerable beings should be allowed or assisted to meet a certain level of adequacy with regard to the fulfillment of their capabilities (Nussbaum 2006, 383). Nussbaum is deliberately elusive about whether every animal has an *equal* entitlement to be assisted to fulfill these capabilities; perhaps possessing extra capacities—as humans do—might give one priority, in a situation of conflict, in having one's capabilities adequately fulfilled. But what is clear is that capabilities determine whether you count morally at all, how much you count, and how you should be treated. So, while manifested somewhat differently, as with utilitarianism and rights theories, the capabilities approach remains capacity oriented.

The Plasticity of Capacities to Human Actions

One question that might be raised with respect to moral status–marking and interest-marking animal (and human) capacities is whether these capacities are fixed and innate or whether they are—at least to some degree—plastic. If capacities are fixed and unchangeable, then (on this view) so would be anything owed to beings on account of their possession. But if capacities are plastic—for instance, if humans could change animals' capacities—this could, in part at least, affect what would promote or detract from their well-being. Irvin (2004, 63) raises some thought-provoking questions about this. In the human case, capacities, she maintains, are not straightforwardly genetic "givens"; they are shaped and developed by *context*. We accept, for instance, that some human capacities, such as those for social relationships, if not developed at an early age, may always be limited or stunted. Other human capacities will develop—or fail to develop—depending on their environment (perhaps the capacity for swimming in humans is like this). Further, the roles that different capacities play in promoting human flourishing may depend on the environment in which an individual is situated. The capacities I need to develop in order to live as a hunter-gatherer are unlikely to assist my flourishing much in urban London, but, equally, capacities developed in urban London will be woefully inadequate in the bush. Capacities, then, can be *context related*.

It seems right to suggest (as Irvin does) that at least some animal capacities are also context related in this sense. And this is of relevance here. For if humans form part of the context of capacity creation—if they can influence the formation of animals' capacities in one way or another—then even animals' capacities have some human relational elements to them. We are not just responding to "what animals are like" in terms of their capacities; we are actually in part *creating* "what animals are like."

We can think about this in terms of the two important roles that I suggested that capacities play: marking moral thresholds and marking welfare-relevant interests. Moral-threshold capacities—such as the capacity to feel pain or the various abilities that constitute being "subject-of-a-life"—are not (at present) substantially open to human influence or intervention.[2] Irvin suggests a possible (though somewhat implausible) counterexample to this, however: suppose humans teach apes to sign, giving them and teaching them to use certain tools. These apes then form their own colony where some adult apes develop signing and tool use to new levels, making technological advances because they can now communicate complex things more effectively. Such technologically communicative apes contrast with those who lack such skills. The developments in the first set of apes' capacities, Irvin suggests, may be morally relevant; that is, these capacities may be threshold ones, making the lives of the apes more valuable. (Indeed, she suggests, their lives might be of more value than those of humans who have not developed such capacities.) If one accepts the controversial view that the capacity for communication and technological development marks a moral threshold, then this conclusion seems to follow. So context *could* influence capacity and be important in determining moral significance; it is conceivable, at least, that human relations with animals could actually raise (or, alternatively, lower) their moral significance by altering their capacities.

But the plasticity of welfare-relevant capacities looks more significant here. For, as Irvin maintains, human beings can act on animals' capacities, directing their capacities in particular ways or preventing them from developing at all. So, for a normal wild monkey, particular close relations with its social group are essential to its welfare. However, if a monkey is brought up in experimental isolation (as in the Harlow monkey maternal-deprivation experiments), its capacity for social relations is permanently stunted; for such an isolated monkey, interacting with a normally social monkey group is not in its interests, since social interaction generates negative, not positive, experiences. Of course, whatever context a being is in, some capacities will be developed, some will remain latent, and some will be stunted. There is no context in which every capacity can be developed; this is likely the case for animals as well as humans. What I take to be important here is the way in which capacity development affects experiential welfare. I may do well experientially whether I am brought up in London or the bush. But the monkey brought up in isolation will do badly in terms of its well being whether it remains in isolation or mixes with its fellows.

47

Irvin's account of the plasticity of animal capacities takes human influence on capacities to be *external*: that is, humans may act from outside to shape, influence, repress, and develop particular innate animal capacities. However, in the case of domesticated animals at least, some capacities have been *internally* created, or at least influenced and shaped, by human beings. Domesticated animals are created in ways that accentuate particular capacities (playfulness, gentleness) while downplaying others (such as the capacity to hunt or fight—though, of course, in some cases these characteristics are bred for rather than bred out). In these ways, humans can actually change animals' innate welfare-relevant interests as well as changing their expression after birth. So in this sense, with respect to many domesticated animals, human relations actually form and shape capacities and interests; they do not just act upon them when they already exist. Relations, then, can *precede and produce* certain capacities rather than only adapting and responding to them; human relations to domesticated animals, at least, influence what beings are actually like and, indeed, whether they exist at all. To explore this further, though, I need to say something more about what I take "relation" and "relational" to mean.

THE IDEA OF "RELATION"
The Meaning of Relation

The terms "relation" and "relational" are central to this book but open to wide interpretation. "Relation" can be construed in ways that exclude nuances I want to emphasize and that may imply a restriction to other meanings that, while certainly relational, are not all that I am construing "relational" to mean. In particular, I do not intend the word "relational" to refer exclusively or necessarily to a *felt* relation or to a relation of *affect*; that is, such affective relations do not *constitute* what I understand by a relational approach. Thus, my interpretation differs from that of some ethicists of care (such as Nel Noddings) who take relational just to mean an affective connection. I intend "relation" in this context also to include *having an effect, potentially having an effect, or having had an effect* on another, or the *existence of an interaction* between one being and another, such that the effect or interaction makes a difference in states of affairs.[3]

The broadness of this definition allows that there are relations between the wind and the roof when the wind blows off a tile, or that the sea relates to the sand when moving it on the beach. I cannot exclude these from falling under this definition of "relational" without excluding aspects of "relation" that I wish to retain. For instance, I do not want to maintain that "relation" in this sense must be one of conscious awareness on either or both sides. This would exclude some relations (in my terms) in which I am interested. My focus, however, is on where relations become of *ethical* concern. In this sense, the tree and the roof tile, the sea and the sand, are excluded from consideration since no moral agency is involved in these cases. The relations with which I am concerned must involve human beings (either individually or, more problematically, collectively) as moral agents interacting with other moral agents or moral patients (that is, beings that are morally considerable, even if they are not able to act as moral agents—such as animals). Not all relations between moral agents, or between moral agents and moral patients that are not also moral agents, are *actually* of ethical interest, but they all *potentially* are. Someone who adopts a relational approach, then, takes the view that in at least some way, human interactions with and influences on animals are relevant to thinking about moral obligations toward them; that is, something else is morally important along with animals' *capacities*.

Relation and Universalizability

One worry immediately raised by the suggestion that relations as well as capacities are morally important is that such a view fails to take seriously a principle of universalizability, since it suggests that different moral obligations might be owed toward beings with similar morally relevant capacities. The principle of universalizability has different definitions, but I'll take something like Gewirth's (1978, 104–105) interpretation: universalizability is the principle that "whatever is right for one person must be right for another person under similar circumstances."[4] A principle of this kind is frequently regarded as a fundamental feature of ethical theory, and to deny it would certainly be problematic. Singer, for instance (following Hare), defines a form of universalizability as the *very idea* that distinguishes the moral from the nonmoral. Regan (1983, 2001) argues that universalizability is the bedrock of ethical theory. Indeed, his affirmation of it is what underpins his vigorous rejection of certain relational approaches to animal ethics (those advocated within an ethics of care). Both utilitarian and rights theorists are committed to a formal normative principle of universalizability. For those who regard some form of universalizability as the defining feature, or one of the defining features, of ethical theory, a denial of universalizability is a denial that the approach falls within the boundaries of ethics at all.

Of course, not all ethicists take this view.[5] But I am not, anyway, about to deny the importance of a principle of universalizability. Some ethical accounts have difficulty accommodating it, including some forms of moral particularism, certain versions of an ethics of care, and some other highly particular accounts of affective partiality. The care ethicist Nel Noddings appears to adopt such a view, maintaining that "in order to accept the principle [of universalizability], we should have to establish that human predicaments exhibit sufficient sameness, and this we cannot do without abstracting away from concrete situations those qualities that seem to reveal the sameness" (1982, 85). So, she says: "A and B, struggling with a moral decision, are two different persons with different factual histories, different projects and aspirations and different ideals. It may indeed be right, morally right, for A to do X and B to do not-X" (1982, 85–86).

But this kind of relational view is extremely particularist. Other relational accounts—including the one I will develop—are neither necessarily nor essentially affective, nor particularist to this degree. Gewirth's definition, after all, does not require us only to look at capacities in order to identify "similar circumstances." The question his definition raises concerns what constitutes sufficiently similar circumstances. What kinds of contextual details are sufficient to make individuals' situations and relations similar or dissimilar in a way that matters morally? After all, as Sher (2001, 637) argues, all moral theories must take account of *some* contextual details in decision making: "It is hard to see either how all contextual features could ever be irrelevant to a moral decision, or how they could all be relevant to it." For a utilitarian, details of context—relating to the expected consequences of particular actions, for instance—can be highly significant too.

The key question for the kind of relational approach I will develop concerns the *scope* of universalizability: more specifically, under what circumstances a moral agent may universalize from (say) moral patient X to other moral patients that may be thought to be relevantly similar or in relevantly similar situations (say, Y and Z). That is, if A ought to behave in a particular way toward X, in what ways would Y and Z have to be sufficiently X-like that, faced with a similar decision in other respects, A should also behave in the same way toward Y and Z?

Regan, for instance, answers this question by focusing on the *capacities* of moral patients. In Regan's case, all beings that possess the capacities that make them subjects-of-a-life fall into a class that should be treated in the same way. A should not kill either Y (a wild moose) or Z (a domesticated cow) for food, because they are both subjects-of-a-life. The relational account I will adopt, in contrast, takes a much narrower view of what constitutes sufficient similarity across groups for universalizing to be appropriate. Capacities such as sentience are, as we have seen, morally relevant. But so (I will argue) also are particular prior commitments of the agent (the commitment to a companion animal, for instance),[6] and other backward-looking relations, such as whether some agent was causally responsible for creating the current situation of a particular animal. This means that more factors are likely to be morally relevant on this account than in (unmodified) rights theory or utilitarianism. The animal "groups" across which universalizations hold are liable to be narrower and more richly described than the capacity-oriented animal groups across which utilitarians' and rights theorists' universalizations standardly hold. But the adoption of a more contextual, relational approach to animal ethics, therefore, need not deny a principle of universalizability, even though the *scope* of the principle shifts.

MORALLY SIGNIFICANT RELATIONS IN ANIMAL ETHICS

There is a substantial and highly varied body of work already in existence that might be described as adopting a "relational approach" to animal ethics, where although animals' capacities might still be important, aspects of humans' *relations* to animals generate or remove, strengthen or weaken what is morally owed to them. There are, for example, accounts based on *social* relations (Francis and Norman 1978), *kinship* relations (Steiner 2008), *affective* or *sentimental* relations (which can be understood in very different ways), *causal* relations (e.g., Rolston 1988), and *contractual* relations. Although all of these relational accounts are interesting (and I will return to some of them at various points in the book), I will consider only three such accounts here: affective relations, causal relations, and contractual relations. (Actually, there is no clean divide between these three accounts—for instance, affective relations underpin some causal stories—but this rough division is adequate for now). However, I will not give anything like a comprehensive overview of these approaches here. Instead I will tease out of them some useful ideas for thinking about how human-animal relationships might ground different moral responsibilities toward animals in different contexts and relations to humans. Where necessary, I will also explain why I have not adopted these approaches in their entirety, and I will outline in what way I think they might be developed.

Affective/Sentimental Relations

One claim shared by a number of ethical approaches that are, in other ways, very diverse is that moral emotions are highly significant in underpinning moral obligations. The moral emotions—such as care, sympathy, and empathy—are clearly relational and provide the best-known basis for a relational approach to animal ethics. Two rather different forms of such an affective approach should be mentioned here. The first—most prominently manifested in versions of an ethics of care—focuses on relations between humans and individual animals. The second—primarily advocated by J. Baird Callicott—emphasizes the affective basis of community membership, including membership in mixed communities of humans and animals.

Care ethics take many different forms; indeed, "care" itself can be interpreted in very different ways (Curtin 1996, 67).[7] But all forms of care ethics emphasize relations instead of, or as well as, capacities. Characteristic of care ethics is the idea that one's moral obligations are stronger toward those to whom one is emotionally close in the right sorts of ways and correspondingly diminish—or even vanish—where one's emotional responses are weaker or nonexistent.[8] For this reason, as Michael Slote (2007, 11) argues, such positions are "avowedly partialistic."[9] On most accounts of caring, distance and closeness—interpreted in terms of states of care—are of ethical significance.

Care ethics can be used to underpin a claim that there are different moral responsibilities to animals with whom one has different *emotional* relations—such as, for example, wild animals in a nearby forest and one's own companion animal in the home. Wild animals are emotionally distant; people generally do not care for them as particular individuals. On the basis of affective closeness alone, there might be either very weak obligations, or none at all, to assist or provide for such wild animals. However, one is likely to have strong, close emotional relations to one's companion animal, so moral obligations to look after and provide for that particular animal might be correspondingly strong. Plainly, this could provide a basis for something like the laissez-faire view I outlined in the introduction and could ground a distinction between what is owed to wild and to (some) domesticated animals.

It certainly seems plausible that sympathy, empathy, affection, and other sentiments do have a role in human ethical relations with animals, just as they do in ethical relations with people. Living with an animal, for example, can create an emotional relationship of a very particular kind, establishing a practical kind of "trust" or "expectation."[10] Situations of encounter may throw us in contact with animals in states of particular suffering and distress; our sympathy may move us to feel a moral imperative to assist (a situation I will discuss later). However, difficulties arise when moral obligations toward animals—or people—are based on emotions alone (although not all ethics-of-care approaches do this). Emotional closeness to some being does not necessarily give us appropriate moral guidance about how we should treat it (and, even more so, about how to treat those for whom we lack such feelings). This is especially pertinent given both the opportunities we have to actively ensure that we do not encounter or develop emotional relations with some animals and the ease with which we can passively accept social separation from them (as in the case of laboratories or confined animal-feeding operations) in order to prevent ourselves from developing sympathy or empathy. So I will not *base* my general arguments about the role of relations and contexts in animal ethics on these moral emotions. Nonetheless, as I argue in subsequent chapters, these emotions certainly have a place in developing a relational approach.[11]

Ethicists of care also draw attention to other important features of certain human-animal relations that, I will argue, are of moral relevance. In particular, Donovan and Adams (1996) contrast their relational account of animal ethics with rights theories that, they argue, emerge out of the misguided idea that all individuals are best conceived of as rational, autonomous agents, the kinds of beings that "require little support from others, who need only that their space be protected from others' intrusions" (Donovan and Adams 1996, 15). Even were this "autonomous-rights" model to work well for humans, they maintain, it does not work well for animals. "Animals are not equal to humans; domestic animals in particular are dependent for survival on particular humans. We therefore have a situation of unequals and need to develop an ethic that recognizes this fact" (1996, 15). Such unequal relations between humans and animals, they suggest, resemble the unequal relations between carer and cared-for, such as the relations between mother and child or nurse and patient. Caring, with its "relational ontology," they argue, can recognize the power imbalance in the relation between carer and cared-for in a way that the discourse of rights finds hard to accommodate.

Donovan and Adams are surely right in part at least; domesticated animals *are* frequently dependent on and vulnerable to humans in ways that wild animals are not, and dependence is rightly understood to be a relational quality, not a capacity. This idea that dependence and unequal relations might be of moral significance is, I think, highly suggestive. However, moral concerns about responding to dependence and vulnerability could operate in parallel with, rather than in contrast to, negative-rights theory, and they need not rely on the affective aspects of an ethics of care. I will pursue this further in the next couple of chapters.

The second kind of affective relational approach might be called a kind of *affective communitarianism*, where the focus is on membership of relevant affective communities. Mary Midgley is perhaps the originator of this view in animal ethics; describing humans as "bond-forming creatures, not abstract intellects," she suggests that it is natural for humans to feel special bonds toward their own children and for people *in extremis* to rescue those to whom they are close rather than strangers (Midgley 1983, 125). And, she maintains, human beings also have bonds to other human beings, just on the basis of their species membership, an "emotional, natural preference for one's own kind."[12] Humans are bound together, on Midgley's account, in a "community of kin." However, this human-specific community is just one of the communities of which humans are members. Humans also belong to communities comprising members of other species. In these "mixed communities," humans maintain different degrees of closeness with different animals; we recognize their communicative signals, live alongside them, and importantly from an ethical standpoint, we can feel sympathy for them. Such sympathetic community bonds, on Midgley's account, explain why animals matter to us.

J. Baird Callicott (1992) develops this idea, also arguing that humans and animals live in mixed communities, where domesticated animals have relations of different degrees of closeness and intimacy with people. These communities are nested within one another; we might model them as concentric circles. The family is the closest, most intimate circle, and the widespread practice of keeping pets in the home means that even this most intimate of circles is often a mixed human-animal community. Agricultural animals are members of a less intimate mixed community, but one that is still a shared community with humans. Wild animals, however—while still community members—are part of the furthest, least intimate community: the biotic com-

53

munity.[13] Like Midgley, Callicott maintains that humans are bond forming (for which he provides an evolutionary account) and that these bonds of sympathy, trust, and affection form the basis of ethical obligation. These bonds are felt, he argues, toward communities of which we perceive ourselves to be members, and they are felt more strongly toward our more intimate communities and more weakly toward distant ones. So, Callicott maintains, on the grounds of their intimate familial relations, pets "merit treatment not owed either to less intimately related animals, for example to barnyard animals, *or*, for that matter, to less intimately related human beings" (1992, 256). Wild animals, however, are still primarily members of a *biotic* community, and although they should be treated with respect, we owe them nothing *qua* individuals (though we should protect the wild communities of which they are members).

Callicott's account of affective environmental communitarianism—an account that he traces back to Darwin and Hume—has been widely criticized (Lo 2001a; Shrader-Frechette 2002; Welchman 2009), and I will not rely on it as my theoretical basis here. However, his account is important inasmuch as it explores ways of conceptualizing different moral responsibilities toward animals in different contexts, on the basis of our relations with them. Even if we reject the kind of affective grounding on which Callicott bases his community attachment, his work begins to make clear the way in which animals can become entangled in human lives and how such entanglements may create some kinds of special obligations, obligations that do not exist toward animals with whom we lack such entanglements. However, as I will argue, it is the human *causal role* in these entanglements, rather than human affective attachments (at least, as understood either in care ethics or in Callicott's communitarianism) that provides a better focus for thinking about the moral significance of human/animal relations.

Causal Relations

By causal relations, most simply, I refer to cases where human beings have caused, or partially caused, animals to be in the particular situations and contexts in which they are. Put so baldly, this raises a whole host of questions, ones that it will take much of the rest of the book to answer. Temporarily, though, I will put such pertinent questions to one side in order to outline some of the key ways in which existing ideas about causal relations could be central in constructing a relational account of animal ethics.

The idea that causal relations may be of moral significance has been endorsed by some ethicists of care. Michael Slote (2007, 44), for instance, maintains that as a matter of psychological description, our empathetic care is more aroused by distress or harm to which we are causally related—however physically distant it is—than by distress or harm that we allow or merely know about. Now, this is dependent

CAPACITIES, CONTEXTS, AND RELATIONS

on an empirical claim about which Slote might be wrong—perhaps this emotional response is not standard, or perhaps it is not so much to do with empathy as guilt.[14] But the basic claim here—that special moral obligations may be generated by our actions, especially where we have some responsibility for past harms—seems to have bite even without the psychological thesis that Slote endorses. This idea is certainly influential in the human case—for instance, as the underpinning for the view that there can be a special moral obligation to make reparation for harms one has had some responsibility for causing. And—although there is no well-worked-through account in animal ethics of which I am aware—some suggestive ideas about the moral significance of our causal relations to animals do exist. I will note two such ideas here.

I suggested in chapter 2 that the relational view I am developing here might work as an addition to a rights view. Some support for this emerges in Regan's (2004, xl) more recent work. Regan maintains that we accept the idea of *compensatory justice* for past harms to humans. Since justice (on his account) also applies to animals, we can make sense of compensatory justice in their case too. More particularly, compensatory justice should be applied to animals—such as black rhinos—who belong to species that are declining in number on account of past injustices. This is about as far as Regan's existing argument goes. Although it is not entirely clear how the argument might be fleshed out, presumably it is something like this: all animals that are experiencing subjects-of-a-life have negative rights; we should not take their lives, liberty, and so on, but there are no duties—as part of the rights argument, at least—to assist such animals. However, we can, in some circumstances, have special obligations of compensatory justice to assist individual animals when we would not otherwise have such obligations—for instance, where animals are members of species we have endangered. This account, though suggestive, is problematic in its current form (how could "being of the same species" be relevant for Regan when only animals' capacities are of moral significance?).[15] However, it gives us some guidance on first steps toward a backward-looking account of special obligation generated by past harms. I will be developing this further, especially in chapter 6.

Holmes Rolston III provides a more wide-ranging causal account of differing moral obligations toward wild and domesticated animals. He locates animal ethics within a dichotomous view of "nature" and "culture," where "nature" is understood as being "outside human control" (Rolston 2003, 108)—that is, nature consists of processes that are spontaneous, nonreflective, and independent of humans, such as evolution and speciation.[16] Wild animals, in wild nature, exist independently of humans, although they may encounter humans moving through or acting in wild nature. Other animals have been "captured for food, domestication, research or other utility" and "transformed by culture" (1988, 79); they require human action to survive and sometimes to reproduce. In this respect, humans are *causally responsible* for the existence and situation of domesticated animals in ways that they are not responsible for the existence and situation of wild animals. And while Rolston accepts that animal sentience provides a baseline of moral considerability, on his account, it is crucially *context* that gives guidance about one's duties (1988, 61). Duties toward similarly sentient animals vary, in part at least, according to whether previous human actions have had an effect on the animal's current situation.

Wild animals, then, come into being and live independently of humans. While Rolston objects to gratuitously harming them, he also argues against assisting them by, for instance, attempting to reduce their pain. Human intervention, he maintains, both changes wild patterns of evolution and speciation (perhaps preserving individuals with weaknesses that otherwise would not have survived and allowing these weaknesses to be genetically inherited) *and* humanizes wild nature. "Pain in nature is situated, instrumental pain; it is not pointless in the system, even after it becomes no longer in the interests of the pained individual" (1988, 60). Wild-animal pain, then, can be outweighed by other ecological and evolutionary values relating to the systems in which the animals are embedded. Central to this part of Rolston's view is the protection of a valuable, untouched, and wild sphere from human activity. But Rolston also hints at something else that is important here. He also says that humans have "no obligations to help wild animals; we are obliged to leave them alone" (1989, 134). *This* looks rather like the laissez-faire intuition that I identified in the introduction, since it suggests not that obligations to assist wild animals are outweighed by other environmental values but that we *just do not have such obligations*. In fact, Rolston might be saying several things here (which, I will suggest in chapter 4, correspond to two possible versions of the LFI): either that we have *no* obligations to assist wild animals, and we should not interfere with them in other ways, or that we are obliged *not to assist* wild animals (a stronger claim about the *impermissibility* of assistance). This begins to raise some critical questions about whether, when, and why assistance to wild animals is required, permitted, or impermissible.

Rolston's arguments about what is owed, in terms of assistance, to domesticated animals are complicated. But—in summary—he notes two key points. First, domesticated animals are in a different context from wild animals because they are "no longer in the context of natural selection." For this reason, allowing them to suffer is pointless, and suffering should be removed "in as far as it can." But—second—Rolston gestures toward another possible causal argument about what is owed to domesticated animals: "In taking an interest in them humans have assumed a responsibility for them" (1988, 79). The domestication of animals, Rolston suggests, gives humans special, additional responsibilities that they do not have toward wild animals.

Rolston's account of assumed responsibility for domesticated animals should be taken, I think, as an account based on causal relations. Because humans have caused certain animals to exist, and to exist in certain ways, they have assumed responsibility for them. This kind of view is developed in much more detail by those who argue that humans have a special contractual relationship with domesticated animals, a contractual relationship that does not exist with wild animals. This *domesticated-animal contract* can provide an explanation and a moral justification for something like the laissez-faire intuition. And it is this contractual approach that has most influenced the arguments that I will develop in the rest of the book—although I will maintain that the idea of a domesticated-animal contract is, in itself, fundamentally flawed. But the arguments made by those who advocate this view are very important for the position I will develop, both in terms of what these arguments affirm about the meaning of domestication and in the ways in which the arguments go wrong.

Contractual Relations

A variety of attempts has been made to find a place for animals within hypothetical contracts between humans.[17] But I am concerned here with the idea of a *special* contract relationship between human beings and some animals; specifically, domesticated animals. The idea of such a contract has a long history: Larrère and Larrère (2000) trace it to Lucretius, Montaigne, and Dupont de Nemours, and a version is (skeptically) discussed by Salt in the 1890s.[18] More recently, there are accounts in Morris (1990), Budiansky (1992), Callicott (1988), Larrère and Larrère (2000), and Telfer (2000). My engagement with the domesticated-animal contract here will be relatively restricted (but see Palmer 1997; 2010, for a wider-ranging view). Here, I will pick out some important and useful features of the idea of the domesticated-animal contract while arguing that, in its existing form, it faces insuperable difficulties—difficulties that explain why I am not pursuing it as the basis for this relational approach. How did the domesticated-animal contract arise? What is the deal? What about those outside the deal? Can the deal be broken? Answering these questions give us some sense of what kind of human-animal relations are supposed to be involved here.

    How is the domesticated-animal contract supposed to have come about? Most accounts give a backward-looking, historical story about the increasing entanglement of humans with animals. Prior to domestication, on this view, animals had to obtain vital scarce resources and protect their lives against a range of threats—hunger, storms, disease, predators. Domestication marks the transition, a change of state, a crossing from "wild nature" into "human society" or "culture." This historical story, however, varies in terms of how active or passive animals' engagement in the process is thought to be. Budiansky's (1992) account—perhaps the best known—argues that the process was voluntary; animals *chose* to associate with humans to gain the benefits from the association. On his account, animals can be thought of as collaborators in domestication.

This leads to the second question: what are the terms of the deal? Domesticated animals, it is maintained, gain provision of food, predator protection, and medical care. But these come at a price. Animals' physical liberty is restricted, constrained by walls, fences, tethers, stalls, and so on. In addition—and this is of deeper significance—domesticated animals are changed internally. Budiansky (1992, 16) notes: "The defense mechanisms that allow a species to survive on its own, but likewise make it fearful of associating with others, are dropped." More generally, many domesticated animals lack a wide range of capacities once possessed by their wild ancestors, including in some cases the capacity to survive, or at least to flourish, in the wild. This could be seen as a loss of *options* (though this is not an unproblematic description, as I will shortly suggest). It is also worth noting that domesticated animals in different contexts seem to have different "deals" (something that it is difficult for any unitary idea of the domesticated-animal contract to accommodate). The lives of agricultural animals, laboratory animals, and companion animals are marked by rather different costs, and for both agricultural and laboratory animals, being killed is a cost that is normally built into the deal.[19]

On the human side of the deal, it is widely (though not quite universally) accepted that humans gain from domestication in terms of convenient and nutritious food, labor, companionship, and so on.[20] It is less clear what the human costs are, apart from the obvious ones of providing for the domesticated animals. This is itself interesting, since in social-contract theory broadly construed (on which the idea of the domesticated-animal contract is usually modeled) a contract generally requires "equal relative concessions" from all parties. It is unclear that the deal here involves the same kind of cost to people as it does to animals, and certainly, no human social contract creates the kind of internal change in human beings that domestication does in animals.

What about those animals outside the contract, in particular, wild animals? Their situation, as it were, remains unchanged. The domesticated-animal contract just makes special terms with some animals—the domesticated ones—offering them assistance or benefits not available to those animals outside the contract. So, whatever might be thought to be owed to all animals on the basis of their capacities remains the same, but this is added to by the extra benefits conferred by the "deal" of domestication.

Finally: can the contract be broken? Most arguments for a domesticated-animal contract accept that it can be broken, although usually only humans are thought capable of doing so. Budiansky maintains that the contract is broken if domesticated animals are worse off, in terms of shelter or protection, than they would have been in the wild (though this is a problematic comparison, as we will see). Callicott (1992, 256) suggests that the contract is broken if its relational basis is undermined—for instance by the depersonalization and mechanization of domesticated animals in industrial farming. Larrère and Larrère (1990) argue that the contract is broken if humans put domesticated animals back into the wild, treat animals poorly in intensive farms, or fail to protect them from predators (and, conversely, that animals who revert to a wild state have themselves broken the contract).

The domesticated-animal contract, then, does provide both explanation and justification for something like the laissez-faire intuition: we have obligations to assist domesticated animals that we do not have toward wild ones, because of the contractual relationship we have with domesticated animals. However, as I'll argue below, the idea that we have a contract with domesticated animals is fundamentally flawed. But thinking about what such a contract would mean and why it is problematic opens up questions that are central to any relational account of animal ethics.

Why is the contract idea flawed? First, the idea of an "animal contract" is intrinsically problematic. Contracts are normally made between free and equal rational agents who understand and assent to them. This, of course, raises major questions about the idea of a domesticated-animal contract. Taken in any literal, historical sense, animals could not have understood contracts of any kind, let alone the kind of contract involved in domestication. Since they could not understand such a contract, they could not have consented to it, and so there was not, as Pateman (1996, 72) points out, the freedom to refuse to enter it.

But perhaps this is too literalistic; we could think of "consent" in a different way here. It is possible to make practical sense of animal consent: we could say that the cat "consented" to have its fur brushed, meaning that if an animal does not display behavioral objections to a particular human practice when it is free to do so (by struggling, scratching, etc.) it is consenting to the practices—a kind of *tacit* consent. Budiansky's (1992, 24) account of collusive domestication, where "animals chose us as much as we chose them" looks as though it would fit the idea of tacit consent well. Could the domesticated-animal contract be seen as one to which animals tacitly consented?

An account of tacit consent would certainly seem to require a collusive historical process such as Budiansky's. But Budiansky's account is contested and tendentious (as Cassidy 2007 makes clear). Accounts of how domestication came about vary, some focusing on human responses to environmental change, some on protecting crops, some on the production of special foodstuffs for feasts, some on a human penchant for taming animals as pets, and some on animal scavenging.[21] It is likely that different historical instances of domestication (such as the domestication of scavengers and grazers) and the domestication of different species happened in diverse ways.[22] Whatever immediate interactions animals might have "consented" to (petting, being fed, etc.), they could not, after all, realistically be construed as tacitly consenting to the process of domestication. The dramatic, generational changes involved could not be reasonably thought to be tacitly consented to by eating a crust of bread thrown in a doorway.

Alternatively perhaps—rather than looking back at the history of domestication—we should instead think about a *hypothetical* contract: what it is reasonable to think that animals *would* give consent to, were they able (Narveson 1983, 49). For hypothetical consent to be plausible, we would have to believe that domestication is a good deal for animals; they could not be supposed, hypothetically, to agree to a contract in which they would lose out. This leads us to ask whether animals have really gained from domestication and whether the benefits have outweighed the costs. Historians of domestication here disagree: Zeuner (1963, 37) and Harris (1989) describe domestication as symbiotic—Zeuner argues that both partners "gain without suffering." Clutton-Brock (1994, 27), on the other hand, argues that domestication works to human, not animal, benefit.

There is one sense in which domestication appears to benefit animals—at least some domesticated animals are members of the most dominant breeds and species on earth. Budiansky notes that, from an evolutionary, species-oriented perspective, domestication was an excellent strategy. But—aside from the difficulty of making sense of the idea that a species as a whole could be described as better or worse off at all (see Norton 1987, 171)—contracts, at least in the social-contract tradition that the domesticated-animal contract follows—are made by *individuals*. We might be able to stretch this to include corporations or nations—but "breeds" and "species" are quite different kinds of entities. What lies at the heart of the issue here is whether some animal individual would, hypothetically, agree to the deal that domestication offers. But even if we could think of domestication as one single "deal," this question is deeply and importantly problematic for two main reasons.

First, if we take domestication to be a contract, it is a peculiarly dramatic one. A large group of the contractors (i.e., all the animal contractors) are, as it were, brought into existence by the contract. And domestication shapes their bodies, temperaments, and capacities and (unlike contracts between humans) changes their natures. This has several implications. The domesticated-animal contract is in some senses irreversible. Even if animals colluded in their own domestication, this could only apply to the first few generations of animals. Since domestication often includes the loss both of some capacities to resist (by fight or flight) as well as the loss (to varying degrees) of the capacity to flourish (by foraging, hunting, scavenging, and resisting disease) independently of human beings, once entering into the domesticated-animal contract, there is no obvious way out for many animals—even if those with whom the contract is made subsequently systematically breach its terms. The mountain sheep could graze elsewhere if humans turned hostile—but that is not an option for Dolly, the cloned sheep. And it is indeed advantageous for humans to later break the contract (or some parts of it), because all and only those who could punish the contract breakers (that is, humans) have something to gain from the contract being broken, and because someone who broke an animal contract would not be regarded by other humans as someone with a disposition to break contracts with other humans (see Gauthier 1986, 162)—and animals are not able to reflect on humans' contractual dispositions at all. Even a hypothetical animal contract means that animals are buying into a contract from which they cannot individually ever escape. Domestication forecloses alternative ways of life. Even recent attempts at de-domestication depend on human, not animal, agency: those animals involved are not free either to stay in or to opt out of the contract.

Second, there is yet a further level of complication here. If domestication is a contract, then domesticated animals are products of that contract. This seems to raise a kind of *nonidentity* problem. No currently existing domesticated animal, on the contract account, would have existed without the contract. There would instead (perhaps) have been an entirely different population of wild animals. So no particular domesticated animal that exists can be thought of as having been made worse-off because of the contract, since without the contract it would not have existed at all. It would be strange to ask of any particular domesticated animal—say Daisy the cow—whether domestication is something that, hypothetically, she would have agreed to. Daisy cannot be conceived of outside the context of domestication, for this is just what makes Daisy the being that she is. There is no possible "wild" or "nondomesticated" Daisy. To say that existing domesticated animals have given hypothetical (or, indeed, tacit) consent to the contract is rather as if, by being born, it were to be said that I had given tacit consent to being a human being. But, of course, I could not have existed as anything else.

These questions about a domestic-animal contract highlight the peculiar and under-explored nature of animal domestication. Domesticated animals have capacities and natures often deliberately shaped by their interactions with humans. They have, in this sense, human relations built into their very being. The language of contract fits awkwardly here, because contracts are commonly things that we can agree to, even if the agreement is tacit, and from which we normally have some kind of exit. But no animal can agree to or exit from domestication; the deep, fundamental ways in which domestication constructs beings makes domestication stand out from any standard understanding of a contract. Domestication is not, in any straightforward sense, a contract entered by free, equal, and rational beings to secure their own interests. It is not obviously something that animals would—or could—give tacit or hypothetical consent to, nor is it even clear that such an idea makes sense. In addition, there is a further worry that (as Pateman 1988 argues with respect to the "sexual contract" and Mills 1997 with respect to the "racial contract") the language of contract *could* serve as a blind for a power relation of domination, about which I will say more in chapter 7.[23] In implying free consent and animal benefit, the language

61

of contract might be used to legitimate a relationship of increasing human control, including not only the labor and lives of domesticated animals but also their genetic fabric.

For all these reasons, I will not develop a contractarian relational approach in this book, although this idea is highly suggestive. Indeed, it includes key insights on which I will build in chapter 4. In particular, it takes as foundational the idea that domestication fundamentally changes humans' ethical responsibilities toward the animals concerned and that this change entails additional obligations to benefit or assist domesticated animals in particular kinds of ways. I will also argue for something like this. But rather than constructing arguments based on contractual claims, I will instead develop arguments drawing on the causal relations and ideas of dependence that I sketched earlier in this chapter. I will also pursue questions, raised here by the domesticated-animal contract, about what domestication *means* and what its role in animal ethics is.

4

Wildness, Domestication, and the Laissez-faire Intuition

This chapter begins a more systematic attempt to develop a relational approach to animal ethics. It assumes the account of animal well-being and what it is to harm and assist animals that I outlined in chapter 1. It assists in clarifying how the relational approach I am developing might relate to the capacity-oriented accounts in chapter 2, and begins to flesh out support for at least some of the important relational ideas in chapter 3. The main purpose of this chapter is to look closely at what I called, in the introduction, the laissez-faire intuition (LFI)—that is, roughly, the idea that, while we have obligations to assist and care for domesticated animals, we have no such obligations toward animals in the wild. To make headway with the LFI, though, I first need to give a more careful account of what is meant by "wild" and "domesticated." In fact, I will suggest that a wide range of human-animal relations needs to be considered here; the LFI is the expression of just one way in which human relations to animals may be ethically relevant. However, as I also noted in the introduction, the LFI itself is not entirely straightforward. I will consider different possible forms of the LFI here, discuss how these forms might relate to different ethical theories, and then think through what an endorsement of those different forms might mean.

WILDNESS AND DOMESTICATION

The use of the terms "wildness" and "domestication" in the context of animals is by no means simple; the terms can be used in different senses to emphasize different things.[1]

Wildness

Wildness is used, both in the animal context and elsewhere, in several importantly different ways. Hettinger and Throop's (1999, 12) claim that "something is wild in a certain respect to the extent that it is not humanized in that respect" seems broadly right. But there are (at least) three different senses in which animals can be "not humanized," senses best understood by thinking about different possible *negations* of the relevant senses of wildness. Further, wildness (in each sense) should be thought of as constituting the end of a spectrum, not as one of a dualistic pair; it is possible to be more or less wild in all these senses.

Constitutive wildness: where wildness is understood on a wild/domesticated spectrum. I will say more about this below, since domestication is itself such a contested term.

Locational wildness: here wildness refers to an uncultivated place and is understood on a wild–developed spectrum (or, perhaps, a wild–urban spectrum—the distinctions here are inevitably fuzzy). Wildness is about *place*. Animals at the wildest end of this spectrum live in environments on which humans have had relatively little effect, such as wilderness; the negation of wildness in this sense would be an animal that lives around human settlements or in a human home.[2]

Dispositional/Behavioral wildness: Here wildness is understood on a wild–tame spectrum. This use of wildness refers to animals' dispositions and behavior toward some or all human beings. A tame animal shows little fear of humans (interpreted behaviorally, primarily in terms of flight) nor aggression toward humans in (nonexceptional) circumstances of encounter. (By nonexceptional, I mean encounters that are not immediately and obviously threatening to the animal; humans and animals alike, of course, may be fearful or aggressive in strongly threatening situations.) "Tamed" is sometimes more specifically taken to mean a reduction in fearful or aggressive behavior after human intentional action to achieve this end; I take this as a subset of "tame" more broadly understood. Wild animals, on this account, are animals that are fearful or aggressive around humans: they are dispositionally and behaviorally wild. This sense of wildness I will set to one side here—not least because humans can create animals that might be thought of as wild in this sense (aggressive dogs, for instance), which makes this aspect of "wildness" particularly complicated.

Of course, it is possible—indeed, likely—for an animal to be wild in all of these ways. A constitutively wild animal may well live in a relatively undeveloped area and behave in either fearful or aggressive ways toward human beings. However, the three do not necessarily coincide. An urban squirrel is usually thought to be constitutively wild but not locationally wild, and it may not be behaviorally very wild either. And even these senses of wildness—while more finely grained than is usually made explicit in work in animal and environmental ethics—poorly accommodate some cases. For instance, there are animal populations that are not selectively bred, but human activities may have substantially affected individual animals' genetic make-up (for instance, animal populations where individuals with particular characteristics have been systematically hunted or culled by humans).[3] These animals are in one sense constitutively wild—since they have not been selectively bred—but nonetheless their genetic make-up has at least been affected by human activity. Further, more generally, it may be argued that no animals are, any longer, locationally wild in a strong sense, since there are no longer any wild locations (an implication of McKibben's 1989 argument that Nature has ended).[4] So, for instance, if—as is likely—humans have influenced global climate, then there are no locations on Earth (except, just possibly, some deep parts of the oceans) unaffected by human activity. I will consider the practical question of all-pervasive human environmental effects in chapter 8.

Some idea of wildness, usually understood in a fairly imprecise sense, underpins any kind of intuition about differential human obligations to wild and domesticated animals. And the term is useful in signifying a cluster of characteristics. So I will continue to work with an idea of wildness in the context of the LFI, to discuss an in-principle case of an animal that is wild in both the locational and constitutive senses. When I refer to "wild animals" from now on, this "full wildness" is what I will have in mind. Even if (implausibly) no animals meet this description of being fully wild, considering this in-principle case will help us think about animals in "less-wild" relations with humans.

Domestication

Most frequently the term "domesticated animal" is used to mean something like Clutton-Brock's (1989, 21) definition "bred in captivity . . . in a human community that maintains complete mastery over its breeding, organization of territory and food supply." But even this definition can be parsed in different ways, since some accounts emphasize the economic benefits of human control over animal lives, while others focus on the biological effects of human control over breeding. Yet other accounts of domestication, in contrast, emphasize animals' property status. Russell (2007, 36), for instance, maintains that "the most crucial thing about animal domestication is that 'wild' animals are converted to property." Finally, other interpretations of domestication focus on cooperation and exchange, taking domestic animals to include (for instance) urban sparrows or squirrels—a sense that fits the original meaning of the term "domestication" as "becoming accustomed to the household" (see Cassidy 2007, 3). And these interpretations of domestication, of course, correspondingly suggest different interpretations of wildness: for instance, as those animals from whom humans do not benefit economically, those that do not cooperate with people, or those that are not property, but I will not pursue these interpretations here, since they are further away from our more standard uses of the term.

All these different kinds of relations are important. However, I will generally use the term domestication for a subset of them, a subset close to Clutton-Brock's definition. I will take "domestication" to refer to animals intentionally controlled by humans with respect to breeding, in particular by deliberate selective breeding, and I will work within the context of relatively recent human activities (given the disputed history of domestication and animals' roles in it). This means that I will not include as domesticated either behaviorally tamed animals whose breeding is not selectively controlled nor animals that have co-evolved alongside people, without any deliberate human intervention, but that live successfully in human communities (such as the grey squirrel). I will also exclude the more difficult case of animals that have become, due to human intervention (in particular, confinement), genetically isolated from wild populations, even though their breeding has not been deliberately controlled by humans.[5] Of course, this definition is somewhat arbitrary, but not very much hangs on it. Other human-animal relations are, of course, important to the analysis here. This merely serves to clarify how I will be using the term.

Domesticated animals—using the sense of domestication adopted above—tend to display specific physiological characteristics, in particular a decline in body size from the bodies of their wild ancestors, accompanied by smaller cranial capacities and smaller teeth. It is sometimes argued that domesticated animals are characteristically neotonous—displaying the persistence of youthful characteristics into adulthood. Of course, particular domesticated animal species have, in addition, been bred by humans in ways that exaggerate or diminish a variety of other characteristics (fattiness, the possession of horns, muscle, appearance of fur, etc.). And sometimes selective breeding can produce unintended effects: for instance, the deliberate breeding for large breast size in turkeys had the unintended effect of making it impossible for turkeys to copulate normally (Price 1999, 253). In chapter 5, I will suggest that some of these changes brought about by domestication are of moral relevance.[6]

Wildness and domestication, understood as I have outlined above, are not the only human-animal relations in which I am interested here, however. As Russell (2007, 30) argues, it is probably better to think of a spectrum of different kinds of relationships. Many of the relations between humans and animals involve animals that are neither "fully wild" nor domesticated. Roughly, we could say that these animals fall in some sense into a "contact zone."[7] Such animals are not much discussed in animal-ethics literature, even though they may be the animals that we most frequently encounter. And there is no widespread agreement on terminology to describe animals that live in the contact zone. Some of them—in particular, the ones that live around human settlements but that are not domesticated—may be helpfully described using the language of mutualism, commensalism, and contramensalism. Taking humans as one "party" in these relations, mutualism refers to situations where both parties (in this case, humans and other animals) benefit from the association, commensalism when one party (in this case, usually the animal) benefits while the effects on the other party (here, humans) are neutral, and contramensalism, unsurprisingly, occurs where one party (in this case, the animal) benefits at the expense of the human (see Leach 2007, 89). Of course, it is not possible to say that one species—or even, on occasion, one individual—always remains securely in one of these associations. After all, a garden squirrel might have a mutualist relation with a small child, a commensal relation with the child's parents, and a contramensal relation with the neighbor who cultivates delicate garden bulbs. Some species, though, are generally thought to occupy one role; nondomesticated rats are almost always thought of as contramensals, although there are exceptions even to this, as in some Indian temples.[8]

These do not, of course, exhaust the kinds of relations humans may have with animals. For example, either through accidental or purposive human agency, animal populations have become established outside the habitat in which they were ecologically located. Such exotic animals may be constitutively wild, but they clearly have a historic relationship to humans. Feral animals may have, at some time, been bred by humans and may still be dependent on them as scavengers; most carry a human-generated story of abandonment or transposition that explains their current location. Animals kept in captivity—in zoos, for instance—have been isolated by humans from wild populations; they are dependent on humans insofar as they are confined, and this may be a permanent state if survival behavior needs to be learned in habitat. In all these cases—ferality, captivity, displacement, domestication—humans are tied up in animals' lives.

FORMS OF THE LFI

So far, I have provided only a bare outline of what I have called the LFI. Now I want to think more closely about the LFI and, in particular, to identify some different possible forms it might take. To do this, some further thought about "positive" and "negative" duties in the context of harm and assistance is needed.

What's meant by "positive" and "negative" duties is much debated (a debate similar to that about positive and negative rights, discussed in chapter 2). Most simply, negative duties are usually taken to mean duties not to act, that is to abstain from certain kinds of actions (usually interventions or interferences with others). Positive duties, on the other hand, are usually taken to be duties to act in particular kinds of ways, standardly to aid or to assist others.[9] There are a number of complicated philosophical problems about the uses of these terms (see, for instance, Scheffler

67

1994; Kamm 2007; Goodin 1985). However, I will still use them, although with some reservations in mind (some of the reasons for the difficulties that emerge here will become clearer later).

What does the LFI imply about negative and positive duties? In the simplest version, which I outlined in the introduction, the critical concern was with the presence or absence of positive duties to aid or assist. It is in these that I am particularly interested, but I will first say something briefly about negative duties. If someone accepts that animals have moral status and that we can have direct duties toward them, then the most obvious duty that follows is not to harm. All the capacity-oriented views considered in chapter 2 share this view, though they disagree in terms of what constitutes a harm and whether benefits to people or to larger numbers of animals could justify outweighing any particular harm. And even in relation to the LFI, the duty not to harm is capacity oriented. It applies to all animals that have the capacity to be harmed, whether wild or domesticated. To accommodate differences with respect to when, if ever, such negative duties can be outweighed (for I do not need to adjudicate between these views here), I will say, for now, that all versions of the LFI hold that there is at least a prima facie duty not to harm animals in any context.[10]

What is peculiar to the LFI concerns additional *positive* duties to assist. Here, as noted in the introduction, the LFI could have several possible and importantly different variations. It may be taken to mean that we have duties *not* to assist wild animals—that is, assistance is *impermissible* (as Rolston's view seemed to suggest); it may entail not having positive duties to assist wild animals, though assistance is nonetheless (sometimes or always) *permissible*; or it may mean that there are *no general presumptive* duties to assist wild animals, but that special obligations to do so could be generated in some (special and specified) circumstances. All these are compatible with the LFI in its most general sense, but are rather different in form. These alternatives can be summarized more clearly as follows:

A. One should (prima facie) neither harm nor assist wild animals; rather, one should not interfere with them at all. Call this Strong LFI.

B. One should (prima facie) not harm wild animals and there is no presumptive duty to assist them—but it may be (sometimes or always) permissible to assist. Call this Weak LFI.

C. One should (prima facie) not harm wild animals and there is no presumptive duty to assist them, though assistance is (sometimes or always) permissible. But positive duties to assist may be generated in some circumstances. The most plausible version of this is the No-contact LFI; this will be explained later.

And A, B, and C are all conjoined with the view that there are at least some duties to assist domesticated animals that do not apply in the wild case (except for some special cases falling under the No-contact LFI).

What is distinctive about all the forms of the LFI is that they deviate from capacity-oriented views in their position on assistance. For they affirm that while duties not to harm are capacity oriented, duties to assist derive from some kind of relation in which animals stand to humans (and hence vary according to these relations). This, though, depends on two distinctions, both of which might be regarded as problematic. First, a distinction is being made between animals who have similar capacities on account of their relations to humans, and second, a distinction is implied between harming and assisting (or, more accurately, between harming and failing to assist). Anyone who wishes to defend a reasoned underpinning for the LFI will have to provide support for both these distinctions. I will delay an argument in favor of the first distinction until chapter 5 and spend the rest of this chapter thinking about the second distinction, that between harming and not assisting.

While most rights views, including Regan's and Francione's, do make a distinction between negative/positive rights and thus between harming and failing to assist, for consequentialists, a distinction between harming and failing to assist when one could is famously troublesome. So, how might a consequentialist respond to the LFI? One likely argument runs like this: what grounds are there for distinguishing between *causing* an animal *x* amount of pain (i.e., harming it) and allowing *x* amount of pain to continue if one could relieve it (i.e., failing to assist)? Other things being equal, if it is permissible to allow *x* amount of pain when one could relieve it, then surely it is permissible to cause it. If it is not permissible to cause it, then surely one is required (not just permitted) to relieve it if one can. After all, it is the pain that matters, not its cause; the focus is on *what happens* rather than on *who does what*.[11] So for a consequentialist, at least, the LFI appears to fail.

Consequentialism—in forms such as utilitarianism, for instance—is characterized by this focus on *what happens*, whether one brings what happens about or fails to prevent it. Many forms of consequentialism endorse an aim at achieving the best outcome or states of affairs, even though different versions may differ about what "best" may be taken to mean and whether one should go about reaching the best consequences in direct or indirect ways (see Kamm 2007, 17).[12] However, the aim at best outcomes seems to be explicitly denied by all forms of the LFI. It might be that a better state of affairs (in terms of suffering, for instance) would be brought about in the world if we assisted wild animals. But nonetheless, according to the LFI it is either not *required* that we assist (Weak/No-contact LFI) or it is not *permitted* that we assist (Strong LFI). So, according to the LFI, one is *not* always required to bring about the best state of affairs in the world, impersonally considered. This appears nonconsequentialist.[13] In order to maintain any form of the LFI, then, it seems one must deny the basic premise of consequentialism.

There are, however, some variant forms of consequentialism that might, at first sight, provide an underpinning for some forms of the LFI. Alternatively, there are other more fundamentally nonconsequentialist positions that could underpin the LFI. I'll consider both briefly here.

Consequentialism and the LFI

To make sense of the possible theoretical issues here, I need to outline some of the characteristic distinctions between consequentialism and deontology that have featured in recent debates and then use these distinctions to explain why it might be thought that some form of consequentialism could underpin the LFI. These distinctions may at first sight appear arcane, but they are extremely useful in better understanding what different forms of the LFI might mean.

The forms of consequentialism I have considered in this book—Singer's utilitarianism, for instance—have been what are sometimes called *agent neutral*.[14] That is—taking a fairly simple form of act utilitarianism as an example—in deciding what to do, an agent should aim at bringing about the best state of affairs in the world, impersonally considered. The decision should not be swayed by the agent's particular situation; the impersonal ranking of outcomes should not vary from person to person. Most forms of deontology, in contrast, maintain—for a variety of different reasons—that an agent is sometimes required not to do something that will bring about the best consequences, impersonally considered. For instance, from many deontological positions, an agent is required not to kill one person, even to save five from being killed by others.[15] Such constraints on the agent are often called agent-centered or agent-relative restrictions. There is something about the position of the agent that means, for instance, that he or she should not violate some restriction—such as not to kill—even if by doing so, he or she could prevent a larger number of similar violations and thus bring about a better state of affairs over all. That a better state of affairs would ensue is not enough, for advocates of agent-relative restrictions, to justify an agent in violating those restrictions (though nonabsolutists will argue that there is at least some point—perhaps killing one to save a thousand, or a million, from being killed—where what will happen is sufficiently terrible to justify violating the restriction). The existence of agent-centered restrictions of varying strengths is at least part of what is central to distinguishing deontology from consequentialism.

Agent-relative or agent-centered *prerogatives* or *permissions*, on the other hand, depart from consequentialism in a different way. They respond to the worry that consequentialism turns individuals into constant optimizers, always required to think about their own projects from an agent-neutral, impersonal point of view and, consequently, having to abandon their own projects and commitments where this is necessary to create best states of affairs. This, Scheffler (1994) argues, fails to respect the independence of our own personal point of view. We all care about our own personal projects and commitments far more than can be represented by just factoring them into what will produce the best state of affairs. And, Scheffler maintains, those independent, personal reasons are important in their own right. So, he suggests, we should accept agent-centered prerogatives, where individuals are allowed to deviate from "pure" consequentialism by weighing their own personal concerns more heavily than would be permitted from an impersonal point of view (though this does not become egoism: at some point, impersonal concerns can still outweigh the personal ones). Thus, agents are not required always to aim at producing the best possible states of affairs, though they are still free to do so if they wish.

While arguing in favor of agent-centered prerogatives, Scheffler rejects the idea of agent-centered restrictions. These, he suggests, are paradoxical. How can it be rational to say that, on an agent-centered account, one should not violate a restriction, when doing so would prevent the violation of a larger number of exactly similar restrictions? If all the violations are the same (equal harm is caused by an agent to a similar victim), how can it be rational to prefer, say, six such violations to one violation, where one violation can prevent six (even though one would have to commit the one violation oneself)? And the arguments for agent-centered prerogatives do not support such restrictions, for restrictions actually constrain agents' independence, by requiring them not to bring about best states of affairs (by, for instance, killing one to save five from being killed) on occasions where someone may decide that this is the best course of action.

Obscure as they may seem, these distinctions are very useful in thinking about the LFI. First, they allow us to distinguish the Strong LFI from the other forms of the LFI. The Strong LFI incorporates a *restriction* on assisting wild animals not present in the other forms; assistance is not permitted on the Strong LFI, even if this would bring about the best consequences, impersonally considered. The Weak LFI and the No-contact LFI might be read in terms of prerogatives, rather than restrictions; that is, we are neither forbidden from assisting wild animals, nor are we required to assist them (except in some specified cases in the No-contact LFI), even if doing so would bring about the best consequences. The agent may exercise his or her own prerogative over whether, and when, to assist in the case of wild animals.

Two things emerge from this. In order to provide grounds for the Strong LFI, some argument would need to be made for a *restriction* against assisting wild animals, even where doing so would create better consequences than not doing so. This restriction would, I think, need to rely on an idea—similar to Rolston's—about non-interference in "wild" environments, an argument that is problematic, as I will suggest later. The second issue here is whether an argument about prerogatives could be used to provide some kind of consequentialist support for the other forms of the LFI, since these forms imply that with respect to assisting wild animals, agents are not required to bring about the best outcomes, although they are permitted to do so if they so desire. I will now look at this possibility a bit more closely.

The Possible Role of Agent-Centered Prerogatives

The most obvious way of thinking about the role of agent-centered prerogatives would be as follows. Individuals have their own "ground projects," as Bernard Williams (1973, 116) calls them: their own families, friends, interests, time commitments, and hobbies. These are of central importance to their lives. However, consequentialists are required only to pursue these ground projects inasmuch—Scheffler says "in strict proportion to"—as they matter from an impersonal perspective. Otherwise, individuals fail to bring about as good states of affairs as they could. Assisting wild animals, let us suppose, could be pretty demanding. If we took seriously wild-animal suffering, perhaps we would be required to spend our weekends heading out into the hills to find wounded animals to help; we would need to give financial support to charities whose aim it was to divert animals from forest fires, search the sides of freeways for animals injured by traffic, or vaccinate wild animals against diseases. We would have to pursue our own ground projects "in strict proportion" not only to the demands other human projects and states placed upon us but also to the state of the wild-animal world. Blizzards, floods, droughts, and at least some predation—all would constantly call upon us for assistance, unless a plausible argument could be made that it would bring about better consequences if sentient wild animals suffered and died without our assistance.

One reading of the Weak LFI is that these strong requirements to assist fail to do justice to the way in which the ground projects human individuals have matter to them. These projects are not only important to them from an impersonal point of view; they are independently important, based on their own hopes, desires, commitments, and so on. So, some form of an agent-centered prerogative should exist, meaning that agents are permitted to weigh their own projects more heavily than would be permitted from an impersonal point of view. And since assisting wild animals is likely to be demanding, perhaps this is a case where assisting them could almost always be outweighed by one's own projects. Wild animals that need assistance may be far away, finding them is likely to be time consuming, and assisting them may be difficult and expensive. To be required to do so would constantly interfere with an agent's commitments. So, on this account, agent-centered prerogatives provide both an explanation and a justification for at least the Weak LFI. The explanation why the intuition that there is no requirement to assist wild animals seems so widespread is because the requirement is extremely demanding. And the justification is that such highly demanding requirements fail to respect the independence of our personal point of view. Of course, someone who took this view might say that if rescuing wild animals is one of our personal projects in life, then we are permitted to do so. But for those of us who have other ground projects, we have the prerogative to pursue those and not constantly be at the call of suffering in nature.

Now, it is possible that some version of this view could be made to work here, and I do not want to rule out a consequentialist grounding of this kind for the LFI. But there are difficulties here, some of which are more easily overcome than others. If we look more closely at the Weak LFI, we find a combination of requirements, prerogatives, and restrictions. There are restrictions on harming all animals, prerogatives not to assist in the wild case, and requirements to assist in domesticated cases. This fits uncomfortably in several respects with a view such as Scheffler's, which denies that a sound case can be made for *any* restrictions. And while his view does not eliminate the possibility of requirements (since there may be some actions that generate such good states of affairs that—even having weighted our own projects more heavily—we are still required to do them) the existence of prerogatives at least reduces our requirements. And assisting domesticated animals is not necessarily a requirement of consequentialism, even before thinking about the tempering effect of introducing agent-centered prerogatives.

Indeed, this point leads to another. What is key to the worries about standard forms of consequentialism from this perspective is the way in which such consequentialism fails properly to acknowledge the independence of the agent's point of view, and bringing about consequentialist goals constantly interferes with the agent's projects and concerns. From a revised consequentialist perspective—the form we are looking at here—in the case of assisting animals, if assistance were difficult and would interfere substantially with an agent's projects, this would outweigh any requirement to assist. It is only where assistance is relatively easy, does not interfere with the agent's ground projects, and where the beneficial outcome is great that the agent should assist. But this is not obviously going to map onto the LFI and other positions that I am arguing for here—for instance, with respect to wildness and domesticity—very easily. Wildness is, after all, orthogonal to easiness of assistance. While it is often going to be the case that assisting wild animals will be more challenging than assisting domesticated ones, it is easy enough to think of counterexamples where assisting wild animals would be easy but assisting domesticated animals would interfere with one's ground projects. So it is not clear that in this respect (as well as that concerning the existence of restrictions) the "hybrid theory," as Scheffler calls it, relates all that well to the Weak LFI (or any other form of the LFI).

There are ways of tweaking the Weak LFI to make it seem more compatible with some form of consequentialism. What I have called a "restriction not to harm" could just instead be seen as a general "rule of thumb" acceptable to consequentialists as well as deontologists (after all, harming usually does generate worse states of affairs). And the Weak LFI could be thought of as a very fuzzy intuition not so much about wildness and domestication but really about the disruptive human effort that might need to be engaged in order to assist animals, combined with the thought that it is easier to assist in the domestic case than the wild case. However, even if this works as an explanation, it seems unsatisfactory as a justification. A more complicated version of a hybrid view, one involving special obligations, might possibly help here, but I am not going to pursue this further.[16] Instead, I will turn to alternative deontological ways of thinking about justifying the LFI.

Distinguishing Between Harming and Not Assisting

Consequentialism, as we have seen, focuses on producing (and allowing) best outcomes and states of affairs. That is, the focus is on what happens, rather than how things came about and who is responsible for them. Scheffler (and others) adopt a form of consequentialism that allows agents to weigh their personal concerns more heavily. Deontologists—while except in the most absolutist cases still paying some attention to outcomes—focus on other features that relate to the moral agent. For most deontological views, it is morally relevant that it is the particular agent (for instance, *me*) that acts, since one is peculiarly responsible for what one does, in a way one is not for what one fails to prevent (a distinction not available to consequentialists). For a consequentialist, the agent's permitting x amount of wild-animal suffering when he or she could have relieved it is indistinguishable from the agent's causing x amount of suffering (provided that, of course, the effort of going to the trouble of causing the suffering does not make a difference to the calculated outcome).[17] Deontologists, in contrast, generally argue (though for a variety of reasons) that harming another is prima facie wrong—but they distinguish this from a failure to assist, even where assistance may bring about the best state of affairs.[18] Of course, most deontologists do argue that assistance is required in some cases, but the relationship of the agent to situations that are not of her own making differs from the relationship of the agent to situations that she herself had a hand in creating, in particular where the agent intended such situations.

This kind of approach looks to be a more plausible underpinning for the LFI than at least standard forms of consequentialism. It has a clearer place for restrictions on actions, it can make distinctions between harming and failing to assist, and (as we will see later) it may have an important place for certain special obligations that are also difficult to accommodate in many forms of consequentialism.

But why might there be a distinction between our responsibilities not to harm and those to assist? Consequentialists begin by looking at *what happens*. But this is not the only place to look. Frances Kamm (2007, 386), for example, makes the following suggestion: "In standard cases in which we harm someone, we deprive her of something she would have had independently of our aid." To deprive someone of something she would otherwise have had, Kamm suggests, is to impose on the person we harm. If we had done nothing, the person would have been better off. Our action has made them worse off by taking away some good of which they were already in possession, a good that they had independently of us and unrelated to us. We have, on deontological accounts, at least prima facie duties not to carry out these kinds of deprivations. Assistance, on the other hand, makes someone better off; indeed, to assist is an imposition on the agent rather than on the person being assisted (assuming that we are not wholly or partly responsible for their situation).[19] If we did nothing, that is, if we failed to aid, a person would remain in the same situation as they were in originally (*ex hypothesi*) independently of us and unrelated to us.[20] In harming, we change someone's situation for the worse. In failing to aid, we just do not change it for the better; we merely fail to improve on what the person (or, for the purposes of this book, the animal) would have independently of us. If one only looks at the "happenings," these two situations look the same. But if we look at other factors—such as the responsibility of the agent—then the distinction between harming and not assisting seems much clearer. Consequentialism normally entails negative responsibility, where one is responsible not only for what one actually does but also for what one fails to prevent. Of course, this in itself is problematic in terms of the hugely expanded scope of moral responsibility it seems to imply. And without denying that there are special cases of negligence (which I will consider later), it seems reasonable to reject such a strong idea of negative responsibility.

This is, of course, a complex and difficult area. A number of supplementary arguments can be made to support an agent-centered view. Nagel (1986), for instance, argues that deliberately to harm is to be personally causally responsible for inflicting pain on another, pain that would not otherwise be brought about; this is morally worse, with respect to the agent, than not relieving pain that exists independently of the agent, where the agent had no causal role in the creation of the pain.[21] I am going to assume that these kinds of arguments about the moral distinction between actively harming and not assisting are at least plausible and turn to think about how this kind of view might relate to the versions of the LFI.

Upholding a distinction between harming and not assisting of this kind might suggest that, while we have negative duties not to harm, we do not have any positive duties to assist, unless some kind of special relationship holds between us and relevant others that generates such duties. A second possibility is that we have duties both not to harm and to assist, but that the duties not to harm are stronger than, and (normally) take priority over, weaker ones to assist.[22] All forms of the LFI fit more comfortably with the former position. I will consider how this might work out in subsequent chapters.

The LFI and the Actions of Other Moral Agents

One further point should be addressed here before moving on: is there, on any form of the LFI, any duty to prevent *other* moral agents either from harming or (on the Strong LFI) assisting wild animals? After all, although a wild animal may be threatened by "natural forces" (storms, predators, floods), it may also be threatened by the actions of other moral agents. This question is important to negative-rights theorists such as Francione or Regan. As we have seen, Regan argued that assistance is owed to a rightsholder if his or her rights are being violated by a moral agent, on the basis of that right, even if one is not oneself the violator. If rights should be protected, then they should be protected from other moral agents' actions. Since I have suggested that the relational view I am developing is at least compatible with this kind of negative-rights view, then it would seem as though any form of the LFI that I might endorse should not rule out assistance to wild animals in the case of harms committed by other moral agents.

Accepting this again separates the Strong LFI from the Weak/No-contact forms of the LFI. The Strong LFI rules out assistance even in the case of harmful actions by other moral agents. The duty generated by the Strong LFI is *not to assist* rather than to protect rights. The Weak LFI and the No-contact LFI, however, at least permit assistance; the No-contact LFI requiring it in some special cases—and, as I will argue, these cases may include acting in response to some or all instances of harmful actions by other moral agents.

For the time being, I will keep all three versions of the LFI in play, although I have already suggested significant problems with the Strong LFI (these three versions are likely not exhaustive of possible versions of the LFI, but they are all I will consider here). In chapter 5, I will indicate which form of the LFI I consider to have the most plausible underpinning and provide some reasons for thinking so. Of course, there are difficulties with the reasons that could underpin all the versions of the LFI. Indeed, part of the task in chapters 6 and 7 is to consider whether such difficulties are so insurmountable that arguments to support even the most plausible form of the LFI cannot be successfully maintained.

5

Developing
a New,
Relational
Approach

In this chapter, I will further develop a cluster of arguments to support a relational approach to assisting animals, arguments that could underpin a form of the LFI. In the last chapter, I noted two potential problems with the LFI: one concerning the justification for distinguishing harming from not assisting, and the other concerning whether human relations with animals are relevant to requirements to assist them (or otherwise). I considered the first problem in chapter 4. Here I will (primarily) consider the second problem: how relations might generate or fail to generate duties to assist in the animal context. There are, I think, three kinds of arguments here that might underpin the view that we are not required (or not permitted) to assist wild animals:

A. All suffering, including that of wild animals, generates duties to assist. But in the case of wild animals, any duty to assist is always overwhelmed by *other* moral concerns about the consequences of assistance.

B. There is a sense in which not harming individual wild animals, but also not assisting them, is *best for them* given their *wild-animal natures*. So we should not assist.

C. Although we should (prima facie) not harm individual wild animals, we do not usually have the kind of relationships to them that generate duties to assist. This is the case irrespective of whether assistance would be good or bad for them as individuals and independent of any other concerns about the consequences of assistance.

Some of this chapter will be spent developing arguments for C, which, I will suggest, is the most secure underpinning for the LFI. But in adopting C, I also commit myself to developing another parallel argument: that we do, in contrast, usually have the kinds of relations to domesticated animals—and some others in the "contact zone"—that generate duties, or at least special obligations, to assist. I will spend the latter part of the chapter making arguments to support this position. First, however, I will consider arguments A and B above, which both have existing advocates, and I will explain why I will not be adopting either of these views.

A. LFI on the Grounds of Consequences

One consequentialist argument of this kind has already been discussed. Singer's argument runs something like this: Assistance to some wild animals may in the long run make animal suffering (or preference frustration) worse overall; so better not assist. Adopting this consequentialist underpinning for the LFI would avoid having to make any distinction between harming and not assisting, for in cases where not assisting is mandated, it is because assisting would (in the long run) cause more harm. I have already pointed out weaknesses with this as a reason to support the LFI in chapter 2, and I will not reiterate them here. But other arguments—primarily based on ecological concerns—might also be made here. For example, it might be argued that to assist wild animals (say, by reducing predation) would have bad ecological consequences, even if it did, in fact, reduce overall suffering. That is, there are other kinds of ecological values, not based on the experiences of sentient beings, that should be taken into account here. (Of course, such ecological values—if they are not human-instrumental—are likely to be difficult to defend.) Consequentialist environmental-ethics accounts of this kind would reflect what might be called a *contingent* LFI. For they accept that all wild-animal suffering does, prima facie, make a claim on us for assistance, in just the ways that domesticated-animal suffering does, but that this claim is overwhelmed by other morally relevant consequences, in particular ecological ones. If those consequences did not follow in some particular case, then assisting wild animals would, other things being equal, not just be permitted but be morally required. This might work as a justification for the LFI in some cases, but the LFI would be *contingent*, depending on the most plausible outcome in each particular case. As I argued in chapter 2, there will be some cases where wild animal assistance *is* required on such a view. I am looking for a stronger, noncontingent justification for the LFI than this (though no doubt some readers will conclude that a contingent LFI is as good as it gets).[1] So for now I will move onto justification B.

B. LFI on the Grounds of Wild-Animal Natures

Several accounts have suggested that something like the LFI can be justified on the basis of the *kinds of beings (fully) wild animals* are. Exactly what is meant by this is somewhat murky, and may veer close to—or be conjoined with—a relational argument of the kind I'll develop in C, below. I will consider two versions of these kinds of views: Jennifer Everett's (2001) and Bryan Norton's (1995).

Everett (2001) proposes a rights view that includes some additional duties of assistance to humans and animals that were undeveloped in Regan's account (see chapter 2).[2] Such duties of assistance, she argues, could be posited without implausible implications in the wild; to maintain that there are duties to assist both humans and animals need not mean that there is a duty (say) to intervene in predation to assist prey animals against predators. Her argument runs as follows: Wild animals that are subjects-of-a-life have inherent value and deserve respectful treatment. But respectful treatment does not entail rescuing prey from predators or, more generally, assisting wild animals. For example, the flourishing of wild animals such as deer "is generally thought incompatible with widespread human intervention" (Everett 2001, 54). If humans regularly assisted deer, it is "questionable whether they could flourish according to their natures." Assisting domesticated animals, in contrast, may allow them to flourish according to their natures.

Something like this view could lend support to a form of the LFI. But it does not obviously flow from the individualist, inherent value-centered position being advocated. It is certainly plausible to maintain that the flourishing of a wild deer *species* is advanced by human noninterference in predation (though this would require a particular interpretation of what it is for a species to flourish). But for an animal-rights theorist such as Regan, the flourishing of a *species* is not a reason for action; indeed, the promotion of the flourishing of a species at the expense of the individual lives of its members is something to which he strongly objects, for this treats individual subjects-of-a-life solely as a means to an end, where the end is the flourishing of the species.

But there may be other ways of working through this argument. After all, it is plausible that an individualist argument like this could work in the human case. Suppose A desired to commit her life to dangerous high-altitude mountaineering. B could interfere with the fulfillment of this desire on the grounds that thereby A would be protected from threats to her life. But it might be argued that to interfere in this way would be to prevent A from flourishing, even if A might thereby live a longer, physically healthier life. For A will not have fulfilled her deepest desires, and it is the fulfillment of these that (to A at least) constitutes "flourishing according to her nature." (Of course, it is possible to counter with an "objective-list" account of flourishing in which A's deepest desires do not play a dominant role. I will put this to one side for now.) Arguably, a case like this parallels the deer-flourishing case, where a deer is taken as desiring to be wild or to be left alone, even where interference would lead to the deer having a longer, healthier life.

But it is hard to see how this kind of account would work. For desires such as "to be wild" or "not to be interfered with" are conceptual and are implausibly attributed to animals (and depend on a more sophisticated view of animal minds than I

79

outlined in chapter 1). Of course, it is likely that animals have immediate, practical, behavior-oriented desires to get away from imminent threats. If human interference is of this sort, they will escape if they can. But equally, if a wild animal is hungry and a human provides food, the animal will (in most cases) desire the food and eat it; if an animal is being chased by a predator and a human deflects the predator, the animal will take advantage of the opportunity to escape. So it cannot easily be maintained—in terms of the animal's subjective experience—that the wild animal cannot subjectively flourish because human interference frustrates their desires for wildness or for noninterference.

Two further proposals might be made here. One appeals to subjective well-being over time. The other proposes an objective-list account of animal well-being. The latter is not consistent with the experiential account of animal well-being I have given in this book, but I will nonetheless consider it. The former is consistent with my subjectivist account, and I will look at it first.

80

The argument here must run something like this: Although human action in the wild may not, in terms of the short-term subjective experience of animals, cause them pain or other aversive feelings—indeed, perhaps quite the opposite—in the long term, their experiential welfare as individuals will be better without intervention than with it. Individual wild animals are harmed by human interference; it sets back their experiential interests considered over time.

Clearly, this is an empirical claim, and it may be right in some cases. For example, the rules against the feeding of wildlife in U.S. national parks may work in some such way. Suppose an otherwise hungry (though not starving) bear becomes dependent on food assistance from humans. The bear begins to seek out human food over the food it would normally eat. Clashes between humans and the bear in the national park become increasingly common; in this situation the prognosis for the bear is bad. It will be relocated or killed; neither is a good subjective experience for the bear. So although over the short term humans assisted the bear—it was better off than it would have been if humans had not acted to feed it—in the long term, its experiential interests were set back by becoming dependent on human food; the bear was harmed by human actions and did not flourish according to its nature.

The problem is that not all cases of assistance look like this. Suppose that a sheep in an isolated population of wild mountain bighorns contracts a kind of highly infectious *Pasteurella*, a pneumonia that sweeps through wild bighorn herds. If humans do nothing, most or all of the population will become infected, and many of the individuals will suffer and die; the mortality rate for such outbreaks can be as high as 75 percent. Research suggests that if the infected sheep is removed and all the remaining sheep are vaccinated with a *Pasteurella* vaccine, suffering and subsequent deaths can be substantially reduced or averted.[3] Certainly, the disturbance and stress of pursuit, capture, and vaccination would be unpleasant to the sheep, but let us assume that they are vaccinated and (as is plausible) over time each individual's experiential interests are promoted by the vaccine, while no ill consequences (such as starvation due to population increase) follow from its use. In this case, human intervention seems beneficial to each of the wild individuals—they are experientially better off and more able to flourish than they would have been had the humans concerned not taken these actions. So it is difficult to see how in the bighorn case an argument like Everett's could stick.

These contrasting cases suggest that it is impossible to maintain any *general principle* that human actions in the wild set back the flourishing of individual wild animals, where flourishing is understood in terms of experiential well-being over time. On some occasions, it might have this effect; on other occasions, however, experiential well-being over time would be *enhanced* by human assistance—most especially in cases of disease and disaster.

The alternative possibility here—as in the human case—is to propose an *objective-list* account of what it is for an animal to flourish. Taylor (1986, 174) for instance, maintains that there is a duty to allow wild animals the freedom to continue to live out their lives in a wild state. Everett claims that for a wild animal to flourish "according to its nature," humans should not interfere with it. Let us take this in an objective-list sense: what it is for a wild animal to flourish is not about how it feels to an animal from the inside. There are different ways of interpreting this kind of claim with regard to an animal's "wild nature." One suggestion—that I do not think succeeds—would be to maintain that wildness is itself a kind of capability (in Nussbaum's sense) that it is good for an animal to manifest, rather like (say) running, or howling, or grooming. This seems to be a very strange way of thinking about wildness. Wildness (with the possible exception of the dispositional sense of wildness, which is not the sense at stake here) describes a kind of *relation* that some animals are in vis-à-vis humans, not a capability those animals manifest. But then, perhaps some relations are objectively essential for a wild animal to flourish according to its nature. So, for instance, one might say that an infant mammal requires particular relations with its parent in order to flourish according to its nature. This seems right. But it does not help us much with the *particular* relation of wildness, because wildness is a *negative* relation to humans—it is specifically about human absence. One way of interpreting this claim could be that the expression of the negative relation "wildness"—taken as noninterference in genetic origin and place by humans—allows wild animals to flourish by leaving a space in which they can manifest their objective natural capabilities without being inhibited by human activity. And certainly, for many wild individuals, for much of the time, this is the case. But at the point where an animal needs assistance—when it is sick or starving, for instance—its ability as an individual to objectively flourish according to its nature is *already* inhibited. And human intervention in many of these cases *could* restore that ability. An objective-list account, then, does not seem better placed here to ground any general principle of nonassistance than an experiential account of animal welfare. Human intervention would sometimes help individual wild animals flourish objectively according to their natures, although there are other occasions when it would not. So it does not seem possible to maintain any general principle of human nonassistance to wild animals on the ground that this infringes on their ability to flourish according to their nature. This kind of argument does, however, start to close in on one that is more successful. Norton (1995) gets nearer to the argument that I will develop.

Norton (1995, 105–106) defends what looks like a version of the LFI, although he uses a number of different arguments—some of which work better than others—to support his view. His basic claim is that in "most situations they [wild animals] are not morally considerable to humans." It is important to note that this does not form part of a broader view that *no* animals are morally considerable, for "the content of the experience of some animals is surely rich enough to make them candidates for moral considerability" (1995, 106). Indeed, Norton clearly accepts that in some circumstances—such as in captivity—an animal *is* morally considerable. On Norton's view, whether humans should take animals into account morally depends on their location. Indeed, his account has the interesting and important implication that one and the same animal may or may not be morally considerable depending on its context. Animal X in the wild may not be morally considerable, but the same individual, when in a zoo, generates a number of obligations.

Norton's use of "moral considerability" is somewhat misleading here. For he is not advocating the view that moral agents can do anything they like to individual wild animals, since the animals do not matter at all; we could not wander through the forest torturing wild animals at whim with no moral qualm.[4] Rather, he takes "nonconsiderability" to mean *not having responsibility for* wild animals, which in turn seems to cash out as *noninterference*, in particular a lack of responsibility to intervene to prevent the deaths of wild animals. At first sight, what he argues for looks like the Strong LFI: humans should prima facie neither harm nor assist wild animals. But closer scrutiny of Norton's argument suggests that his view is nearer to the Weak LFI. He accepts that there may be cases where assisting a wild animal (for instance, a drowning bison), though not morally *required*, is at least morally *permissible* (1995, 120).

What is interesting here is how Norton underpins these claims. He uses several different but related arguments. One closely resembles the argument we have already seen: that we should respect the wildness of wild animals, and to respect wildness means nonintervention. But given that Norton accepts that sentience or "richness of experience" makes a creature a candidate for moral considerability, what could justify this? One kind of justification seems to revolve around an idea that wild animals have a kind of *autonomy* (thus, resembling one version of Everett's argument above). Norton (1995, 106) suggests that "the forbearance we exercise here is very similar, psychologically and perhaps morally, to the attitude of wise parents who, after the time of maturity, let their children live their own lives."

But this comparison is problematic. First, even wise parents should, presumably, assist their independent children in life-or-death situations (of disease, or accident, or attack) where the children could not help themselves—that is, the kind of situations with which we are concerned here. But even if they should not, it is not clear that this argument can be successfully extended to wild animals. For wild animals do not have the kind of rational decision-making autonomy that independent adult humans have (as Norton accepts, in fact, in the rest of his paper, which in part concerns the inability of individual animals to volunteer to sacrifice themselves for their species). Since wild animals are not concerned about their rational decision-making autonomy, any worry about autonomy cannot be one about how an animal's life goes from the inside. But perhaps this was not what Norton meant. Perhaps in the case of the independent children, the argument is that it is good for the adult child not to be assisted by the parent, even if the child has no desire about this one way or another and even if the adult child might die without parental assistance. That is, the state of autonomy is an objective-list good, one that outweighs other objective-list goods such as health and even continuing to live. It is difficult to see how this could be maintained, even in the human case, as a general principle. But in the animal case, since animals are not capable of autonomy in a conceptual sense, it is hard to see why this would be an objective-list good for them at all (even if one accepted objective-list goods for animals). Of course, it is plausible to suggest that (in a practical, not conceptual, way) a wild animal wants to be able to move around its habitat, to eat what it wants and to sleep when it wants, and that constraints on these might constitute a harm. But freedom to do these things cannot easily be cashed out as autonomy, or only in such a restricted sense that the comparison with the human case is lost.

Perhaps this strand of Norton's argument could be better interpreted as being about the protection of wildness understood in a sense detached from either internal or objective-list goods for individual animals. Whether or not noninterference in wild animals' lives is good for the individual animals, it preserves wildness, and on Norton's account, wildness is valuable. The claim that wildness, or wild ecosystems, are valuable (independent of the goods of individual wild animals) is obviously important to some forms of environmental ethics (it is fundamental, for instance, in different ways to accounts such as Rolston's, and to Elliot's [1997] argument that human restoration of nature fails to restore the wild value lost in human destructions). One way of reading Norton's discussion might be to see him as claiming something like: "Animals can have high levels of richness of experience, which makes them morally considerable and might suggest that there is some duty to relieve their suffering. But there is also this other value, wildness. In the case of wild animals, protection of

83

wildness trumps the goods of individual wild animals, so we should not intervene in the wild to protect individual wild animals." And certainly—if one could defend wildness as a trumping value—then an argument of this kind could produce the Strong LFI. Since wildness must be protected, no actions that might compromise wildness—which includes both harming and assisting wild animals—are (prima facie) morally permissible.

I am not going to try to defend that difficult argument. For Norton himself ultimately seems uncomfortable with this view; wildness *does not* seem to be a trumping value on his account, since one may intervene in the wild to cull, to promote species diversity, etc. Instead, he hints at another rather different argument for nonintervention to assist wild animals, one that stems not from the general value of wildness but from the kind of (or rather, lack of) relation that humans have with wild animals themselves. For Norton also suggests that the context of wild animals is such that they *just do not trigger* the kinds of positive duties of assistance that we have toward captive or domesticated animals (or, more generally we might say, toward animals in the contact zone). This is not a trumping argument, where one moral concern (for wildness) trumps another (rich individual animal experience), but rather an argument that, in the wild, rich individual animal experience just *does not generate positive moral duties to assist at all*. I am going to develop a case for this kind of view further, for if it can be maintained, it provides an underpinning for a noncontingent LFI.

C. LFI on the Grounds That Duties to Assist Are Absent

Distinctive to the LFI is the absence of duties to assist in the wild (broadly speaking) and the presence of such duties to assist in the domesticated case (again, broadly speaking). Two related questions need to be answered: Why might there be no duties to assist fully wild animals? And why might such duties, or special obligations, exist in the domesticated case, even though such animals may have very similar capacities to fully wild ones?[5]

As we have seen, a number of arguments can be made that distinguish between duties not to harm and duties to assist. Those who make such distinctions—most commonly, libertarians—often argue that although we always have duties not to seriously harm others (their rights, for instance, should be seen as side constraints on our actions), assistance is a special obligation only generated by agreements (such as promises or contracts) or by other kinds of special relations. In the absence of these kinds of special relations, we have no duties to assist others. It is immediately obvious why these arguments might be relevant here. For if we could use this kind of reasoning in the context of human relations with animals, we could argue that wild animals lack the kinds of special relations with people that generate duties to assist, while domesticated animals do have such special relations. This could underpin a noncontingent LFI. Below, I will suggest some arguments in favor of this view. These arguments are not bombproof; indeed, there are very strong objections to them, which I will consider in the remaining chapters. But still, I think a plausible case, at least, can be made here.

One starting point is a related family of arguments in the human case, arguments that focus on the significance of *distance*. Even if these arguments are not fully persuasive in the human case, they might nonetheless have some power in the animal case. After all, one way of interpreting wildness is in terms of distance. Constitutive wildness can be seen as bodily distance from human interaction. Locational wildness is a kind of physical distance from human interaction, or at least from human locational impacts. And distance has had an important role to play in recent discussions of morality: in particular, in debates over the duties of the affluent toward distant impoverished people.

One well-known and powerful set of arguments here maintains that distance should be regarded as morally irrelevant. Singer (1972, 229–243), for instance, famously claims that just as we should rescue a drowning child at our feet, so we should assist a starving distant child to eat. Likewise, Peter Unger (1996) maintains that the widespread intuition that we have much stronger duties toward those whom we physically encounter than toward those who are needy but physically distant is actually the product of psychological tricks relating to salience and conspicuousness. (The LFI, then, could be just another of these psychological tricks.)[6] We might take these kinds of accounts as focusing on spatial distance. And that "bare" spatial distance should be morally important does seem implausible. Parfit (1984, 486), for instance, dismisses the idea; indeed, he claims—in response to arguments about temporal discounting—"*no-one* thinks that we would be morally justified if we cared less about the long-range effects of our acts, at some rate of n percentage per yard" (emphasis mine).

On most accounts where distance matters morally, there's a much "thicker" sense of distance at stake. Some accounts of care, as I indicated in chapter 3, understand distance in an *emotional* sense and argue that we can distinguish morally between those to whom we are emotionally close and those from whom we are emotionally distant. Alternatively, distance is sometimes thought to be morally relevant in a cultural, community, or nation-state sense, as advocated, for instance, in the work of some communitarians. Here, those who are distant fall beyond the boundaries of some cultural group, community, or nation; for instance, those who do not make or have not made a contribution to the establishment or maintenance of the group or who fail to share some characteristic perceived to be central in common with other members.[7]

Another sense of distance—one that is a factor in, or closely related to, several of the senses above—is distance understood as, in some way, the *independence* of individuals and groups from one another. This independence is usually construed as an actual (or perceived) lack of entanglement with others, generally in terms of having had, or having, no causal influence on the circumstances of others. Individuals or groups distant in this sense are, thus, those not responsible for, nor contributors to, the state of affairs (in particular, the state of well-being) of those that are distant: they may indeed—initially at least—know little or nothing about them. The greater the level of contact, entanglement, and influence—that is, the less distance, in this *causal* responsibility sense—the more *moral* responsibilities are thought to be generated.

So, there are many ideas of morally relevant distance: those who are just spatially distant, those who live beyond a certain significant boundary (such as that of community or nation), those for whom one has no personal feelings of affection, those with whom one has no causal entanglement—and indeed, more generally, as Narveson (2003, 429–430) argues, those whom it is more costly to help. Many of these ideas about distance in the human case can be transferred in somewhat related forms to thinking about animals, especially if we think of distance in terms of wildness. After all, "fully" wild animals are usually distant from all humans in a number of the senses above. They are often spatially distant; they are part of no human community or nation; they have no affective relations with individual humans; it is likely to be costly to help them, the more distant, the more costly; and they are independent of humans—that is, there is a lack of causal entanglement. In particular, humans are not causally responsible for the situations that fully wild animals are in. So arguments made about the moral significance of distance with regard to diminishing or failing to trigger moral obligations in the human case might transfer to arguments to support one or more forms of the LFI. I will try to develop this kind of argument below. My concern here will primarily be to engage with ideas about causal entanglements and responsibilities that support—broadly speaking—the case that wild animals can be thought of as *distant* in morally relevant ways while, conversely, domesticated animals are relevantly morally *close*. Note that there are two claims here. The first is the *denial* that we are required to assist fully wild animals. The second is the *affirmation* that we are required to assist domesticated animals (and additionally, some animals in the "contact zone"). I will try to make the best case for these positions here, in turn. To make the strongest case, I will defer until chapters 6 and 7 a number of critical challenges to these arguments.

One claim sometimes found in the human case is that we do not have duties, or we have very weak duties, to assist distant human strangers with whom we have never, even indirectly, had any interaction. So, suppose we discovered a community of hungry people on Venus (or on a hitherto undiscovered island, etc.) whose crops had failed because of climate change, caused by a shift in that planet's axis or some other factor entirely unrelated to us. Is there a duty to assist these Venusians and to relieve their suffering? The Venusians are distant in a number of senses, not just physically: they are beyond any boundary of community or nation, they share no common institution with other humans or indeed with human society more broadly construed, and there has been no interaction with them from societies on Earth. Those on Earth carry no possible causal responsibility for the Venusian situation. Utilitarians of a Singerian stripe would claim in such a case that distance is irrelevant; suffering Venusians should be taken equally into account with suffering Earthlings. However, there is widespread dissent from this view among both ethicists and political philosophers, many of whom would argue that while it would be seriously wrong to land on Venus in order to torture and eat the suffering Venusians or to destroy the few crops they have left, if there are any duties to assist at all, these are *very much weaker* than duties to assist comparably hungry humans on Earth.

One classic statement of a claim like this, in the human case, can be found in Nozick (1974). Suppose a number of Robinson Crusoes each individually occupy separate islands. These islands differ with respect to the natural resources they have available; in addition, the Crusoes have differing abilities and dispositions for work. Later, the Crusoes discover one another through radio transmissions; not only do they discover each other's existence, but they also have the ability to transfer resources between themselves, allowing better-off Crusoes to assist worse-off Crusoes. Is there any *duty* for the better-off Crusoes to assist the worse-off Crusoes? Nozick argues not. In particular, since the Crusoes have lived independently of one another, no question of *justice* is raised by the differentials in each Crusoe's holding (and hence in his well-being). Nozick (1974, 185) maintains: "In the social noncooperation situation, it might be said, each individual gets what he gets unaided by his own efforts: or rather, no-one can make a claim *of justice* against his holding."

Now, a number of difficulties are raised by the importing of claims about justice from human/human to human/animal relations, and, of course, even in the human/human context, the term "justice" can be used in a number of different ways. This notwithstanding, accounts like Nozick's can provide a helpful way into thinking about problems raised in the animal context. There is at least something that *resembles* this kind of justice—call it an analogy to justice—that it is useful to explore further here in the human/animal case.[8] Concerns about "justice" and "injustice" of this kind emerge out of social and/or political contexts, contexts that involve human intentions and moral responsibility. We might say, for instance, that there is something unjust about access to healthcare or the redistributional effects of a taxation system within some state. But we would not say that in *this* sense it was unjust that it rained on a picnic, or that a baby was born with a cleft palate, or that (as in the case above) a planet shifted on its axis and damaged the growth of a crop. These events fall outside the realm of human intention and moral responsibility; they are not, in this sense, injustices. This thought about justice helps in considering the situation of fully wild animals, for fully wild animals are outside of human social/political contexts. Even if there is a sense in which something resembling justice could be relevant to animals, it does not apply in *their* case. If they are hungry, or suffering, or being preyed upon, there is nothing *unjust* about the state of affairs. And one, at least, of the major grounds for arguing that there is a duty to assist other humans— whether distant or otherwise—is that they find themselves in particular bad situations because of an injustice.

A useful view to consider here is that of Thomas Pogge—widely accepted to be one of the philosophical champions of assistance to the distant poor. In general terms, Pogge accepts that duties not to harm are much more stringent than duties to assist (2007, 633). Indeed, he comments: "I reject such recipient-oriented approaches [as utilitarianism and Rawls' veil of ignorance] and agree on this point with libertarians . . . I agree that the distinction between causing poverty and merely failing to reduce it is morally significant" (2002, 13). Both "human rights and justice," as Nozick agrees, involve "solely negative duties."

But this claim does not mean, for Pogge, that we lack or have merely very weak duties to assist the (physically) distant poor on Earth—quite the contrary. For (according to Pogge) no people in the world are in the situation of the Venusians (or the Crusoes). Even if the poor are spatially distant, they are not distant in what Pogge understands to be a morally relevant sense: the sense of entanglement and causal responsibility that underpins social justice. On Pogge's account, the affluent are at least in part, even if indirectly, *causally responsible* for the situations of the poor and suffering on Earth; that is, they are failing or have already failed in their negative duties not to harm. The poor on Earth, unlike the poor on Venus, are *victims of injustice*; injustice that has three possible forms (it is not necessary to accept all three; any one will do the job for him): the effects of shared institutions, the uncompensated exclusion from the use of natural resources, and the effects of a common and violent history (Pogge 2007, 634). The better-off shape institutions that benefit them while harming the worse-off, and/or enjoy advantages from which the badly-off are excluded without compensation, and/or benefit from a violent history that gives them a good start in life, while depriving others. The wealth of the affluent has not been achieved *independently* of their relations to the suffering poor; though physically distant, the affluent and the poor are causally entangled, in particular via common institutions. This entanglement, in which the affluent violate their negative duties to those who are poor, in turn generates positive duties to end such harms and to compensate those who have been harmed.

These kinds of arguments cast light on a plausible underpinning for part of the LFI. Humans, I've claimed, have prima facie negative duties not to harm all sentient animals. Requirements to assist them, however, must be generated by some kind of relationship. One key way in which such requirements could be generated is by human/animal entanglements, histories, and shared institutional frameworks where humans are, or have been, either responsible for harms to animals or for the generation of particular vulnerabilities in animals. Indeed, some such entanglements might take similar forms to those for which Pogge argues in the human case. He maintains that the affluent have moral responsibilities to the distant poor because of shared institutions, entrenched deprivations, and histories of domination and colonization that disadvantage the distant poor and render them vulnerable. These are claims of social justice in the human case; there may, at least, be an analogous pattern of shared oppressive institutions, entrenched deprivations, and relations of domination in the animal case.

Fully wild animals, though, do not have such relations with humans; so duties to assist them are not generated on these grounds. There is no analogy to current or historical unfairness or injustice (or, indeed, fairness or justice) about the states in which wild animals find themselves. Inasmuch as they live without human contact, they are outside the realm of justice altogether.[9] And this starts to make sense of the idea that they are, as Regan (1984, 357) following Beston (1971) suggests, in some sense members of "other nations." If moral agents act to harm wild animals or create/render them vulnerable to harm, then duties toward them may be generated. But where animals are living, as it were, in an independent wild state, these kinds of duties to assist, at least, are not generated.

Some form of this argument provides, I think, the strongest support for the intuition that we should have a broadly laissez-faire moral attitude toward assisting fully wild animals: prima facie we should not harm them, since they are sentient and morally considerable, but we have no duties to assist them, because their situation, even when they are suffering or starving, reflects no injustice, and no moral agents were involved in bringing it about.

A number of questions, though, are raised here in particular about *other* grounds for assistance—including in the human case. For one might ask: does this view, then, imply that there is a duty to relieve the suffering of the distant poor on Earth when suffering is a product of some injustice, but no duty to rescue the drowning child at one's feet, since the child's situation is an accident and not an injustice? Does this leave the LFI in the position where there are no duties to assist *anyone* when the cause of need is not an injustice or a preexisting harm, when humans are needy due to accidents or nonanthropogenic forces? And, on the other hand, if there are such duties, how does this play into the argument about the LFI? I will address this problem in chapter 7. However, I will consider further two issues here. First, I will say something about what this argument suggests with respect to the three forms of the LFI that I outlined earlier. Second, I need to say something about the *other* claim that forms part of the LFI: that humans *do* have the kinds of relations with domesticated animals that generate special obligations to assist them, obligations that do not apply in the wild.

IMPLICATIONS FOR FORMS OF THE LFI

In chapter 4, I outlined three alternative forms of the LFI: the Strong LFI (neither harm nor assistance in the wild permitted), the Weak LFI (harm not permitted, assistance permitted in the wild but not required), and the No-contact LFI (harm not permitted, assistance permitted but not required, contact with wild animals may generate special obligations to assist). I have now suggested arguments that might underpin part of the LFI. None of them, alone, offer obvious support for the Strong LFI. The argument above does not entail that it is *morally impermissible* to assist wild animals (it was not *required* for the well-off Crusoes to assist the poorly-off Crusoes, or for the Earthlings to assist Venusians, but, on the other hand, it was not *forbidden*). Even if there were no obligations to assist, one might feel sympathy for a poor Crusoe or a wretched Venusian and offer them assistance (there might be an argument here grounded in human virtue—I will discuss a case of this kind in an animal context in chapter 8). Assistance would certainly be *permitted* on both a Pogge- or a Nozick-style account. Some environmental ethicists, as I noted earlier in the chapter, maintain that wildness is itself a value that should be protected, and this looks as though it is going to be the best (and perhaps the only) argument that would support the Strong LFI. I am not convinced, however, that such an argument could be made to work, and I am not going to attempt to develop it here. Someone who developed such a wildness view might nonetheless accept many of the arguments that underpin the No-contact LFI, as the kinds of contact involved will have already compromised animals' "full wildness," so there's likely to be less concern that intervention in these cases does not preserve wildness. On the basis of the case that I have proposed above, however, either the Weak LFI or No-contact LFI could be supported: that is, assistance in the wild is permitted but is not required.

What, then, of the No-contact LFI in relation to the Weak LFI? Given what has been suggested above—that entanglement, in particular, causal responsibility or something analogous to justice is of moral significance—this case would tend to support the No-contact LFI. Where there is no human/animal contact, then a laissez-faire approach to assistance prevails; there are only negative duties toward fully wild animals. It is forms of contact, in particular the creation of vulnerabilities and earlier violations of negative duties, that generate special obligations to assist. I will consider more about how this works out in the rest of this chapter and the remaining chapters of the book. But what does seem to emerge here is that the No-contact LFI looks to be the most defensible form of the LFI.

WHY DOMESTICATED ANIMALS MIGHT BE *CLOSE* IN MORALLY
RELEVANT WAYS

In chapter 4, I outlined a variety of human/animal relations, including the "fully wild" (where animals are constitutively and locationally wild), domestication, mutualism, commensalism, contramensalism, and other kinds of potentially relevant human contacts including captivity, relocation, and displacement, which together constitute the human-animal "contact zone." Here, I am going to focus primarily on domesticated animals; in later chapters, I will consider animals differentially located in the contact zone.

Even if (as discussed in chapter 3) domesticated animals "colluded" in their own domestication, the existence of most domesticated animals today is the result of human decisions and actions, in multiple ways. Humans are responsible, at least in part for (a) the *actual situation* in which many domesticated animals find themselves, a situation that often involves being closely confined in spaces that prevent them from finding food, mates, etc. for themselves; (b) key facets of domesticated animal *natures*, including in many cases an inability to be self-sufficient; and (c) the *very existence* of most individual domesticated animals—a stark contrast with fully wild animals.

The first two of these factors make domesticated animals peculiarly vulnerable in comparison with wild animals. In order to flourish well at all, and particularly in order to flourish in the situations in which humans put them, such animals need human support. As Goodin (1985) maintains, "A is more vulnerable to B (1) the more control B has over outcomes that affect A's interests and (2) the more heavily A's interests are at stake in the outcomes that B controls." For most domesticated animals, humans have almost complete control over their most basic interests, making them, on Goodin's terms, supremely vulnerable to people and frequently wholly dependent on them.

Of course, all animals—including humans—are always vulnerable to particular kinds of threats, such as those from internal disease and external disaster. Vulnerability is, as Fineman (2008, 8) rightly maintains, to some extent ineliminable, a consequence of being embodied, "a universal, inevitable, enduring aspect of the human condition." However, for most people most of the time, and equally for wild animals, this enduring vulnerability is not *realized*; it does not, for instance, generate strong and ongoing dependency on others for care and provision. Although humans are dependent as infants and often dependent when aged, their dependency is "episodic, sporadic, and largely developmental in nature" (Fineman 2008, 9). This is not so for domesticated animals. Dependence on humans, for most domestic animals, is permanent, enduring, and lifelong.

It is useful here to distinguish between two forms of dependence, which I will call "external" and "internal" dependence, corresponding to (a) and (b) above. Captive wild animals provide a good example of external dependence: such animals might be able to provide for themselves in their native species habitat, but in confinement they are circumstantially dependent on humans to provide food and shelter. Their dependence is an external, human-imposed effect of captivity (though over time it might become learned dependence, so that if released such animals could no longer be self-sufficient). Equally, some domesticated animals might be able to survive without human care if placed in appropriate environments. But they lack access to such environments and so are also externally dependent on humans for food and shelter. As Burgess-Jackson (1998, 168–169) argues of companion animals—but the argument can be extended more widely—once animals have been taken into our homes or confined in some other way, on farms or in labs, their alternative options for living have been shut down. They can access neither other humans who could support them nor resources to allow them to support themselves. Part of what constitutes human responsibility to provide care here, then, is the creation of animal dependence by denying an animal access to other possible options for survival. And this kind of dependence, while external (i.e., not necessarily flowing from the animals' *nature*, though the animal may be dependent in this way as well), is usually permanent.

However, domestication is a process that often also produces *internal* dependence, dependence that is constitutive and inevitable in a deeper sense than that generated by external confinement and other restrictions and that has limited parallels to dependence in human cases. Domesticated animals are deliberately shaped by humans, in terms of factors such as bodily form, fur or hair production, susceptibility to disease, reproductive capacity, and temperament. For this reason, many domesticated animals need humans to survive and certainly to flourish. Without humans to provide for and to protect them, many would die (though some would survive—perhaps with poor welfare—in a feral state); there *is* no wild environment in which they could be self-sufficient. This is particularly true of animals bred in ways that meet very specific human requirements—such as cows that can only give birth through caesarean section, cats bred without fur or claws, turkeys bred to gain so much fat that they cannot walk, or genetically modified laboratory mice created to be susceptible to specific cancers. But even less dramatic forms of domestication can make survival without human care highly tenuous. For example, domesticated horses released into the wild are often attacked by wild horses and fail to grow a sufficiently thick winter coat to protect themselves; they are unlikely to live long in the wild. So, in these domesticated animals, we might say, vulnerability is always realized; this is the root of their dependence on humans.

Goodin (1985, 195–196) provides a useful way of thinking through dependence of this kind. Dependence (in the human case) embodies, he suggests, an *asymmetry* of power: the subordinate party *needs* the resources provided by the relationship, the relationship is the *only source* of such resources, and the superordinate party controls the resources. Goodin's account of the human case fits the created dependence of many domesticated animals well, though in a domesticated-animal context we might add that the "embodiment" of the power relationship can be quite literal; the superordinate party actually created the subordinate party *in order that* they should be in this subordinate situation, and, in many cases, there could be no alternative, nondependent arrangement by which the subordinate could survive.

Based on this account of vulnerability and dependence, a relational argument about the creation of special obligations to assist animals could take this form: When humans deliberately create morally considerable, sentient animals who have no other ways of fulfilling their needs and are constitutively profoundly dependent on and permanently vulnerable to humans, then humans create special obligations toward those animals. Likewise, where humans close down animals' options by external constraints on their movements and environments, preventing them from fulfilling some or all of their needs in other ways—then by making animals' potential vulnerability actual, humans create special obligations to assist them. (The latter cases could include some human effects on wild animals, such as the devastation of their habitats, as I will argue in chapter 6.)

There is nothing unusual about the general claim—in a human context—that vulnerability and dependence create special obligations (irrespective of whether one had a hand in creating it). In some forms of interhuman ethics, just being a member of a vulnerable human population (irrespective of the *origin* of the vulnerability) is standardly thought to mean that special protections are required. Take, for example, the approach to vulnerable populations adopted in the Belmont Report (1979), the document that provides "ethical principles and guidelines for the protection of human subjects of research" for the United States. Here, the "involvement of vulnerable subjects"—such as the very sick or those in prisons—in medical experiments raises the possibility of "special instance[s] of injustice." Because the vulnerable have "dependent status" and a "compromised capacity for free consent," they are "easy to manipulate" and thus need special protection. Likewise, children used in medical research must be offered special protection because of their heightened vulnerability. For although children share the same general vulnerabilities as the rest of us, their lack of understanding or ability to resist can make it easier for those vulnerabilities to be realized. In addition, they have *special* vulnerabilities that arise from their inability to be self-sufficient. This combination of vulnerabilities provides the basis for the argument in the human case that members of vulnerable groups need special protection. What is interesting is that arguments of this kind are rarely ever made in the case of sentient animals. Indeed, animals are *created* to be more vulnerable in these ways just in order to make them easier to manipulate—so the very same

93

arguments that work in favor of special protection in human cases seem to work in favor of fewer protections and greater availability for harms in animal cases.[10]

However, the domesticated-animal case introduces additional factors here that are not applicable, or not applicable in the same way, in most human cases. The realized vulnerability of domesticated animals is not serendipitous or unfortunate, and neither is it something merely temporary, passed through as part of a developmental process. It is voluntarily and intentionally created by people. It is not, for instance, as though people have just stumbled upon mice populations especially susceptible to forms of cancer or hairless cats that burn with any exposure to the sun. Animals have been shaped that way by people; people have voluntarily created animals to be vulnerable and dependent.

The closest human parallel—where humans create vulnerable and dependent beings—is choosing to have a child. This choice is widely thought to generate special obligations toward the resulting child, not just because a child is needy and vulnerable, but because *it is your child*; you have obligations toward your own child that you do not have toward children in general.[11] So, if a couple voluntarily decides to procreate, they undertake obligations to care for their child, either themselves or in some other way that will be good for the child. As O'Neill (1979, 26) maintains: "a standard way of acquiring obligations is to undertake them, and a standard way of undertaking parental obligations is to decide to procreate." Suppose someone decides to procreate but denies any obligations to the infant, neglecting it or failing to provide for its basic needs. The neglectful parent is morally culpable in a way that would not apply to some other adult who, though knowing that there are neglected infants nearby and being able to adopt one of them, nonetheless chooses not to do so. The decision to procreate brings with it moral responsibilities to the offspring that results from that decision, responsibilities that look backward to the decision itself.[12]

Human procreation is particularly relevant here because, as with the creation of a domesticated animal, it concerns the coming into being of a particular sentient being that would not otherwise have existed. Further, the sentient being created is dependent on others to survive and flourish—dependent in particular on his or her creators to care for him or her or to organize care for him or her. In the case of human children, physical dependence generally diminishes over time, and children (usually) eventually become independent of their parents. And, of course, human children are not usually deliberately created in particular ways. Though some forms of human-embryo selection and gene modification occur—and may be on the increase—these are generally morally justified on the basis that they will enhance the welfare of the child produced and add to its possibility of a good and independent life. While "savior siblings" may be selected for the good of a sibling, this is not to the disadvantage of the selected embryo, and the deliberate creation of deaf children by deaf couples

94

in part follows from the argument that a deaf child would fit more easily into deaf family culture than a hearing child. In the case of domesticated animals, however, effects of breeding and genetic modification are only occasionally in the interest of enhancing the individuals' welfare; they instead generally increase individual animals' dependence on humans and vulnerability to environmental stress. Where welfare is improved by particular breeding practices, this is usually to allow animals to live better only within the context of the closely confined and stressful conditions of intensive farming. This deep involvement in the creation of the very nature and capacities of a sentient being, in turn, I suggest, creates an intensified moral responsibility for its welfare.

However, these claims create complications—and problems, some of which I will consider in the next couple of chapters. For instance, someone might say: "Sure, a parent has special obligations to care for his or her child. And if I bred kittens, I would have a special responsibility to those kittens I'd bred. But presumably you want to do more with this argument: you want to say that 'we' have special obligations toward domesticated animals, whether we personally bred them or not. And justifying that leap is going to be a problem."

Someone who raised this question would be right. There are two related problems here. One concerns *voluntarism*: normally, special obligations are thought to be the kinds of obligations that must be voluntarily assumed. But the way this view is shaping up, we seem to have obligations to which we never actually agreed. And second, problems are raised about what might be thought of as *group responsibility*. Full wildness was characterized by "no contact" with humans. But in thinking about domestication, I discuss the actions of a "we," and it is unclear to whom this "we" refers. After all, processes of domestication, of developing animals' habitat, etc., have happened over long periods of human history. Who is responsible? "Humans" includes human structures, practices, and institutions over time and individual humans past and present—farmers, breeders, lab technicians, consumers—all of whom played and still play some role in the creation of dependent sentient animals and benefit from their existence. But still, responsibilities here seem diffuse, smeared over time and space, and even if one could allocate them in any satisfactory way, the relationship between causal and moral responsibility seems unclear. These are important difficulties with the view I am developing. I will discuss these problems (among others) in the following chapters.

95

6

Past Harms and Special Obligations

In chapter 5, I considered reasons why we do not (normally) have the kinds of relations with wild animals that generate obligations to assist and why we *do* have special obligations to assist and provide for domesticated animals that have either been created to be vulnerable and dependent or placed into situations where they have no other options but to depend wholly or partially on human support. In this chapter, I will consider another context that can also create special obligations toward animals: where there has been past infliction of harms that generate ongoing negative effects on their lives. While domesticated animals may be placed in such situations, the scope here moves beyond domestication. Animals that are constitutively wild may be harmed by humans in relevant ways, and as a result their vulnerability over time may be enhanced and their ability to be self-sufficient compromised. One way into thinking about special obligations created by past harms is to look at the idea of *reparation* in the human context—since most accounts of reparation depend on the idea that special obligations can be generated by past harms. I will suggest that although the idea of reparation in the human context and backward-looking special obligations to animals do not map onto each other exactly, some of the questions raised by human reparation cases parallel those in animal cases. I will think this through by using *Coyotes*, a case study of negative human effects on constitutively wild animals.

However, these kinds of reparation-like special obligations—as well as the special obligations that arise from the processes of domestication and captivity—raise a series of complex questions about who has moral responsibility to do what, and why. For instance, there may be multiple perpetrators of harms and multiple beneficiaries from such harms; who has a special obligation to do what in such cases? And what of individuals who claim neither directly to have harmed an animal, nor to have benefited from any harm to an animal, nor to have directly or indirectly created any animal? Does this mean that they lack any special obligations to assist animals harmed or created by other people? I will consider these questions both in relation to *Coyotes* and to a second case, *Dumpster Kittens*—a case that, additionally, helps clarify the way in which, even though animals with similar capacities may be in similar situations, we may still have different obligations with respect to assisting them, providing that our relations to them are relevantly different.

SPECIAL OBLIGATIONS CREATED BY PAST HARMS
The Idea of Reparation in Human Cases

Over the past half century, the idea of reparation has become increasingly important in national and international politics. The idea presupposes some past wrongful harm or injustice; reparation is always, in some way, backward looking. Such past harms may take different forms: causing avoidable and intense suffering; enslaving; displacement; violating rights, including rights to land; the confiscation of material assets; and a variety of other serious offenses. It is generally agreed in such cases that some moral wrong has occurred; disputes about reparation usually concern what (if anything) should be done to "make good" a past harm, not whether any harm occurred—although since shifts in moral view occur across time, sometimes the harms were not widely accepted as wrong when they were carried out. Reparation combines recognition of a past harm, acceptance of some kind of responsibility for or relation to the past harm, and acknowledgement of a moral imperative to attempt in some way to repair or make good the harm—that is, the recognition of some special obligation toward those affected by the harm, or to their descendants. If no reparation occurs, on this view, the harm sits as a kind of persistent debit in a moral ledger.[1]

That *some* action should be taken to make good, however, does not identify *whose* responsibility reparation is. There are two leading accounts of this, which, following Caney (2006, 467), we can call a "causal account" and a "beneficiary account." Causal accounts focus on perpetrators: those who commit an injustice are liable to carry out reparation. There are good reasons for seeing this as appropriate; in particular, because the liability of perpetrators appeals to our morally important sense of desert (Rachels 2007). However, causal accounts also generate difficulties, since perpetrators may be multiple and—over time—pass out of existence, or (in cases of collective perpetrators, such as states) be transformed in ways that make claims against them inappropriate. Beneficiary accounts, on the other hand, maintain that those who benefit from some injustice are responsible for reparation. This may identify at least a partially distinct set of individuals from a causal account (since both perpetrators *and* nonperpetrators may be benefited, or perpetrators may not be benefited at all). Here the thought is that beneficiaries are enjoying an unjust gain; without good reason, their interests have been advanced at the expense of others' being set back, even if the beneficiaries are not directly responsible for having set those interests back. Indeed, this kind of backward-looking beneficiary account is not only given by those strictly concerned with the idea of reparation. Thomas Pogge—whose work I considered in chapter 5—for example, gives something like a beneficiary account of affluent individuals' special responsibilities to assist the poor. The affluent, he maintains, benefit from arrangements that impoverish others, authorize the institutions that produce such arrangements (presumably, in part at least, by voting for them, as well as by paying tax to them), and neither take compensating action nor shield victims from the effects of these global systems. Inasmuch as benefits could be refused (but instead individuals eagerly accept them) and the systems involved could be opposed and the victims protected (but individuals do not act to do so), on Pogge's account some *moral* responsibility for these harms fall on such affluent individual beneficiaries. They therefore have an obligation to try to improve the circumstances of those whose interests have been thus unfairly set back.

Both beneficiary and perpetrator accounts run into difficulties when *intergenerational* reparative claims are at stake, as they often are. Not only do perpetrators, original beneficiaries, and original victims disappear over time, but nonidentity problems start to arise. The sense of "benefit" and "harm" at stake here seems to imply that those concerned are either "better off" or "worse off" because of the past harm. But in intergenerational cases, the killing, dislocation, etc. caused by the perpetrators may actually create the very circumstances in which those particular individuals that now exist are born. As particular individuals, the offspring of those harmed are not worse off, since these particular individuals would not have existed at all without the past harms; they are produced by the harmful acts.[2] Intergenerational-reparations accounts have to take some account of nonidentity arguments (perhaps by moving to group-based rather than individual-based claims for reparation).[3] In addition, claims about being "better off" or "worse off," Waldron (1992, 8–10) plausibly argues, imply that we can know what would be the case now had some past harmful event that did occur not happened. But the status of such counterfactual reasoning is—at best—unclear.

Identifying perpetrators, disappearing perpetrators, the relation between causal and beneficiary accounts, and, in intergenerational applications, nonidentity and counterfactual problems all raise substantial difficulties for reparation accounts in the human case. And there is (at least) one further problem: The contentiousness of reparations claims varies partly in relation to what would *constitute* reparation. A formal apology for the past, for instance, is likely to be less contentious than reparation that involves land transfers. This is not surprising. While formal apologies may set back no existing person's or group's serious interests, land transfers almost certainly will. If those interests belong to nonperpetrating beneficiaries, especially where the land concerned has become critical to the beneficiaries' well-being and identity, a new set of claims about wrongful harm could be triggered in attempting to resolve the already existing claims. Reparations settlements that generate plausible new reparations claims surely look as though they should be avoided.[4]

Although these factors seriously complicate reparations claims, these complications do not provide sufficient reason to abandon all backward-looking justice claims of this kind. If some have unjustly been made much worse off while others have unjustly harmed them or have benefitted from the unjust harm, there does seem to be a moral case for some form of reparation.

"Reparation" in Animal Cases

Since I have argued that animals can be wrongfully harmed, a question about reparation—or at least some kind of backward-looking special obligation—is not ruled out in principle. And this is a form of relational obligation that could fit well with accounts of what is owed to animals in rights theory. Indeed, as I noted in chapter 3, Tom Regan (2004, xl) has raised the idea of "compensatory justice" for past rights infringements. But a number of general difficulties about extending the idea of reparation to animals arise.

One difficulty concerns the possible offensiveness of an animal comparison with human reparation. It might be argued that talk of reparation to animals, implicitly and perhaps explicitly, implies that human comparison classes are animal-like. This is especially problematic where a focus on displacement appears to draw a parallel between displaced peoples and displaced animals. But—although perhaps a claim for animal reparation *could* be expressed in offensive ways—this is not good reason to accept a more general "offensive comparison" argument. If animals share certain morally relevant capacities with humans, and these shared capacities underpin moral status, a certain kind of human-animal sameness has to be accepted. Once *this* sameness is conceded, it would be inconsistent to say that (for instance) a forward-looking utilitarian approach (thinking about consequences of possible actions on animals) is inoffensive but a backward-looking approach (looking at the effect of past actual actions on animals) is offensive. If harms of particular kinds are of moral concern, then they are of moral concern whenever they happen. Of course, there might be key differences between human and animal cases that make animal cases weaker or not morally relevant at all. But then it is these factors, not the very business of making the comparison, that are important.

A second kind of objection—one that seems more powerful—maintains that human and animal cases are dissimilar in morally relevant ways, because claims for reparation in human cases always come from those directly, or indirectly, harmed. If

99

reparation is dependent on the harmed party's *recognition* of the wrongful harm or the harmed party's *actively making a claim* for reparation with respect to the harm, or both, then reparation cannot apply to animals, who can do neither.

I will think this through with a human case: Suppose Group A is violently and forcibly displaced from its land by the more powerful Group B. Group A is forced to live (and die) in marginal areas where food, water, and shelter are sparse and inadequate. But let us say that the violent history is concealed by the conquerors from Group A's children. *They* do not know how their impoverished situation came about, nor that they are much worse off than they would otherwise have been, although it is no secret among the land's new occupants (Group B). Not knowing their situation, Group A's children can neither understand it nor protest about it and make demands for reparation. Does this mean that they are not *owed* any form of reparation?

If one accepts reparation at all, it would be strange to reject a claim here. Suppose the children subsequently found out that they had been wrongfully harmed and demanded reparation. Would reparation only be owed because now the children know about the harm and ask for compensation? Surely it is the wrong way round to say that their *awareness* of harm grounds claims for reparation (though the social discord generated by the demands themselves might provide an additional and forward-looking reason to justify such reparation). It is the existence of the wrongful harm that grounds the reparation. But if the harm itself, not the awareness of the harm, is the ground for reparation, then the animals case cannot be excluded on this basis. Animals may need human guardians or trustees to represent their claim, but the need for representation does not mean that they *could not have* a claim; claims can be made on behalf of humans even when they need representation.[5]

But perhaps a crucial difference is being passed over here. The children may have lacked the *awareness* of the harm, but they at least had the *capacity* to recognize it once they reached a certain age. Animals always lack that capacity.[6] This difference does stick. But is it of moral relevance? Suppose instead some humans with severe cognitive disabilities had been displaced from their land; they would also always lack the capacity to understand that they had been unjustly harmed, but would they thus be owed no reparation? This seems implausible; an injustice would surely have been committed against them even though they lacked the capacity to understand it.

Perhaps the thought here, though, is that while this was a wrongful harm, and some sort of "making good" *is* required, calling this making good "reparation" is mistaken. It may be that bound up into the use of the term "reparation" is the psychological understanding on the part of those involved that some offered and received benefit, compensation, or recognition *is* reparation. If this is right, then the term does not transfer well over to animals or to any other beings that could not psychologically recognize what reparation *is*. However, this is not sufficient reason to say that animals could have *no* claim on humans for *any kind* of backward-looking assistance in the case of wrongful harms, even if reparation is not the right word, and even if it is accepted that the extra psychological benefits gained from recognizing reparation *as* reparation do make reasons for reparation in (normal) human cases stronger than in animal cases. Since animals' interests have been wrongfully set back, it can still be argued that something is now owed to them. We could, instead, use the language of *special obligation* based on special relationship, rather than the language of reparation.

A third general concern about reparation claims is that they only hold good where harm was *intended*; accidental or unintentional harm cannot provide grounds for reparation. Of course, some harms in both human and animal contexts are intended, so this concern, if upheld, would merely serve to limit the scope of reparations claims in both human and animal cases rather than serve to reject them altogether. What is at stake here is what we *ought to know* about the nonmoral facts of situations in which we find ourselves. Someone persuaded by this view would need to think that we do not have to trouble ourselves at all to find out whether our actions might cause harms. But this is not a view that is widely held in the human case. Unger (1996, 32), for instance, plausibly maintains: "In an area frequented by little kids, when you park your car quickly, without taking care to know the space is free of kids, then, even if you cause no harm, there's something morally wrong with your behavior." That is, to use Raz's (2009) terms, there is a duty of care in such circumstances. But then, equally: wild areas are known to be frequented by sentient wild animals; when there are plans to develop such areas, not to try to find out what animals are there and not to consider how to protect or at least to accommodate their vital interests to some degree is also (I suggest) to breach a duty of care.[7] The developers could easily have known about the effects of their actions on wild sentient animals, even if they did not directly intend them, so there may still be grounds for special obligations to these animals—although lack of intention to harm on the part of perpetrators may plausibly *weaken* claims to assistance.

These points certainly suggest that claims for assisting animals on the basis of past harms must be carefully framed and may be weaker than comparable human claims to reparation. But this does not completely undermine the claim that we can have backward-looking special obligations to animals.

However, not all cases of human harms to animals are very amenable to accounts of this kind. Agricultural animals, for instance, are generally brought into being by humans and are substantially dependent on humans. While such animals can be (and frequently are) harmed in very serious ways, it is difficult to talk about reparation-like obligations to them, because paradigmatic reparation cases have two features not well replicated in agricultural animal cases. Reparations cases usually involve harms to independently existing individuals (or, on some accounts, groups) that are made worse off by the morally unjustifiable actions of others, and they are usually harms that have now ended but that have persisting negative effects on the victims or their offspring. Neither of these features comfortably apply to agricultural animals. These animals are not independently existing beings made much worse off than they would otherwise have been, or not in any standard sense. They have been bred by humans for the conditions in which they actually are. This raises such peculiarly complicated nonidentity and counterfactual problems that it is hard to make sense of any reparation-like claims here. Second, inasmuch as there are concerns about wrongful harms to agricultural animals, these are generally about *ongoing* harms. In that case, an argument to stop harming, rather than an argument for reparation-like responsibilities, has priority; it would be strange, after all, to recommend reparation for a harm that is still being committed, if there is some way of stopping the harm.[8]

However, cases where constitutively *wild* animals have been negatively affected by people look much closer to paradigmatic reparations cases, since these animals are independently existing and could have had other, better lives. Let us now consider this case study: *Coyotes*.[9]

Coyotes

A number of coyotes have been displaced from their habitat by a large residential housing development; they have lost access to much of their hunting territory and their denning areas have been destroyed. They cannot move elsewhere because other coyotes already occupy contiguous territory (and coyotes are territorial). The building of the housing estate has harmed the coyotes (setting back their serious experiential interests in ways that would not otherwise have occurred); they are now much worse off. They continue to suffer in the present from these past setbacks.[10] And they are vulnerable to new, related hazards: road danger has intensified, and the new residents of the housing estate are trying to trap or shoot them. At no stage have any interests of the coyotes been taken into account.

This case resembles, in structure, certain human reparation cases, where land has been taken from existing inhabitants, displacing them or making it much more difficult for them to live. While, as I have suggested, claims in the human case may be stronger than in the animal case—not least because of the ways in which humans can be aware of the unjust nature of past harms—this does not mean that, if we accept that the coyotes have moral status, their interests can be completely disregarded. Human activity has had the effect of making the coyotes more vulnerable (by exposing them to new threats such as road hazard and hunting) while at the same time compromising their ability to provide for themselves by building on their habitat, reducing the numbers of their prey animals, destroying denning areas, etc. In this sense, the human effect on coyotes (in intensifying vulnerability and reducing self-sufficiency) seriously sets back their interests, in an ongoing way. If we take their interests with moral seriousness, these harms should generate some backward-looking special obligations to assist.

However, even if we accept that animal cases generate weaker special obligations than human cases but otherwise no *special* difficulties, *Coyotes* still generates many of the same problems that human-reparation cases do: identification of perpetrators, disappearing perpetrators over time, receding victims over time, nonidentity problems, counterfactual claims, and the possible creation of new offenses toward nonperpetrating beneficiaries. How can these be dealt with in animal cases?

In the context of *Coyotes*, we can simplify by dealing with a (roughly) same-generation case: the original population of displaced coyotes and their immediate offspring (since immediate generations co-exist). So, we are considering coyotes that are the *very same ones* whose habitat once was what is now Wilderness Road and Coyote Close. This avoids both nonidentity and receding-victim problems.[11] The coyotes are now both absolutely badly off and worse off in morally relevant ways because of the residential development. So: there are past morally relevant harms with persisting negative effects and enhanced vulnerability (through road traffic and hunting), *and* we can identify "victims" to whom some kind of special obligation is owed. This tells us some of what we need to know, but two key issues remain: *who* should assist the coyotes, and *what would count* as doing so? Dealing with both these issues is problematic.

Suppose we adopt a causal account and focus on perpetrators, that is, that those who displaced the coyotes are responsible for assisting them. We face two difficulties: *identifying* the relevant perpetrators and dealing with *disappearing* perpetrators. Identifying perpetrators is difficult because so many different individuals were involved: the former owners of the land, the developers, the architects, and the construction workers. And even if one could identify such perpetrators in theory, it may no longer be possible to track them down: perhaps the architects, developers, and construction workers have now moved elsewhere; the companies have gone out of business; and some individuals have retired. Although perpetrator accounts have obvious advantages, it can be very difficult to pursue perpetrators, even over short periods of time.

The alternative, then, is to turn to a beneficiary account: those who gain from some wrongful harm (which may include but not be limited to perpetrators of the harm) have some special obligations toward those whose interests are being set back by the harm in an ongoing way. Beneficiary accounts, of course, have difficulties too. The main ongoing beneficiaries are the new residents of the housing estate. But (let us assume) these beneficiaries acquired their land with justly earned money at market prices. If the new residents were to suffer substantial losses from reparation claims, it would not be unreasonable of them to claim that *they* had now been harmed.

One way of thinking through the impasse here is to begin from a different place: what kind of assistance is appropriate, given the setbacks to the coyotes' interests? What would really help them and at least begin to "make good" some of the ongoing negative effects from which they are suffering?

As I have already noted, there are some standard human gains from reparations that coyotes cannot experience. They cannot gain psychologically from knowing that reparation *is* reparation; anything like an apology or a memorialization would be wasted on them. They lack concepts of justice, bear no grudges against either perpetrators or beneficiaries, and seek no satisfaction from either. They cannot analyze why they might have been thrown into such a vulnerable position. They cannot be resentful, blame others, campaign for change, nor seek retribution. And there is no reason (unlike in the human case) to prefer to seek reparation from perpetrators on account of the satisfaction that this would give the victims, nor to be concerned about the effects on social disharmony if reparation is not extracted from the perpetrators. And there is perhaps a further sense in which coyote claims are weaker than human ones would be, deriving from the idea of property rights. In comparable human cases, it is often argued that reparation is required because those forcibly displaced had property rights to the land (even if these were not recognized at the time). Some recent work in environmental ethics *has* argued that sentient wild animals should be accorded property rights to their habitat (Hadley 2005). But I am not going to defend this difficult claim; it may be that property-rights arguments provide extra reasons for reparation to displaced humans but not for animals. The wrongful harm to the coyotes that I am interested in was not an encroachment on their property rights but of making their lives painful, miserable, and vulnerable, both absolutely and relatively.[12]

The weaker nature of animals' claims provide grounds for thinking that "making good" need not mean (as it might in a comparable human case) restoring the coyotes to their land by, for instance, removing buildings and rewilding the land. Rather, it primarily requires the conferral of practical benefits that make living easier and less dangerous for them, so that the coyotes' lives now are relatively and absolutely better, closer to their lives before the development. Since it is highly unlikely they could benefit from being relocated, this means accommodating them better where they are.[13] One of the reasons why the coyote case is relatively easy is that such accommodation is possible—though it can be difficult, both for coyotes and for humans. Land can be (and frequently is) open to multiple uses by a number of species, including humans, simultaneously; these species include coyotes. What is needed, given the relatively weak nature of the coyotes' claims and the kind of assistance from which they could actually benefit, is that the coyotes are able to become less vulnerable and more self-sufficient right where they are. After all, unlike the vulnerability of domes-

ticated animals, the vulnerability of these coyotes is contingent and external; changing their environments can reduce their human-originating vulnerability. This is the
nearest to "making good" that is possible for the coyotes. And it also helps to resolve
the problem about who should assist them. Given what the coyotes need, they can
best be assisted by the ongoing beneficiaries: those who live in the housing development that was built on their former habitat.

What does this mean for these human residents? They have (like everyone else)
general, prima facie duties not to harm the coyotes, since the coyotes are sentient,
morally considerable creatures. So (unless there are extremely serious conflicts between the residents and the coyotes, far beyond their just being a "nuisance") they
should not trap, hunt, or otherwise cause suffering to the coyotes. But *these* residents, I am suggesting, *also* have special obligations to *these* coyotes, because they
are benefiting from the coyotes' past harm, ongoing vulnerability, and constrained
self-sufficiency. This does not mean that the residents should directly provide for
the coyotes, since the provision of food, while this might help in the short term, is
unlikely to advance their longer-term interests; in promoting habituation, feeding
would produce dependence and thus heighten, not reduce, vulnerability. Rather, the
residents should *tolerate* the coyotes and to be willing to live alongside them, thus
reducing at least the most potent threat to the coyotes' well-being and allowing the
coyotes to make the best life they can in their reduced circumstances.[14] The benefits
of the land should be shared with the animals whose habitat it used to be, perhaps
involving messier land use, some restoration of coyote habitat, fencing, and traffic
calming. This might generate inconvenience and irritation to human residents and
would require close monitoring of domesticated animals and teaching children how
best to respond to coyote encounters. But it would not involve relinquishing and destroying the humans' property.

So there are several reasons, in this case, for moving to a beneficiary account. This
beneficiary focus, though, need not be a prescription for *all* animal-reparation cases,
although it does follow the trend in recent debate over *human* reparation that repa-
ratory responsibilities should shift over time from perpetrators to ongoing beneficiaries (Mamdani 2001, 59). But where perpetrators are plural or disappearing while
(other) beneficiaries are easy to identify, best placed to bring about the benefit, and
can do so at relatively low cost, it makes pragmatic sense for these beneficiaries to
be assigned the responsibility to assist. Were the situation different—for instance,
were the fulfillment of these kinds of special obligations extremely costly—then the
original developers, if still in existence, could be held responsible for contributing to
the costs of "retrofitting" the housing estate for wild-animal habitat. It would be better, of course, were developers required to accommodate the basic interests of sentient wild animals by design or (if necessary or possible) relocation in their original
plans. That is, it would be better to avoid the relevant harm in the first place. But my

105

concern here, as in this book more generally, has been to think about assistance—in this case what should be done after a harm has been committed—rather than about preventing the harms themselves.

A number of questions remain about intergenerational animal cases or instances of sentient animals whose habitat cannot be shared with people. I do not have room to consider these complications here. However, there is one other important question I want to explore further in the next section. Suppose I were to buy a house in the new housing estate, and some ethicist comes by one day, telling me I have a "special obligation" to displaced coyotes, from whose former habitat I am benefiting. One (printable!) kind of response might be: "But aren't special obligations things to which one voluntarily agrees? Sure, I may have some general duty not to *harm* sentient animals, but I never signed up to *assist* any of them! I can't have special obligations to which I didn't agree." This question is very similar to the one I raised at the end of chapter 5: whether we can have special obligations that we have not voluntarily assumed. In the rest of this chapter—using another case study, *Dumpster Kittens*— I want to consider a number of further problems about backward-looking claims, including this concern about voluntarism, and—additionally—possible ways to deal with claims that look as though they rely on a kind of "group" responsibility.

VOLUNTARISM AND GROUP RESPONSIBILITY
Dumpster Kittens

Suppose the owner of a pedigree cat decides to breed from her. However, once born, the kittens turn out to have various breed imperfections and are unlikely to sell for a profit. So the breeder takes the week-old kittens and leaves them in a dumpster. Even if—had they been older—these kittens might have lived feral lives, they are too young right now to survive; left in the dumpster, they will die unless assisted. Out for an evening stroll, Peter passes the dumpster. Hearing noises, he looks in and sees the kittens. Should he assist them? Consider a variation on this case: Suppose instead Peter chances upon a nest of week-old urban *rats* in a dumpster, apparently abandoned by their mother and also too young to survive without assistance. Should he assist the baby rats? Are his responsibilities different in the two cases, and if so, why?

First, I want to think about this case from a capacity-oriented perspective. Here we have animals with similar capacities: both the rats and the kittens are sentient and suffering. In both cases, Peter can assist and is well (and best) placed to do so. From a utilitarian or capabilities view, it looks as though Peter should assist both cats and rats. (There *might* be an argument for differential treatment of the kittens and the rats based on consequences, but I am unsure how this would go). On some forms of the negative-rights view, both cases should also be treated the same, though the prescription would be reversed: since negative rights alone do not provide for duties to assist, there is no obligation on this basis to assist either the kittens or the rats. A rights view, on the other hand, that calls on moral agents to assist in cases of prior rights infringements is likely to maintain that Peter should help the kittens but not the rats, as does a relational approach of the kind that I have been developing. These latter views give us grounds for discriminating between these cases, by maintaining that the "back story" in the case of the kittens is rather different from that of the rats. However, this claim about morally relevant back stories, as we will see, raises a series of further questions—also raised by *Coyotes*—about how an individual like Peter could be related to harms committed by others and whether he could have special obligations to which he has not explicitly consented.

Let us begin by thinking about the back stories here. The kittens are in the dumpster because of the actions of the breeder. But it is not, solely, the actions of the individual breeder that have led to this situation. The breeder is also part of a larger, institutional history of domestication and pet ownership—in this case, the deliberate human creation of breeds as companion animals. The kittens are bred, after all, because they can be sold; there are other people who would buy the kittens, people who would show the kittens, corporations that would feed the kittens, and so on. While being a fine example of a pedigree breed can, in one sense, make an animal constitutively more vulnerable (for instance, the common phenomenon of deafness in white Persian cats makes them more vulnerable to road traffic), breed perfection can also *protect* an animal, since its marketability (as in this case) may be a matter of life and death. The breeder's decisions are at least influenced by the market for pedigree companion animals, so there is some sense in which responsibility for these kittens' fate is broader than the actions of the individual breeder herself. But however we read this responsibility, it is clearly humans—primarily the breeder, but other humans too—who are responsible both for the *existence* of the kittens and for their current suffering and ongoing realized vulnerability.

Compare this with the back story for the urban brown rats. Urban brown rats are (usually) contramensals, living alongside humans despite deadly discouragement. They are constitutively wild, not domesticated: their populations have expanded into and benefited from human societies, but humans have not deliberately invited them in—quite the contrary. The back story here, then, is rather different from the kittens' story. (However, I should note that any claims about urban brown rats are not intended to extend to *all* rats, since some rats have very different relations to people. The relation of companion fancy rats to humans is very like that of pedigree kittens, and the relation of experimental rats in laboratories to humans is quite different again. Although all rats are categorized as *rattus* and share similar *capacities* to one another, the claims here are *not* species oriented; different members of the

107

same species may be in very different relations to people.)

Peter—out for his evening stroll—then, is located differently with respect to the kittens and rats, because of these differing back stories. When Peter chances upon the kittens, they are already victims of another human's unethical actions—and Peter knows this just by seeing the kittens, even though he does not know exactly how they got there. He also knows that the kittens are members of a breed and species from which humans derive benefit (including, plausibly, Peter himself). This, I'll argue shortly, gives Peter some weak moral reason to assist, even though he did not *himself* breed or harm the kittens; the kittens have been harmed by a human and have been created, more generally, within a human-directed institutional framework that brings gains to people through making vulnerable animals. What of the rats? Urban rats live and flourish alongside humans; they are adapted to the human world, and do not strictly fall under the "No-contact" part of the LFI. But, on the other hand, these rats have not obviously been harmed by any person, they do not have a deliberately created constitutive vulnerability, and they have not been spatially constrained by humans.[15] If urban rats are dependent on humans, this is not because of any individual or group decision to *make* them that way (indeed quite the contrary). In this sense, then, the situation of urban, constitutively wild animals like rats is rather like that of fully wild animals: there are prima facie negative duties not to harm them but no special obligations to assist them, even when they are needy and suffering (though assistance is permissible and may be required in cases of preexisting harms or if dependence-creating relations of assistance have intentionally been established). So, Peter is *not required* to assist the rats, even if we took painless killing to be a form of assistance in such a case. He could walk on by without having done anything wrong. It would be permissible for him to assist—indeed, it might be argued that it would be a supererogatorily good action if he did (though he probably would not get much support from an animal-rescue center for showing up with the nest of a wild rat)—but he is not morally required to do so.

However, claiming that, in such circumstances, Peter has a special obligation (albeit a weak one, as I will explain) to assist the kittens is highly contentious. And it is contentious for some of the same reasons as *Coyotes* was contentious. Can we say that Peter has special obligations that he has never voluntarily assumed? Does the claim that he has any kind of moral obligation imply that there is some group responsibility to assist companion animals, in which Peter cannot help but participate? How could such claims be justified?

One part of the challenge to the view I am proposing is a voluntarist one. Voluntarists argue that "all special responsibilities must be based on consent or some other voluntary act" (Scheffler 2001, 1998). Indeed, some philosophers distinguish between the terms "duties" and "obligations," maintaining that obligations, unlike duties, must be voluntarily assumed (see, for example, Brandt 1964). The relational view for which I have been arguing looks as though it would be in trouble if we took a voluntarist approach. For a voluntarist, there are general duties and relational, special obligations for which consent is needed. But I am suggesting that there are relational special obligations to assist—alongside general duties not to harm—that do not require an individual's consent, at least not in an explicit sense. So, Peter has special obligations to assist the kittens to which he never assented.

It is helpful here to consider different forms of voluntarism, since these understand "voluntariness" somewhat differently. Some argue that one must have explicitly consented to each particular special obligation, others maintain that by entering particular "relationship roles" one consents to the obligations that go along with the role, and still other forms of voluntarism maintain that explicit consent to obligations in either of these ways is not needed if there is voluntary acceptance of the benefits that come from a relationship. On this latter view, by voluntarily accepting the benefits, one has implicitly consented to the relationship and thus to the special obligations that may then flow from it. For those who take the view that explicit consent to special obligations is required, *promise making* is a central model, since a promise is a voluntary commitment that sets up a special obligation to the promisee with respect to the matter of the promise. Those who argue in favor of "relationship roles" see *parenthood* as the paradigm case; in voluntarily taking on the role of "parent," one agrees to assume the corresponding obligations of care for a child. On the third view, *friendship* might constitute a core case: if one voluntarily accepts the benefits of a friendship, then one is accepting the relationship of friendship and the special obligations to the friend that come along with that relationship. Underlying all these voluntarist claims is the view that people do not have special moral obligations arising from memberships of groups, the actions of others, or from situations or relations to which they have not in one of these senses consented. So it looks as though Peter could not have obligations to the kittens based on the breeder having harmed them nor on the basis that he is the member of a group that produced and upholds an institution that led to the harm. Equally, the residents of the housing estate could not have special obligations to the coyotes that the estate displaced merely on the basis that, as residents, they are benefiting from the harm to the coyotes. Special obligations may, after all, impose severe constraints on one's actions and require considerable sacrifices. One cannot just discover that one has these constraints; consent is required to assume them.

Of course, some of the obligations toward domesticated animals outlined here *are* voluntarily assumed by individuals, perhaps falling into the category of "role" voluntarism—owning a companion animal being a paradigm case. The cat breeder, for instance, in taking on the role, should have assumed the obligations of care for the kittens that come with this relation. But Peter does not have the same relationship to the kittens as the breeder: he did not cause them to come into being; any obligation he has to assist does not seem to be voluntarily self-assumed at all.

I will argue below that his obligation to assist—as with those living on the housing estate in *Coyotes*—could be made to work with the idea of voluntary acceptance of benefits. But the voluntarist premise can be more fundamentally questioned. It is not obvious why one should accept the view that all special obligations must be voluntarily self-assumed (Kagan 1992, 230). Some relations usually thought to establish special obligations are *not* entered into voluntarily. Siblings do not voluntarily enter the role of being a sibling, and children do not voluntarily enter the role of "being X's child," but being someone's sibling or someone's child are usually thought to be relations that carry obligations. Other relations—like parenthood—that are thought to establish special obligations may be *entered* voluntarily but do not offer the possibility of voluntary *exit*. This raises questions about their voluntary nature in the longer term; they are not, for instance, like standard contractual relations. Most generally, as Scheffler (2001, 64) argues: "We are, after all, born to parents we did not choose at a time we did not choose; and we land in some region of a social world we did not choose. And from the moment of our birth, and sometimes sooner, claims are made on us and for us and to us." Although the obligations that arise from relations may be burdensome (as well as beneficial), this does not necessarily mean that they must be self-assumed. After all, general duties—primarily duties not to harm—are often burdensome, but no one argues that *they* must therefore be voluntarily self-assumed; it seems strange to use burdensomeness as a reason for arguing that special obligations, unlike general ones, must be self-assumed.[16] Thus it is not convincing that the voluntarist argument about special obligations should be accepted at all.

Nevertheless, an argument about voluntary acceptance of benefits—rather like Pogge's argument with respect to obligations to the globally impoverished—is worth pursuing here and may help cast some light on Peter's obligations to the kittens. Of course, Peter's encounter with the kittens is certainly involuntary, and it is unlikely that any relationship with these particular kittens will ever benefit him. But if we broaden the relevant back story, we can see that there's a story to tell about how Peter may benefit from the institution of pet ownership, of which the kittens are a manifestation.

Pet breeding[17] and ownership is a deeply rooted institution in many human societies. But there's more to say here: in developed Western societies such as the United States, at least, research indicates that those who keep companion animals benefit from their presence. Companion animals seem to bring a variety of health gains, including a reduced risk of cardiovascular disease (Anderson et al. 1992), lower blood pressure, reduction in instances of depression, reduction in stress, and, of course, pleasure and companionship (Barker and Wolen 2008; Friedman and Son 2009). They also provide assistance to those who are blind, frail, or subject to seizures.[18] And very many people do live with companion animals; 50 percent of U.S. households kept a sentient animal or bird as a pet in 2007.[19] Relatedly, the presence of companion animals appears to bring benefits to *all* the members of developed societies, even those that do not keep them. The reduction in human health-care costs from pet ownership, for instance, in Australia alone, was estimated in 1995 to be between AUS$790m and AUS$1.5b.[20] In addition—although, undoubtedly there are some social costs from companion animals—there are a wide variety of other social benefits, not least a reduction in social tension, an increase in social-support networks, and the creation of large numbers of jobs.

Pet ownership, then, is a deeply entrenched human institution, closely (though not completely) bound in with domestication. Both institutions benefit humans, and most humans as individuals have at some time in their lives benefited from these institutions. To parallel Pogge's case with respect to other global institutions, such as trade, in accepting the benefits of the institution of pet ownership, actively perpetuating it in one's life, and not disassociating oneself from it or protesting against it, on the arguments I have suggested above, one acquires some share in moral responsibility for it—and for those individuals produced by it. The pedigree dumpster kittens are animals in an extremely vulnerable situation, placed there in part by a human who has abandoned her duty not to harm them, but also created (and rejected) by an institution from which every pet owner has benefited. If Peter is benefiting or has benefited from the institution of pet ownership by having or having had a companion animal of his own, he has, on this argument, an obligation to assist the kittens. It follows, again, that this obligation to assist would be absent in the case of the baby rats, for rats are not the product of a human institution that intentionally produces dependence and vulnerability from which humans have benefited and are benefiting, and from which this particular person has him- or herself benefited.

But now, let us suppose Peter has no companion animal, he has never had one, and he has no particular support for the institution of pet ownership. What should he do, on encountering the pedigree dumpster kittens? (I will say more about *encounter* in chapter 8.) Does pet-free Peter have any obligation to assist the kittens, one that he would not have to the rats?

There are two possible kinds of reasons for giving a positive answer to this question, the first (I think) somewhat more plausible than the second. The first is that Peter gains some small personal benefits from being in a society with the institution of pet keeping. The second is that Peter contributes toward the creation of a shared group attitude toward animals that makes harming them permissible, and that as such, he shares in moral responsibilities to assist those animals wrongfully harmed, even where he himself did not cause the harm. I will take these in turn; the second will need somewhat more explanation than the first.

Personal benefit: Pet-free Peter, as I have suggested above, is likely to benefit as an individual in minor social and economic ways from the institution of pet ownership. This minor benefit is enough to generate a weak obligation to assist the kittens (most likely to alert an animal-rescue organization to assist directly), an obligation he would not have to the rats. However, this claim might be thought to have some troubling implications. After all, it is normally true that we can choose whether to keep a companion animal or not. So in this sense, we can choose whether to gain the direct benefits available from companion animals. Peter has chosen not to gain these direct benefits (perhaps there would not be benefits, given his circumstances). But still, he lives in a society where there are minor benefits to him from the institution of pet keeping. He cannot avoid getting these—they seem to be *nonexcludable* goods, benefits that, to use a distinction of Simmons (1979, 129), one has nonexcludably received rather than accepted. So then, he has involuntarily acquired special obligations, albeit rather weak ones, toward vulnerable companion animals such as the dumpster kittens. Is there nothing he can do about this? Is he, to use Baier's (1991, 209) expression, just "saddled with" these special obligations, rather than choosing to assume them—as we always are in general situations where we should not harm?

But it does seem possible in this case that someone like Peter could, at least, disassociate him- or herself from the institution of pet breeding and pet ownership, even if he or she could not disavow the small and intangible benefits. That is, there is perhaps a possible *exit* from this special obligation—of the kind to which Pogge draws attention—even if we did not choose to get into it and cannot shed the benefits gained from the institution. For instance, supporting policies aimed at reducing the number of companion animals or contributing to organizations that oppose companion animals in principle could constitute sufficient disassociation (although many groups that oppose the institution of pet keeping would still argue that there are obligations to assist individual companion animals that have resulted from it—as, for instance, does PETA). But if pet-free Peter disassociated himself in this way, he *could* walk on past the dumpster kittens, since he is not harming them and they have no special call on his assistance. So the weak obligation to assist is not, I think, completely inescapable.

Shared attitude: For this kind of argument to make sense, it is necessary to maintain that a *group* can, in some way, be morally responsible or blameworthy. This is controversial in application to any group. But it is particularly controversial with respect to *unorganized* groups such as ethnic or national groups, or even "humanity" (as opposed to *organized* groups, such as governments or corporations with formal decision-making procedures).[21] But, of course, for the claims I am interested in here—not only in *Dumpster Kittens* but more broadly—it would be helpful to say something about just these kinds of unorganized groups. I did not, for instance, in the last chapter, say that individuals had to be personally responsible for either harms or the generation of vulnerabilities or that individuals had to be beneficiaries from harms or the generation of vulnerabilities in order to have obligations toward domesticated animals. My original claim sounded more like this (roughly rendered): if *some* humans have created especially vulnerable and dependent animals, *all* humans appropriately placed have obligations to assist them in relevant ways.

"Appropriately placed," however, *could* be filled, as I have suggested, with "who have benefited." But another more controversial possibility would be to make a group claim: that (for instance) humans (or nationals of a particular country, or members of a community, etc.) are a group such that responsibility for the actions of some group members can, at least loosely, though not necessarily equally, be attributed to all the group members. That is, *all* group members would have some (though not necessarily *equal*) moral responsibility for the activities of some members, even though other group members did not themselves act in this way nor (for clarity) necessarily benefit from these actions. This idea of group responsibility is controversial in several ways, particularly in its apparent lack of voluntarism and in the way in which nonactors share in at least partial moral responsibility for actions they did not themselves perform. Despite the controversial nature of such claims, I will develop an argument to this effect, even though the relational approach I am defending does not stand or fall on its success.

An argument by Held (2002, 160) helps develop this idea. She argues that accepting the idea of group responsibility both corresponds to common human practice and "enables us to have a richer and more appropriate understanding of the relevant moral features of human actions and practices." She uses the case of ethnic conflict to support her argument and focuses on the idea of *shared attitudes*.

Suppose all the members of ethnic group A hold the view that members of ethnic group B are inferior, stupid, criminal (etc.). Some members of ethnic group A commit acts of violence toward members of group B; others do not. But all share the same underlying attitudes of denigration and hostility. Is it not the case, Held suggests, that the hostile and denigrating attitudes of members of group A increase the likelihood of harm to members of group B, even though only some members of group A actualize these harms in practice? If this is the case—if all members are responsible for contributing to a climate of denigration and hostility—then this is a reason to hold all members of group A responsible even though some of them did not perform the relevant harmful actions. There is, on Held's account, no requirement that they be held *equally* responsible. And she also allows for possible *exits*: individuals can disassociate themselves from the attitudes of the group and in this way at least reduce the moral responsibility that flows from membership of the group (she notes, however, that one might still be benefiting from the harms to others, in which case disassociation might not be enough to free oneself from all moral responsibility).

How, then, might this kind of approach be relevant here? One possibility is to maintain that humans, or some groups of humans, share attitudes toward animals that create an "attitudinal climate" of risk to animals in which harming animals is

113

likely to occur. A number of different beliefs and attitudes could contribute toward creating this attitudinal climate: beliefs that animals do not or cannot feel pain, attitudes of indifference to animal pain, attitudes of deliberate ignorance about animal pain, attitudes that depend on human superiority and animal instrumentality, strong anthropocentrism, attitudes of enjoyment of animal pain, and so on. These different attitudes patch together a shared attitudinal climate in which, while only some are actually directly responsible for harms to individual animals, many others contribute to creating the world in a way that such harms are sometimes institutionalized (as in the meat industry), encouraged, or at least tolerated. To return to *Dumpster Kittens*, even though Peter himself did not dump the kittens, he likely shares in a variety of social attitudes toward animals from which the production of pedigree animals and the dumping of imperfect or otherwise unwanted companion animals emerges. In this sense, as a member of the group that produces the attitudinal climate, Peter shares in moral responsibility for what it produces. And this gives him a weak moral responsibility to assist the dumped kittens.

Of course, Peter might not share in any of the attitudes that patch together this attitudinal climate of increased risk and acceptability of harm to animals. If that is so—as with the argument from personal benefit above—and he has disassociated himself from such attitudes, protested against them (or aspects of them), withdrawn or refused support for them, and so on, then he does not share in the moral responsibility for harms that the shared attitude at least indirectly produces. In that case—as with the argument from personal benefit—he does not share even very weak moral responsibility for the harms that have befallen the kittens, and he has no special obligation to assist them any more than he has an obligation to assist the rats.

To conclude: In this chapter, by looking at two cases, *Coyotes* and *Dumpster Kittens*, I have tried to develop the relational approach to animal assistance in several ways. I have argued that preexisting, human-caused harms can provide reasons to assist animals thus harmed. And I have suggested that special obligations to assist such harmed animals can be generated either by causing harms, benefiting in some way from the harms, or (more tentatively) sharing in attitudes that, indirectly at least, contribute to the production of such harms.

7

Some
Problems
and
Questions

Here I will tackle some pressing problems and questions that might be thought to undermine this more relational, contextual approach to animal ethics. First, I will consider the possible claim that in defending any underpinning for the LFI, I am relying on a problematic human/nature dualism, a worry that may have emerged at various points in the argument. Second, I will turn to a potentially troubling implication of the No-contact LFI that arose in chapter 5: that it gives no moral reason to assist strange *human beings* with whom one has, as it were, had "no contact." I will then consider two questions that have arisen at various points in the book: first, are there some human/animal relations that we just shouldn't create—and is domestication (given the vulnerable and dependent states it produces) one such relation? And second, going back to chapter 1 and other parts of the book, is painless killing a harm to the individual animals killed? (Important though both these questions are, the No-contact LFI is compatible with different answers to them). Finally, I will briefly tackle one last problem: does the approach advocated in this book require an excessive amount of information, thus making moral decision-making impossibly difficult?

THE PROBLEM OF HUMAN/NATURE DUALISM

This problem might be articulated in a number of different ways, but at its heart is this worry: does the claim that we have no duties to assist wild animals, but special obligations to assist domesticated animals, presuppose a dualistic separation of humans from the rest of nature, between the "wild" and what is "not wild," so that human actions in relation to wild animals are seen as "interference?" That a view implies such a dualistic human/nature separation is commonly thought to render it problematic. So, for instance, Desjardins (2003, 142) says of Paul Taylor's work: "The emphasis on noninterference as a major normative principle suggests a view of humans and nature that is questionable at best. To say that we ought not to interfere with nature implies that humans are somehow outside of or distinct from nature, so we should leave natural processes alone." Perhaps a similar concern applies to my argument?

A more specific—though directly related—problem concerns a possible implication of the view I have been developing for native peoples and other groups following more "traditional" ways of life. Is an unpalatable dichotomy thrown up, whereby either such peoples fall out of the category "human" and into the category "wild," with respect (for example) to their hunting practices,[1] or, alternatively, where such peoples are judged to be acting unethically? This may in turn suggest yet another problem: is the view being proposed here universalistic in a "bad" sense, lacking in cultural sensitivity and indifferent to context in the human case?

Does the No-contact LFI assume some kind of dualistic separation of humans from nature? This question needs unpacking, since different concerns may be at issue here. First, wildness, as presented here, is neither some kind of intrinsic value nor a nonrelational property that is manifested by particular animals. Although I have noted other views that could be interpreted in one of these ways, I have not adopted such a view of wildness myself. On my account, wildness is relational; it signals a lack of interaction between humans and animals, in particular in terms of location and nondomestication. And wildness forms part of a spectrum of possible relations, not one side of a dualism; animals can be more or less wild and more or less wild in different ways. In this sense, there is no sharp, dualistic dichotomy between what is wild and what is not; in thinking about the "contact zone," I have actually tried to undermine such dualism.

Second, my arguments here do not imply any broader claim about the wrongness of "interfering with nature." A defense of the Strong LFI might require such a claim, but neither the Weak nor the No-contact versions of the LFI require it. The argument here is that there is a prima facie duty not to harm wild animals (a duty that applies to all animals, not just to wild ones) and that there is no special obligation to assist wild animals, on the grounds that such special obligations are created by relations that do not exist in the wild case. That we are not required to rescue prey from predators, for example, does not follow from any general, dualistic rule of nonintervention in the wild; it applies because humans do not have the appropriate relations that would generate such an obligation. (And assistance is not *forbidden*, at least not on any grounds I have given here.) If, in the human case, I were to claim that I have special obligations to assist my own children that I do not have toward yours, even if you do not accept the claim, your objection to it is unlikely, after all, to be based on the view that my position is *dualistic*.

116

A third possible dualism a critic might have in mind concerns the attribution of moral agency to (some) humans and not to anything else. This concern would not relate to worries about a wild/nonwild distinction, however, since my account does not presuppose that any animals are moral agents. But still, some kind of dualism between (most) humans and everything else may exist here. This dualism is one I will accept, though noting that all humans for some of their lives—and some humans for all of their lives—are not moral agents, that there may be degrees of moral agency, and that it is possible that nonhuman moral agents exist, even though we do not (with certainty) know of any.

Fourth, an objection that might really bite—and that leads on to the concern about native peoples—can be derived from Val Plumwood's (2000) attack on what she calls "ontological veganism." The particular focus of Plumwood's concern is that arguments for veganism are "ecologically alienated" and fail to acknowledge that all bodies (including our own) are "edible." At the heart of this objection, I think, is the idea that it is "natural" to eat others and be eaten in turn: the denial of this is a denial of one's place in the ecological world.

Although I have not discussed vegetarianism or veganism, there is room for an objection like Plumwood's to the position that I have proposed. One part of Plumwood's argument is that predation—the consumption of others, whether sentient or not—is part of what it is to participate in an ecosystem. A view that eschews consuming sentient others, especially in a wild context, is a view that denies ecological connection, for such consumption lies at the heart of ecosystems. For Plumwood, this is one sign of our ecological alienation, an alienation that is manifested in a variety of other ways, such as locking up our own dead bodies to prevent them from being eaten. But, on the other hand, Plumwood's account also does not deny that wild sentient animals are morally considerable, nor does she suggest that to be concerned about killing or causing wild animals pain is either mistaken or misplaced.[2] Indeed, Plumwood insists that all animal life should be treated with respect—even reverentially—but maintains that killing animals for food in particular contexts should, nonetheless, not be regarded as unethical. The context about which she has particular concern involves the ways of life of native peoples.

Does this relational view suggest that the ways of living of some native peoples are ethically problematic? The ways of life followed by some native peoples pose a problem for a number of accounts of environmental ethics. Some environmental ethicists opt for forms of the view that the hunting practices of native peoples, or sometimes hunting more generally, falls outside human culture and is, in some sense, a "wild" practice. Rolston (1994, 123), for instance, maintains that much hunting is morally unproblematic, because it is an action common across species for survival and is thus, in this very particular sense, "natural." To put Rolston's claim in the terms I have been using: there is a class of human actions that, when carried out in a

117

certain way by humans toward animals, *do not count* as producing human impacts or effects. The species commonality of such actions neuters the "humanness" of their origin. Activities like this, then, collapse into "the wild," into "human as predator," and do not, as it were, stand out as human in terms of being the actions of moral agents. Native peoples' hunting falls into this category of "natural therefore permissible" for Rolston (while trophy hunting does not).

Even without tracking the problems of this view too closely, it has several implications that look well worth avoiding. It is puzzling to suggest that there is some class of voluntary actions that, because it is shared with other species, is exempted from moral scrutiny in the human case (some animals kill conspecifics in mating fights, for instance, so should parallel killings by humans be morally tolerable)? In addition, there is a way of reading this suggestion that implies that the traditional lives of native peoples are in this respect—and presumably in others—"less human" than the lives of urbanites. Of course, Rolston maintains that urbanites *can* hunt "naturally" too. But still, it is at least possible that on this kind of account, traditional native ways of life display more cross-species commonality than urban lives, potentially lending support to a view that they are "less human" or perhaps "less cultured" than those people who live in other ways. Indeed, there is one particular way in which my account might slip into that view: were it to be assumed that the animals that live around the settlements of native peoples are "fully wild" while those that live around urban settlements (for instance) such as squirrels or raccoons are constitutively but not locationally wild. But native peoples, of course, have a variety of relations with the animals that surround them and live among them, just as urbanites do.

Rejecting the view that there is something "wild" about the practices of native peoples, however, moves toward the other worry: that to accept the No-contact LFI is to judge the ways of life of such peoples to be unethical, that the No-contact LFI lacks contextual sensitivity, and that it manifests the kind of cultural imperialism to which Plumwood so strongly objects. However, I do not think these need follow.

The duty not to harm, as part of the No-contact LFI, is a prima facie duty. Since I have primarily been exploring questions about assistance, the focus of this book has not been on how to weigh harms to animals in the context of significant human interests.[3] It is very plausible that for many native peoples, hunting animals for food and fur is a vital interest in a way that eating meat and wearing fur is not normally the case for people living in industrial societies, and that an adequately nutritious diet is not possible for these peoples without the consumption of sentient, morally considerable animals. In such cases, human interests in vital nutrition, warmth, and survival are likely to outweigh animals' interests in not being hunted. In addition (and I will consider this problem further below), where I have worried about harms to sentient animals, I have focused on aversive experiences, especially pain. But— contrasting with the lives of many animals in industrial farming—animals may be hunted and killed by humans in the wild without high levels of pain or sustained aversive experiences; it is not necessary to completely endorse Plumwood's (2000, 300) comment here to see something in it: "In the one case an animal's entire life can be instrumentalized and distorted in the most painful ways in the service of an unremitting, unreflective, and ungrateful human desire for meat . . . in the other case, an animal can be made use of responsibly and seriously to fulfill an important need, in a way that respects . . . both its individuality and its normal species life."

The idea that animals might be treated in any way that people wish—that harming them is of no import or not something to be taken seriously—is, I think, not a view widely held among native peoples themselves. Accounts by anthropologists make it clear that at least some (although not all) native hunting cultures understand hunting to be—to use Tim Ingold's (2000, 47) phrase—a relation of "inter-agentivity." Animals are active and relational, and even sometimes seen as members of other peoples. While this does not make killing animals for food impermissible on such views, it does make it nontrivial; such killings may, for instance, require justification and propitiation. Of course, these perspectives on animals flow from quite different worldviews than the one from which this book originates. It would be a mistake to suggest that some easy unity is possible. But still, it is not clear that anything that I have said so far in the book is necessarily insensitive to the hunting practices of native peoples or automatically renders their actions unethical. The particular contexts and relations relevant to any particular case would need to be considered more closely before judgments could be made.

THE PROBLEM OF HUMAN ASSISTANCE

A significant problem for the relational approach that I have been developing arose in chapter 5: perhaps this relational view suffers from a similar difficulty to the one I attributed to an unreformed negative rights position in chapter 2. That is, one might be convinced that good arguments underpin the claim that there are no duties to assist wild animals, so long as they are in a situation of no contact—that is, where they have not suffered preexisting harms of human origin—when special obligations might arise. But is preexisting injustice, or something analogous to it, the only ground for obligations to assist "no-contact" animals—and if so, does this mean that there are also no requirements to assist "no-contact" people? And if, on the other hand, there *are* requirements to assist in the "no-contact" human case, wouldn't these requirements also apply in the wild animal case, thus undermining the LFI?

We can think about this further by returning to Singer's case of the nearby drowning child versus the distant starving child. Singer assumes that we will intuitively think that there is a duty to save a drowning child at our feet (providing the cost to us is not enormously great) and moves from this intuition to argue that there is no morally relevant difference between the nearby drowning child and the distant starving child. If we accept that we should assist the one, we must also accept a duty to assist the other. Some philosophers, in contrast, argue that we have a duty to assist in *neither* case—so, famously, Murphy (1980, 168) maintains that if we were on a lounge chair by a pool where a strange child was drowning at our feet, and we could rescue the child even without getting out of the chair, still, no right would be violated by not doing so (although Murphy accepts that this would reflect very negatively on our *character*). My account of assistance seems to suggest—in contrast to both of these views—that there is likely to be an obligation to assist the distant starving child, since his situation is plausibly due to an injustice from which we are in some way benefiting, but that there is no requirement to assist the nearby drowning child, because it is not an *injustice* that the child is drowning: it is an *accident*. This position would certainly be—intuitively at least—strange. But for my distinction between assisting domestic and wild animals to hold, if I want to include any argument that there is a duty to rescue an unknown nearby drowning child, the duty will have to apply to the *child* without also applying to (say) a drowning wild *animal*.

This problem is, clearly, a difficult one for the relational approach I have been developing. But it need not be fatal; there are possible consistent responses. I have suggested reasons as to why there is no general requirement to assist wild animals but that assistance is owed to domesticated animals and, where relevant, to other animals that have been drawn into the contact zone. This assistance will include at least some "natural" threats to domesticated animals, because their vulnerability to those "natural" forces is likely to be in part of human origin, as humans are responsible for some or all of these animals' existence, their constitution, and their vulnerable locations in the path of the threat. Indeed, given the degree of control humans usually have over the lives of domesticated animals, it is at least plausible that assistance is almost always required when such animals are threatened by natural forces (though these requirements might be outweighed by other conflicting and stronger requirements). So, the problem is not about justifying when assistance to animals is required but rather that no grounds have been offered for assistance in *human* cases of natural threat or other threats that do not plausibly emerge from social injustices. A defender of the No-contact LFI might not feel the need to find explanations in the human case here, but this response seems inadequate. One reason that it is inadequate is that it implies, at least, that in a lifeboat case—(say) a flood, where a human stranger and a domesticated dog are both trapped, one might have an obligation to rescue the dog but not the human. Although it would almost invariably be argued—even from the strongest animal-rights positions, such as Francione's—that in a forced choice between the life of a human and the life of a dog, the human's life has priority, here counterintuitively there seems to be no duty to the human stranger but a requirement to assist the dog. However, even putting the response like this raises a curious issue: the anthropogenic nature of domesticated-animal vulnerability (for instance) may generate obligations to assist animals, but then, are not humans themselves (obviously and inevitably) anthropogenic?

Although humans are brought into being by other humans, they are not purposefully designed to be vulnerable and dependent, or not (at least) to stay that way. They are frequently located where they are (in relation to natural threats) at least in part by their own choice. (If their location is due to injustice, then duties to assist on this account are likely already to exist.) But nonetheless, there are arguments that can be made for assisting humans in the case of natural threats, based on relational obligations, rather than being (directly) capacity oriented. I will sketch an approach here—one that is consistent with the relational view that I have been advocating—that might at least begin to assuage a worry about the implications of this position for assisting unknown humans.

Scheffler (1997, 190) identifies three ways in which people generally think that special moral responsibilities are generated from relations. These are: (a) moral responsibilities that emerge out of past interactions (e.g., promises, agreements, debts, harms), (b) moral responsibilities that emerge out of special relationships (e.g., children, parents, siblings, friends), and (c) moral responsibilities that emerge out of membership of some common group. Although I have been putting forward considerations that fall under (a) and (b), I have not considered anything that looked like (c). But something like (c) may form a basis for duties to assist humans threatened by natural causes (though these duties might be weak, and, as Pogge suggests, considerably weaker than general duties not to harm). In making an argument of this kind, I take "group" or "community" in the sense of establishing a boundary of membership, where there are either more duties, or stronger duties, to individuals that are members of a relevant group than to those that are outside it. (So I am not meaning the good of a group understood as a *whole* here.)

Although this argument could be developed in different ways, I will draw on Francis and Norman's (1978) "community" relational approach here, since they are concerned with both animal and interhuman ethics. Francis and Norman maintain—in what they accept to be a "rough-edged" kind of way—that because of the relations in which humans stand with respect to one another, it is possible to talk about "a single overall [human] community of a morally significant kind."[4] The relations Francis and Norman identify include mutually recognized communication, the ability of humans to justify themselves to others, reciprocity in economic relations, mutual cooperation, the joint organization of political and other institutions, membership of political communities, the sense of a political "world order," and membership in families. This network of rich interhuman relations, they argue, generates special moral responsibilities to community members that do not apply to those outside the community. They do not explicitly argue that the rich network of relations that constitutes the human community generates obligations of *assistance* to community members, but this is implied in their view. Accepting a view like this provides a reason why the unknown nearby drowning child should be rescued: we should assist members of the richly related human community, at least when we can easily do so and the threat is a strong one. This kind of relational argument as providing grounds for assistance is very widely accepted; even the strongest of capacity-oriented theorists frequently turn to the relations that hold between humans as a way of justifying such requirements to assist. Feinberg (1992b, 180–181) maintains: "Merely being a fellow human being is enough of a 'relationship,' on this view, to ground a duty to rescue when the threatened harm [of drowning] is that severe." This sounds something like the "moderate cosmopolitanism" identified by Scheffler (2001, 115), where membership in the global community of human beings is "one important source of reasons and responsibilities."

122   Of course, Francis and Norman's claims are controversial. One might deny that community membership is relevant to any form of moral obligation, or that if there are duties to assist all humans, these are capacity, not community, generated. Or one might deny that "human beings presently on Earth"[5] could constitute a morally relevant community; one might instead argue that only smaller units such as states, which are more closely bound together (for instance, by shared values) can constitute a community. Since my relational approach itself does not stand or fall by these arguments, I will not consider these objections further here. But there are some problems I do need to consider here, assuming that one accepts at least some aspects of Francis and Norman's case.

The "human-community relations" view adopted by Francis and Norman avoids the concerns about racism or sexism to which group-oriented claims about moral significance are often vulnerable. However (and this is the point of their article), they maintain that *all and only* interhuman relations are sufficiently rich and complex to constitute a morally significant community. Animals are either incapable of participating in rich human relations at all, or they do so only in the weakest of ways, and not in ways that (unlike in the case of children, for instance) involve emotional and intellectual development. But Francis and Norman's argument is problematic both with respect to human beings—raising concerns again about human beings who may be only weakly able to engage in at least some such rich human relations— and with respect to animals. After all, it is not possible, on the grounds offered— mutual recognition, social communication, social participation, familial and economic relations, and so on—to include all humans and to exclude all animals. Some animals—domesticated ones in particular—*do* engage in communicative relations with humans. Animals *are* deeply bound up in economic relations with humans, and animals do live in human families and are usually considered to be members of those families. These are exactly the kinds of relations that Francis and Norman consider to be important. Francis and Norman's global human community should, to be consistent, be extended to a global "mixed" social community, including all humans and the nonhuman sentient animals with whom humans have strong social relations. This provides a basis for maintaining that there are at least weak, community-oriented obligations to assist fellow humans in need, even where there is no causal responsibility for creating such need. And although I have already argued that there are other reasons for assisting domesticated animals, such a social-relations view also provides *additional* reasons to support the idea that there are obligations of assistance to domesticated animals.

Two possible worries remain. The first worry is that the suggestion here—that there are obligations to assist all members of the global human community, duties that extend to domesticated animals, if the boundaries of community are drawn loosely—appears to muddy the usual distinction between "general" and "special" duties or obligations. As Scheffler (2001, 49) characterizes this distinction, "general duties are the duties we have towards people as such, whereas special duties are those duties that we have only towards people with whom we have had certain significant sorts of interactions, or to whom we stand in certain significant sorts of relations." (Scheffler's definition takes no account of duties towards animals.) The No-contact LFI accepts *general* duties not to harm, both toward people and sentient animals. In the previous chapters, I have also argued for *special* obligations of assistance toward animals that have been harmed or made vulnerable by humans. I am now suggesting further obligations of assistance based on something like social relations or global-community membership. These obligations might be thought to be general, in the sense that they apply to all people in the global community and plausibly also to all sentient animals in a "mixed" community. But they *are not* general (unlike those duties not to harm) across the sphere of all morally considerable beings, because wild "no-contact" animals are excluded from them. So, it seems better to think of these morally significant social relations as generating special obligations, not general duties—not least because general duties are usually taken to be capacity oriented, while those being discussed here, in contrast, are relational.

The second worry might be that I have created something ad hoc—the kind of concern, I noted earlier, that Jamieson (1990) had about any "add-on" duties of beneficence to Regan's negative rights position. This criticism would work as follows: there were lacunae in the argument with regard to assisting human beings; therefore I invented, in an ad hoc way, a further category of obligations to assist people. I am not sure how deeply this criticism bites. For while capacities are central in establishing moral considerability and in grounding duties not to harm, I have argued that it is relations of one kind or another that establish what is owed to others beyond this, whether this entails considering past harms and injustices, the creation of vulnerabilities and special relationships, or more generally partaking in social, communicative, and cooperative relations—or indeed, all of these. The emphasis on the moral importance of relations, even though different kinds of relations are at stake, is constant. So this does not seem ad hoc in any strong sense.

IS DOMESTICATION A RELATION THAT WE SHOULD NOT CREATE?

The relational approach, as I have conceived of it, concerns animals that are already in existence. I have argued, for instance, that we have special obligations toward domesticated animals when they have been created to be vulnerable and dependent. But this gives rise to further questions. Are there some animals that just should not be brought into being, because of the kinds of relations into which they will inevitably be born, especially where this inevitability is constitutive? More specifically, is there something wrong with creating a domesticated animal that is inescapably going to live a life of vulnerability and dependence? After all, one claim I might be making is that domestication is, in itself, a harm.

It is not obvious at first sight what it would mean to say that "domestication is a harm." The account of harm that I have given here is individualist and experiential.[6] From this perspective, given my interpretation of harm, to say that "domestication is a harm" must be to say something like: "for all individual domesticated animals, being domesticated sets back interests, primarily by producing pain and/or aversive experiences that the animal would not otherwise have undergone." This claim is doubly problematic. First, although some forms of specialized breeding do cause or create a high probability of physical pain and aversive experience, either from birth or later in life, most domesticated animals do not undergo negative bodily experiences just on the basis of their domesticated constitutions. And many of the psychological problems that realized vulnerability and dependence could create in the human case do not apply in the animal case; domesticated animals do not experience humiliation about their dependence, resentment about their subordination, nor future-oriented anxiety about the long-term consequences of their vulnerability. They are thus not psychologically harmed *merely by being in* such relationships, even though unquestionably some human relationships with domesticated animals do cause them psychological harms. But the harms that happen to domesticated animals are not general harms to be attributed to domestication itself.

Second, a deeper problem is also raised here about the counterfactual condition—that an animal must made be worse off (in terms of its experiential interests and given a foreseeably normal course of subsequent events) by harmful action(s) than it would otherwise have been. It is very difficult to get a grip on how this might work in the case of domestication. For any particular individual, the manifestations

124

of domestication are a fundamental part of the animal's inner constitution. The animal could not be any other way and be that individual, so it is unclear how its interests could be set back in this way, nor what the "otherwise" could be. Although humans could have produced a different animal, this is not an alternative for any particular animal once it exists. No animal has been made worse off by being born domesticated, because if it had not been born domesticated, that particular animal would not have existed at all.[7] (This would apply even if one took a nonexperiential view of animal well-being.)

If domestication rarely in itself produces pain and negative experience, and if any particular domesticated animal could not have an alternative constitution, it is difficult to see how domestication could be seen as generally harmful in the sense in which it sets back the serious interests of particular individual animals. However, there are arguments that maintain that domestication is morally problematic in some other sense. The argument I want to consider here focuses on the kinds of power relations that domestication establishes: that is, the deliberate creation of vulnerable and dependent animals, animals that are shaped for human needs and that bear in their very bodies the impression of human power.[8]

Power Relations and the Creation of Vulnerability

In *Protecting the Vulnerable*, Robert Goodin (1985) argues that vulnerability is the source of human special responsibilities. Goodin accepts that some (human) vulnerability is inevitable and maintains that although some people are especially and permanently vulnerable (their vulnerability is thus "realized"), everyone is vulnerable to some degree.[9] Some vulnerability, such as that of lovers to one another, might be regarded as a good. But not all vulnerability is desirable. Neither is all of it inevitable: at least some vulnerability is socially constructed or exacerbated (1985, 191). So, for instance, those who use wheelchairs are more vulnerable in a society constructed around steps and narrow passages than in one with gentle slopes and wide pathways. This suggests that we should think about different vulnerabilities differently; in some cases, we might want to try to reduce or eliminate particular kinds of vulnerability and dependence; in other situations, the creation of vulnerability is not objectionable; and in still others, the priority might be to better support and assist those who are vulnerable and/or dependent rather than to attempt to eliminate the vulnerability and dependence.

Drawing on Goodin's thinking, one question here might be whether the created vulnerabilities of domesticated animals are the kinds of vulnerabilities we should aim at reducing, removing, and not continuing to produce, or, alternatively, whether they are of the kind that it is morally permissible to produce but that bring about special obligations for care and support. Francione (2000, 172), for instance, objects generally to the creation of domesticated companion animals (and I think, by implication, to all domesticated animals) primarily on the grounds of their vulnerability:

> They exist forever in a netherworld of vulnerability, dependent on us for everything and at risk of harm from an environment that they do not really understand. We have bred them to be compliant and servile, or to have characteristics that are actually harmful to them but are pleasing to us. . . . Humans have no business continuing to bring these creatures into a world in which they simply do not fit.
>
> (Francione n.d.)

While (as I maintained above) I do not think it can be successfully argued that domestication is necessarily experientially harmful to domesticated animals themselves, and Francione's argument about poor "fit" is problematic (what could fit better into the humanized parts of the world than domesticated animals?), Francione may have another significant concern here. There may be something wrong with creating animals to have particular relations of vulnerability to and dependence on us, and this would be the case *even if* such relations did not negatively affect animals' experiential well-being.

Here is an extreme example: Suppose it were possible to engineer an animal (say a pig) that can feel pain, but that, provided it is fed enough, has no social desires and little will or desire to move (say gene-knockout technology has eliminated these); its experiential well-being would be just fine kept in close confinement in a crate. Someone who objected to the production of such an animal might say that such a pig is extremely vulnerable to people, it cannot be independent, it is completely dominated by human beings and has no powers to resist whatever people might do to it, and the production of animals like this is morally reprehensible, whatever we might say about their experiential well-being. This claim is intuitively appealing, but on the basis of the arguments I have made, I have no grounds to say that there is anything morally problematic here. The modified pig is not frustrated nor in pain. To use Rollin's (1998, 156) terms, the *telos*, or nature, of the pig has been altered so that it can have good experiential well-being while closely confined. So why the moral unease about such a modified pig?

Leaving aside problematic arguments about naturalness, one objection to the production of this pig might be that an experientialist account of well-being just misses some of what is important, and that on a nonexperientialist account, this animal's well-being is not "just fine." (This would reject my account of well-being but not a relational approach in itself.) A further concern might be that the focus on the pig's well-being alone is misplaced. The worry is not so much about the animal's well-being but rather about the kind of human-animal relation that is manifest in creating the pig, that is, about the kinds of individuals or societies that would find the creation

126

of animals like this morally tolerable (irrespective of the animals' experiences).

The "wrong account of well-being" objection is interesting. We are not, after all, talking about the well-being of something that is already in existence but rather about creating what the well-being of a creature can be. It might be argued that some kinds of well-being just should not be created (but not because they cannot be fulfilled, because the purpose of creating these kinds of well-being is exactly that they *can* be fulfilled). Why would this be morally problematic? It is difficult to make any intrinsic (that is, noncomparative) reason work without introducing some kind of naturalness or species-dignity argument, both of which are very hard to defend. Any argument that runs something like: "created well-beings should possess x number of psychological capacities" would seem also to count against the creation of animals that have always had less developed psychological capacities, such as shellfish. A Mill-style comparative argument provides another possible way through here: just as it is better to be a dissatisfied Socrates than a satisfied fool, perhaps it is better to breed a dissatisfied normal pig than a satisfied modified pig. But for whom would this be better and who are the competent judges in this case?

Although some argument of this kind may work—and may successfully challenge my experientialist account of well-being—an argument about the kind of power relations involved, and the people or society who would find such relations morally tolerable, is more persuasive here, though still very problematic. Some existing human relations with animals—and certainly the creation of modified pigs of this kind—can be described as relations of domination, by almost any definition of domination that exists. Lovett's (2001) account of domination, for instance, includes three conditions: an imbalance-of-power condition, a dependency condition (where one is not free to exit the relationship without incurring costs, and the more costly the exit, the greater the dependency), and an absence-of-rules condition (where, even if there are formal rules, there is no assurance that in any particular case those rules will be followed). Existing animals in confined-feeding operations or the laboratory meet these conditions; indeed, they are created for them and born into them.[10] The modified pig simply further meets these conditions. And—if we take these conditions to be on a sliding scale, as Lovett does—animals' domination is of the most severe kind: the power imbalance is extreme, exit is impossible, and arbitrariness high.

Even if this does not cause experiential harm to the animals concerned, we can question what this says about human individuals (or, perhaps, groups and societies) that are willing to create completely defenseless sentient beings whose lives are entirely dominated by human interests. One—admittedly contentious—way of thinking about this emerges in various accounts of virtue ethics. Thomas Hill's (2007) version of environmental-virtue ethics, for instance, claims that there are some kinds of behaviors about which we are likely to ask, "What kind of person would do *that*?" even where no one is harmed—for instance, laughing at a news story about a plane crash or spitting on the grave of the grandmother whose fortune one has just inherited. Behaving like this, Hill suggests, indicates the absence of "traits that we want to encourage, because they are, in most cases, a natural basis for the development of certain virtues" (Hill 2007, 683). Likewise, careless environmental destruction, Hill argues, indicates the absence of traits such as humility, a disposition to cherish what has enriched one's life, and an appreciation of one's place in the universe. And worries of this kind—what this behavior says about *us*—might be what underpins the moral unease about the creation of the modified pig. Even though the pigs so created are not themselves harmed, harms (and failures to assist) on this view do not exhaust all there is to say about the moral world. The drive to create such relationships of domination reveals human hubris, an extreme manifestation of the way in which (to use Hopkins' words) domesticated animals must "wear man's smudge and share man's smell," a kind of arrogant and manipulative human importance that "programs animals with ends to suit ourselves" (Cooper 1998, 155).[11]

I put this suggestion forward tentatively, since there is a plausible objection that if animals are not harmed by being produced in these ways, then there are no grounds for thinking that producing them in such dominating ways *would* be damaging to the formation or maintenance of human character or make it more likely that those who create such animals are going to carry out actual harms.[12] If this objection persuades and the experientialist account of well-being holds good, then on this view there is indeed no obvious reason not to modify animals in these ways, provided that their experiential well-being is good.

So, in summary: On an experientialist view of animal well-being alone, domestication is only problematic when animals are created in ways that inevitably cause them pain or frustration. It is not generally the case that domestication is harmful, nor that the creation of dependent animals is intrinsically morally problematic. However, the relational approach that I have been advocating is not necessarily tied to an experientialist account of well-being; this experientialist account could be rejected, or supplemented, without rejecting the broader relational approach that I have been proposing (in particular, the No-contact LFI). This would open the possibility of objecting to certain kinds of dominating human-animal relations, even if they did not cause experiential harm. On either view of well-being, it might still be possible to argue that where vulnerable, sentient animals are created for complete human domination questions may be raised about human character. Indeed, an account of domestication as itself morally problematic is, I think, compatible with the No-contact LFI, even though it is not the view for which I have argued here.

DOES PAINLESS KILLING HARM?

A further question raised by an experiential account of well-being is whether the painless killing of a sentient animal should be viewed as harming the animal. Before attempting to work through some of the difficult issues this raises, I want to make three points. The first is that the relational approach that I have been advancing does not stand or fall on any particular account of painless killing. As noted in the previous section, the No-contact LFI is compatible with different ideas of animal well-being, of what constitutes a harm, and whether painless killing is such a harm. Second, whatever one thinks about painless killing, in practice it is rare and hard to achieve (consider the difficulties that have surrounded the application of the death penalty in the *human* case in the United States). Individual animals are rarely killed without inflicting pain and distress in industrial abattoirs, for instance. So, in most cases of killing, worries about pain and distress are also appropriate and make the process of killing harmful, independently of concerns about the death itself.

A third point here is substantial. A significant group of philosophers (and others) reject the whole approach to thinking about the killing of animals that I adopt below. They suggest that the very turn to reasons and to philosophical argument to address this issue exactly misses the point. Philosophical reflection *deflects* the immediate emotional response of shared vulnerability, the overwhelming nature of identification and painful sympathy for fellow creatures by which we come to understand what death and killing actually *means*. For example, reflecting on a fictional lecture by John Coetzee's character Elizabeth Costello in his novel *The Lives of Animals*, Cora Diamond (2008, 74) comments:

> The awareness we each have of being a living body, being 'alive to the world' carries with it exposure to the bodily sense of vulnerability to death, sheer animal vulnerability, the vulnerability we share with them. This vulnerability is capable of panicking us. . . . Is there any difficulty in seeing why we should not prefer to return to moral debate, in which the livingness and death of animals enter as facts that we treat as relevant in this or that way, not as presences that may unseat our reason?

As with Gaita's concern about immediate recognition of animal suffering, noted in chapter 1, the very emotional distancing involved in philosophical discussion can set us off on the wrong road; it has us asking "one question too many."

Powerful as these objections to philosophical reasoning about killing animals might be, I do not find them wholly persuasive. After all, this powerful experience of animals' deaths as revealing that they are vulnerable "fellow creatures" is not accessible to or shared by everyone (indeed, that Elizabeth Costello's horrified and even "unhinged" response to the killing of animals isolates her from all those who surround her is central to Coetzee's novel). And some people who may or may not be moved by the plight of animals have similar powerful responses of horror, panic, or shared vulnerability to the termination of early fetuses or to the exercise of the death penalty. Indeed, a child may have similar powerful responses to the mutilation of a favorite toy. It is surely important to ask whether there is an appropriate basis for such powerful emotional reactions—bringing reason into play alongside emotion— which moves us immediately into the philosophical realm. The powerful reactions to the killing of animals described by philosophers such as Diamond rest on a kind of imaginative identification with animals as being "like us," being fellows, sharing common vulnerabilities, and so on. But presumably, we could be mistaken about this (as the child about the toy), because the appropriateness of the imaginative iden- tification depends on what animals are actually like (indeed, it presupposes this). But even to ask the question about appropriate identification moves us again into the territory of philosophical debate; from there it is a short step to questions about whether killing animals painlessly harms them at all, and whether, if so, killing some kinds of animals in some kinds of situations harms them more than killing other ani- mals in other situations. While there is a proper place for emotional responses to animal suffering and death, this is surely only part of the story.

It is appropriate, then, to consider central aspects of the philosophical debate about the painless killing of animals and to offer a view about whether painless killing should be seen as harmful in at least some cases. I will do little more than to sketch some alternative approaches and to assess which account seems most plau- sible. I will only be concerned here with killing in respect to the actual creature being killed—as opposed to those animals emotionally attached to, dependent on, or part of a social group with the one killed.

One possible take on painless killing from the experientialist account of animal well-being that I have adopted is that there is nothing wrong with it at all. Since the killing is either not experienced or not experienced aversively, then what's to object to about it?[13] Perhaps all that matters on such an account are experiences that are actually undergone. The end of experience, or lost experience, would therefore not matter morally. On such an account, then, painless killing—apparently of humans as well as animals—cannot be of moral significance (except for its effects on those left behind). However, this view seems extremely implausible, and it is not the only pos- sible interpretation of an experientialist account of painless killing.

A starting point here is to ask: "Why might painlessly killing humans be wrong?" and to work from answers to this question to think about nonhuman animals. This question is itself complex: certainly with respect to painless killing, "humans" are not generally thought to be a unified group. After all, there are cases when it may be argued that painless killing is morally obligatory (when requested by someone in severe and terminal physical pain). There are other situations when many argue that it is at least permissible (in the case of early abortions). There are also the more obvious cases, where it is thought to be absolutely impermissible—indeed, one of the worst possible moral actions. However, thinking about "margins-of-life" cases— such as the killing of fetuses—can help in uncovering what it might be in human life that makes the taking of it seem so problematic, even when there is no associated pain or distress.

Arguments about the wrongness of painless killing take a number of forms. Some seem more compatible with the experientialist understanding of well-being that I have adopted in this book than others. I will divide these arguments into two main groups (although different arguments cluster in each group): those arguments, first, that concern desire (or preference) satisfaction, and then those that concern lost futures.

Desire Arguments

The possession of nonsubstitutable preferences or desires to go on living, or the belief that one is a subject of experience/other mental states, in conjunction with the desire to continue as such, could provide a desire-oriented basis for maintaining that painless killing harms sentient animals. This view, I should note, is not straightforwardly compatible with an experientialist view of well-being. (Experientialist accounts are generally understood as competing with desire-oriented accounts of well-being.) However, given the general significance of this view—in particular to discussions about killing animals—it is important to consider it here.

To maintain that painlessly killing sentient animals is morally problematic on a desire argument, one must accept (a) that an animal has the capacity to possess a desire to go on living and (b) that the premise that what is valuable about desire satisfaction is *not*, or not *only*, how such desire satisfaction feels from the inside (i.e., not the *experience* of desire satisfaction) but rather that desires should be satisfied in some "objective" sense. That is, it must be allowed that one can be harmed by the frustration of a desire even if one never actually experiences the desire frustration or knows that the desire has been frustrated.

First, to (a): What does it mean to have a desire to go on living? There are a number of candidates, some of the most common being (i) actually having such a desire, in the sense of having the capacity to formulate certain relevant concepts and understand them (the kind of view advocated by Tooley 1972); (ii) having sufficiently long-term desires about one's future that they amount, essentially, to having a desire to go on living (e.g., desires to have a career, desires to have and nurture offspring, etc.); (iii) having any future-oriented desires at all, even if these are short term (e.g., desire to eat the bowl of food under one's nose); and (iv) behavioral expressions of resistance to death (e.g., by struggling, fleeing, fighting).

While (i) seems like extremely strong evidence of a desire to go on living (although, of course, one might be lying: one could *say* one had such a desire having just taken an overdose) and (ii) seems like very plausible evidence, since these other long-term desires are premised on continuing to live and their satisfaction provides reasons to go on living, (iii) and (iv) are considerably more controversial. Paola Cavalieri (2009, 39) defends a view rather like (iii); for her, any "intentional being that has goals and wants to achieve them" is the kind of being that wants to go on living, and she explicitly denies that the kinds of wants such beings possess require any kind of self-awareness, as is implied by (i) and (ii).[14] Francione (2006, 240) proposes a position that looks more like (iv), arguing that sentient animals "prefer or desire or want" to remain alive, and that this means that they have an interest in continued existence. After all, "sentient beings use sensations of pain and suffering to escape situations that threaten their lives": consider instances where animals gnaw off limbs in order to escape from traps. Although Francione does not explicitly say this, presumably the thought here is that if animals' desires were only for short-term pain avoidance or pleasurable experiences, then they would not inflict pain on themselves in order to avoid dying.

Although I do not want to dismiss either of these arguments, both are, at best, controversial. As McMahan (2002, 182) argues, the frustration of short-term desires—such as the desire to eat a bowl of food (the kind of desire I attributed to animals in chapter 1) does not alone provide a strong reason to think that death is a harm or misfortune. Such desires do not themselves amount to a desire to go on living and do not seem to provide a reason to live in order to ensure their satisfaction. And many things could be going on when an animal gnaws off a limb in a trap: a response to the pain in the limb, panic at being unable to move, fear at being in a particular unfamiliar place, and so on. That the gnawing is evidence of the desire for continued life as opposed to a response to something more immediate is far from the only possible interpretation of this situation.

Of course, part of what is going on here just is a disagreement about what it means to "desire to go on living" and what concepts, if any, are required to have such a desire. I find it most plausible that a desire to go on living requires at least some conceptualization: that one is a self, that one is alive, that being alive can end (i.e., something much closer to [i] or [ii] than to [iii] or [iv]). But few, if any, animals look likely to meet conditions (i) or (ii). (Nor, indeed, do fetuses and very small infants, as Tooley argues). Some philosophers argue to the contrary, maintaining that at least some animals have desires that amount to a desire to go on living. Singer (1993) in particular maintains that great apes should be thought of as having a sense of self that persists over time, considers it plausible that whales and perhaps other mammals such as dogs and cats do; this long-term sense of self, on his account, grounds a desire to continue living.[15] If Singer were right on this point, then—if one is persuaded by a desire view of the harm of killing—at least some mammals *would* be harmed by painless killing. This part of the claim, then, depends substantially on one's view of animal minds; the less modest the view, the more plausible it is likely to seem that some mammals have a desire to continue to live.

The second concern, (b), forms part of a more general concern about the role of desire satisfaction in well-being (discussed briefly in chapter 1). Characteristic of the desire account is the view that one can be harmed and benefited by one's desires being frustrated or fulfilled even if one never experiences or knows about such frustrations or satisfactions. This is not the place for a substantial discussion of the merits and difficulties of such a view; it has some advantages over an experientialist account, but it also requires one to accept other contentious ideas, such as that one can be extensively benefited and harmed after one's death. Of relevance here is that it is simpler to understand a desire view of well-being in the *human* case, where we can more easily make sense of how desires and experiences may come apart, than in the *animal* case. So, for instance, an experientialist account of well-being may be unable to give a satisfying explanation as to why we would not want to be hooked up for life to an experience machine (but see Bernstein 1998). Humans—or at least, adult humans—it might be argued, desire their pleasurable experiences to be "authentic." That is, faced with a choice between artificially produced pleasurable experiences from an experience machine and similar (or even less pleasurable) "authentic" experiences generated by "real lives," they would desire the latter. It is not only the experiential "feel" of experiences that matters but also that they have the right sort of origin. Humans can prefer, or desire, less good experiences from the right source over better experiences from the wrong source, because good experiences are not all that they value.

It is not obvious, however, how animals could make such distinctions, because bound up in such discrimination is a kind of conceptual world to which animals do not (as far as we know) have access. For an animal—almost certainly, all animals— what matters about desire satisfaction and frustration is surely how the frustration and satisfaction feels from the inside. Given the kinds of desires it seems most plausible to think that animals have, desire satisfaction collapses into the *experience* of desire satisfaction (or frustration). The kinds of desires that relate to experience machines and perfect deceptions—and, I think, the desire to go on living—require a kind of conceptual sophistication that it is hard to imagine that animals have (and of course, some humans also do not have). So, I am not persuaded that, in the animal case, a desire view can provide good reasons as to why painless killing should be thought of as morally problematic (though it might do so for adult humans, if one finds the desire view of well-being itself to be plausible). It is at best very uncertain whether any nonhuman animals can have the relevant desires.

Lost-future Arguments

A variety of different "lost-future" arguments have also been used to underpin claims that painlessly killing humans is wrong. For classical utilitarians, the painless termination of an on-balance more-happy-than-not life reduces the amount of pleasure in the world and so constitutes a loss of that future experience. But this loss is understood in, as it were, an impersonal way; a loss to the world rather than a loss to the individual killed; the state of affairs in the world is less good than it would otherwise have been. However, given the impersonal nature of this loss, the creation of an equal or greater amount of pleasurable experience in the world (e.g., by the breeding of a new individual with at least as good on-balance experience) would make good this loss.[16] So although painless killing does mean a kind of lost future, on this view, the loss can be righted, since individuals are, essentially, replaceable. It is this apparent aspect of the view—that even human adults could be painlessly killed and replaced—that has led to its widespread rejection (see, for instance, Lockwood 1979). This explains Singer's movement toward the preference/desire view discussed above: a view that protects more psychologically sophisticated beings from replacement. The strong "replaceability" view seems so intuitively unacceptable that I will not pursue it here.[17]

Other lost-future accounts maintain that painless killing is morally problematic when it *irreplaceably* destroys an individual's valuable future. A leading account of this kind—though several versions have emerged in discussion—is the "future-like-ours" argument, one version of which has been central to philosophical debates about abortion. Two forms this argument can take are as follows:

1. The loss of a "future like ours" or "a potential future of value" (see Marquis 1989, 2001), where this future is understood *not* to be self-represented but "the goods we would have experienced had we survived" (Marquis 2001, 363).
2. The loss of a "future of value," where this future *is* self-represented (the failure of actualization of present hopes, fears, dreams, plans, intentions about the future, which can be thought of as forming dispositional mental states). (See Marquis 2001; Brown 2002)

We can pass over (2) fairly quickly here—even though it seems plausible. The argument in (2) concerns the loss of futures that an individual has in some way imagined or considered—that is, has represented to themselves. The nonactualization of such futures by premature, though painless, killing is viewed, on this account, as a harm to them. (Of course, various adjustments to the argument must be made to accommodate unrealistic dreams that would never have been realized, etc.) We could concede that the loss of self-represented realistic futures would be harmful, but this would not be relevant in the case of animals, since (as far as we know) animals (like fetuses) are unable to represent their futures to themselves in this kind of way. If (2) were the only basis on which painless killing harmed, then sentient animals are not harmed by being painlessly killed.

So, it is (1) that we need to consider further here. Marquis' argument could be interpreted in an experientialist way, if we took future goods at stake to be experiential ones. Marquis maintains that abortion is, in most cases, morally problematic, because abortion deprives a fetus of what it would otherwise have: a "future like ours" with all the goods of consciousness enjoyed in a typical human life, the things that make life worth living. So, although there are things that I value now, they are only one part of what is lost by killing me; with respect to the future, Marquis says: "I will (or would) value [those aspects of my future] when I will (or would) experience them, whether I value them now or not" (Marquis 2007, 141).

This view, he suggests, fits with other intuitions we have: for instance, it explains why we might think that voluntary euthanasia is permissible for humans who are suffering with terminal illnesses—because they have already lost a future that they will (or would) value. Marquis himself refrains from commitment on what this view might imply for animals; he is undecided as to whether their lives are sufficiently "like ours" to make killing them wrong. But he at least accepts the *possibility* of a parallel argument: that (for instance) in the case of the painless killing of calves, the animals are harmed because they would value the (experiential) goods in their future when they experienced them, whether they value them now or not.

There are many objections to Marquis' argument (in the context of abortion, of course, as well as animals: see, for instance, Brown 2002, Card 2006). However, there is one particular problem on which I want to focus here, because I think it points toward a way in which painless killing of animals harms them—though not as much as it harms adult human beings.

Let us return to Marquis' key remark: "I will (or would) value [those aspects of my future] when I will (or would) experience them, whether I value them now or not." Marquis' use of "I" here expresses a kind of identity. He seems to assume that the "I" in the future that will (or would) experience particular goods is the same as the "I" that exists in the present. But in many cases—including that of a fetus and potential future goods—this "I" relation does not straightforwardly hold. A fetus is not an "I" in the sense in which we usually mean it, and certainly it is something quite different from the future human person that will (or would) exist. Marquis' argument thus depends on precarious ideas about identity over time. In this respect, McMahan's account in *The Ethics of Killing*, which has a different view of identity over time, is more persuasive.

A fetus, or a young infant, McMahan (2002, 170) notes, "is unaware of itself,

135

unaware that it has a future; it therefore has no future directed states." For this reason, "there would be very few continuities of character or belief between itself now and itself as a person. And if it had lived to become a person, it would then remember nothing of its life as an infant." Much of the loss, were it to die, therefore, McMahan maintains, is *impersonal* (as in the utilitarian view above); there is a loss of future good to the world, rather as there would be if one fails to conceive a child that one could have conceived, a child that would have lived a good life. In the case of *nonconception*, no one has been harmed; the loss is purely impersonal. In the case of the infant, unlike the case of nonconception, there is a particular individual, but the infant, in McMahan's terms, "would only have been weakly related, in the ways that matter, to the subject of the good that is lost." The kinds of relations that matter, McMahan (2002, 45) suggests, are "memory, desire, intention, belief and character," for it is these that create psychological continuity. These constitute what McMahan calls the "prudential unity relations," the kinds of unity between oneself now and oneself in the future that form the basis for "rational egoistic concern for the future" (McMahan 2002, 42). Where the relations between oneself now and oneself in the future are strong, the removal of that future is a serious harm. Where they are weak, it is a lesser harm. And if there is no relation between oneself now and oneself in the future, then there is no *personal* harm at all (though there may be an impersonal loss to the world).

How is this position relevant for thinking about animals? It suggests that a key factor in terms of whether we should worry about painless killing concerns the psychological continuity between an animal now and its future self. So, McMahan (2002, 75-76) suggests, if we imagine a (fictional) being that feels pleasure but that lives entirely in the "specious present"—it cannot remember more than a second from the past nor anticipate more than a second into the future—we will not think the *life* of this individual being matters. Though we might think it important that these kind of pleasant experiences continue to exist, it will not be important that *this* particular life continue, so long as some other being continues to have those experiences, for there is no "significant unit" here, no psychological continuity over time. Although on Marquis' terms, this being might have a future of value, on McMahan's argument, the good that is lost in painlessly killing the creature of the specious present is *impersonal* (as would also be true of a fetus, which in its early stages lacks even the pleasures of the specious present). The creature of the specious present, even though sentient, is not *harmed* by being painlessly killed, because it lacks any psychological continuity over time.

For McMahan, then, Marquis' claim suffers from a "missing link"—the link between the organism that is painlessly killed and the future goods that are lost. What Marquis does not establish—in the case of the fetus, anyway—is that there is sufficient psychological continuity between the fetus and the lost future to say that the *fetus has been harmed* by the loss, though there may be an impersonal loss to the world. The question that remains, of course, is how far some or all animals are like this, what kinds of psychological continuity animals can have across time, and how strong those links might be.

McMahan proposes that, in thinking about the misfortune of death or the harm in killing, we adopt a theory of "time-relative interests," in which the strength of an individual's interest in continuing to live is "in effect, the extent to which it matters, for his sake now or from his present point of view, that he should continue to live. It takes into account how strong the prudential unity relations would be between himself now and himself in his subsequent life, assuming he were to live" (McMahan 2002, 105). Thus, two factors are involved in time-relative interests: the loss of future goods and the psychological connection between the present individual and those goods. If we interpret these time-relative interests in an experiential way, this account is compatible with the account of well-being that I have adopted in this book.[18] The harm to a painlessly killed being will vary according to its mental capacities as an individual, with respect to the strength of the prudential unity relations; there is no single "answer" as to whether an animal is harmed by being painlessly killed.

McMahan (2002, 199) presents an account in which the goods that animals can enjoy are relatively limited (in comparison with the human case) and the prudential unity relations are relatively weak (again, in comparison with adult humans). The harm of painlessly killing animals is, on his account, substantially less than is entailed by painlessly killing a human. While details of his account are questionable with respect to at least some animals, nonetheless, McMahan seems right in more general terms. Animals do have time-relative interests in continuing to live if there are experiential goods they could go on to enjoy and if they have some kind of psychological continuity with their future selves. The more goods there might be, and the stronger the psychological continuity, the greater the harm to them of being painlessly killed, although this harm in itself is less substantial (except in unusual cases) than the harm to an adult human.[19] On this view, at least some justification is needed in order to kill animals, even if that killing is painless.

So far in this chapter, I have considered a number of difficulties and questions raised by the view that I have been outlining. Some would be raised by any version of this relational approach to animal ethics; others specifically relate to my adoption of an experiential account of animal well-being. Even if the experiential account of animal well-being cannot withstand these difficulties, I have not uncovered anything fatal to the relational approach to animal ethics more generally. However, I will end this chapter by considering something that might threaten the plausibility of this contextual, relational view. Does this view—given its partially backward-looking, context-oriented, and relational nature—require too much information, so that information gathering would paralyze ethical decision-making?

THE PROBLEM OF EXCESSIVE KNOWLEDGE

Worries about the amount of knowledge needed to make ethical decisions have been leveled at several ethical theories. Most obviously, act utilitarians have been criticized for demanding too much knowledge: an agent must both project into the future a variety of different possible consequences and then become a utility calculator to work out which of these various possible consequences is likely to produce greatest utility. But such criticisms are not restricted to utilitarianism. Waldron raises a similar problem with respect to communitarianism. Suppose a communitarian is in the situation of the Good Samaritan, seeing an injured man at the side of the road. This communitarian, he proposes, "would not immediately pass by on the other side, but his approach would be to stop and try to figure out his relation to the man who had fallen among thieves" (Waldron 2003, 341–342). This is a problematic response, he suggests: it abstracts away from the immediacy of confrontation with a fellow human being and shifts instead to "calibrations of community" (thus falling victim to the same kind of calculative emphasis as utilitarianism).

138

There are different concerns being expressed here: one is about the amount of information needed; another is about the recourse to calculation and a movement away (in Waldron's case, at least) from the personal response generated by encounter (again, a concern that philosophizing is a distraction from an immediate response). I will discuss the immediacy of encounter in chapter 8, so I will put it to the side here. But what about the problem of excessive knowledge? The relational approach to assistance that I am advocating looks just as troublesome as utilitarianism and communitarianism in this respect; it, too, might require large amounts of information. Of course the "not harming" aspect need not require much knowledge other than that relevant beings are sentient (though in specific cases there are questions raised about weighing harms to different beings and the prudential unity relations). But in the case of assistance, this relational approach may require a lot of information—some of which may be difficult, or even on occasion impossible, to obtain, but the lack of which might hinder decision making in terms of speed or clarity. In order to know whether there is an obligation to assist an animal, one is likely to require information about how it got into the situation in which it needs assistance and what role which humans (if any) played in getting it there. In addition, questions are raised about when human engagement triggers obligations to assist in the first place. So, for instance, are individual polar bears owed assistance because of anthropogenic warming in the Arctic (a case I will consider in chapter 8)?

A first (if somewhat trite) response to this is to say that there is no reason to think that many ethical decisions *should* be straightforward. Situations involving exotic sentient animals introduced into fragile ecosystems, native wild animals driven from their habitats by human development, feral animals living in urban areas, and animals affected by anthropogenic climate change all *do* raise complicated questions. It is implausible that a "one-size-fits-all" answer *is* going to be appropriate to these situations; we should surely expect that the historical and relational context would be relevant to making decisions about what to do, just as we usually do in human cases. It is, of course, difficult to make quick decisions using this approach. But it is only on a few occasions that such quick decisions are needed (I discuss several examples of this kind in chapter 8). Many cases, in contrast, will be ones where some kind of policy has to be made about how to treat the animals in question; investigation into the relevant context does not seem to be overdemanding in such cases.

Second, utilitarians have made a number of responses to just these kinds of criticisms. One response that might be appropriated here can be drawn from Hare's "two-level" thinking. Aware of the difficulties involved in always having access to sufficient information to make an informed decision, Hare suggests that utilitarians work with two levels of principle. Level 1 principles are those that should guide everyday actions, especially in situations of stress, where there is insufficient time to find out all the relevant information and a quick decision has to be made. Level 2 principles, in contrast, are those arrived at in a "cool hour" after "leisured moral thought in completely adequate knowledge of the facts" (Hare 1982, 31). These principles, Hare says, are universalizable but may be very specific in a way not possible when operating at level 1. Of course, Hare's approach is designed to facilitate utilitarian judgments. But equally, something like this could work for this relational approach. There will be situations where immediate decisions must be made with respect to how to treat a particular sentient animal. In those situations, where information is sparse, assistance may be the best policy. After all, in the case of a wild animal, assistance is at least not impermissible on the No-contact LFI. (Though if one is already aware of other strong reasons not to assist then this may weight such a case in the other direction.) And encounter itself—which is likely to be what precipitates urgent decision making—may be of some significance, as I will suggest in chapter 8. If it is a domestic animal, the "default setting" should be that assistance is required, though of course (as with a disassociating pet-free Peter) there will be, on occasions when there is time for reflection, some exceptions. But most cases *will* provide time for moral reflection, both for individuals and in social contexts, and in these cases, finding out further relevant information should be part of the decision-making process.

So, as with any approach to ethics that involves looking backward (and some that are forward looking!), this relational approach does require a good deal of information in order to make informed decisions. There are certainly ways in which this is practically problematic. But, on the other hand, the need for information could equally be viewed as an advantage. After all, leading approaches to animal ethics (such as those of Singer and Regan) have been called oversimplifying, one-size-fits-all, applying abstract principles to complex situations without adequate sensitivity to context (for example, Slicer 1991). On the relational account that I am proposing, however, there is a place for complexity, particularity, and close and careful attention to situation that should be welcome to such context-oriented perspectives.

To conclude: in this and the preceding chapters, I have attempted to develop a relational account of animal assistance and to address some of the most pressing questions and problems that have arisen. But perhaps the best way of thinking through such an approach is to consider how it might work out in practice. That is the aim of chapter 8, the final chapter of this book. There I will consider some further cases, think about what difficulties each raises, and outline how someone taking the approach that I have been developing in this book might respond.

8

Puzzling Through Some Cases

The relational approach to animal assistance that I have been developing in this book is not likely to deliver simple answers. Given the importance of context, different situations will throw up a variety of morally relevant factors, only some of which I have been able to explore so far. In this chapter, I will discuss several case studies, all of which raise questions about assistance in relation to wild suffering, human-originating harms, or created vulnerabilities or dependencies. These cases, however, raise or develop issues I have not previously explored in detail. In some of these cases, I will compare the relational approach to animal assistance that I have been developing—most specifically, the No-contact LFI—to what I think would be the response of unmodified capacity-oriented views to these situations. I hope this will give some sense of how these approaches would work out differently on the ground. Each case would undoubtedly benefit from much more detailed examination than I give it here, but I hope that this chapter will provide some indication, at least, of the practical implications of this relational approach for animal ethics.

PERSISTING HARM: POLAR BEARS AND CLIMATE CHANGE

The U.S. Geological Service predicts that Arctic sea ice will dramatically decline over the course of the twenty-first century (DeWeaver 2007, 22), a prediction that has received some support from the record-low sea-ice cover in September 2007 and unusually low sea ice in the summers of 2008 and 2009.[1] Since polar bears hunt, mate, and travel on sea ice, they need it to survive. Earlier ice melt and later ice cover may mean that polar bears have insufficient fat reserves to survive the ice-free season; in addition, as they weigh less, their reproductive ability diminishes. Studies already suggest that some populations of polar bears are in decline and that bears in these populations weigh less than they did several decades ago (Derocher et al., 2004).

It is widely (though not universally) accepted that the decline in Arctic sea ice is a consequence of increasing anthropogenic greenhouse gases in the atmosphere released in part, though not exclusively, by the burning of fossil fuels. I will here assume that climate change is occurring, will continue to intensify in the Arctic, and that it is largely anthropogenic in origin. What does this mean for human moral responsibilities toward polar bears? Should bears threatened by anthropogenic climate change be assisted?

This is an extremely complicated case, for a number of reasons. First, it might be argued that the target of direct moral concern here should be the polar bear *species*, not individual polar bears. For reasons I have given elsewhere (Palmer 2009), I am not convinced by this argument or, at least, not inasmuch as it might be thought that the species "polar bear" is itself an object of moral concern. Second, it might be asked "Why pick out polar bears?"—since there are many sentient species whose members' well-being is threatened by climate change. Of course, this is true: the focus on polar bears is merely an example; they are not special in this sense. Third, climate change itself raises enormously difficult questions about causal and moral responsibility, all of which are relevant to this case, and, additionally, different humans are likely to be rather differently located with respect to their moral responsibilities toward polar bears (for instance, the relation to an Alaskan polar bear of a tourist on a cruise ship is rather different from that of a local Inuit). The polar-bear case could, I think, generate a book of its own. But I will here consider some of the important and challenging questions that climate change raises for the approach to animal ethics that I have been developing.

First, and most generally: does anthropogenic climate change itself present a challenge to the idea of the No-contact LFI? More precisely, does it mean that there are no longer any "fully wild" animals, animals that are "outside contact"? If there is "no more nature," as McKibben (1989) argues, then *all* animals seem to be drawn into the contact zone. And one reading of this might be that humans have some obligations to assist *all* sentient animals, because they are all "contacted."

However, this would be to conclude too much. "No contact" in the case of the LFI has a more specific meaning—no contact in the sense of prior harms or creation of vulnerability or dependency. It is only in these kinds of contexts—where animals' interests have already been set back or are at high risk of being set back due to human actions—that, I have argued, special obligations to assist exist. There will be many animals, even in a world of anthropogenic climate change, who are not harmed or made vulnerable by climate change nor negatively affected by humans in other ways. Some sentient animals may benefit from climate changes; for others, such changes would make little difference. Yet others, in particular human commensals and contramensals, will continue to live well alongside humans so long as humans continue to live well (and perhaps even if they do not). Since humans have not—in general, anyway—harmed these animals or put them at high risk of harm, special obligations of assistance are not created (as we saw with the dumpster rats). So even in a world of climate change, where human use of the Earth's atmosphere, land, and waters is constantly expanding, there will still be animals to whom humans do not have obligations of assistance, even if in a more general sense they are "contacted." Given the growth in numbers of commensals and contramensals, this seems unlikely to change.

A second question here concerns whether climate change should be seen as harming sentient animals at all, in the sense that I have understood harm. That is, even if animals' interests are set back, perhaps such setbacks are more accurately thought of as hurts or misfortunes. This raises even more difficult questions about harms, intentions, and moral responsibility than was raised by *Coyotes* in chapter 6—questions that are unresolved with respect to climate change even in the human case (see, for instance, Garvey 2008, 77). While it is certainly true that with respect to current emissions, climate change could not be called unforeseen or accidental, earlier releases of CO_2 and other greenhouse gases (call this CO_2e) were not *knowingly* risky. Unlike the developers of wild land in *Coyotes*, for instance, who had good reason to think they were destroying sentient-animal habitat, or even the car driver in *Squirrel 2* (below) who knows that cars often cause roadkill, there was no strong reason, until the late 1980s, to think that the emissions of these gases would change the climate; ignorance about these effects was (broadly) unavoidable. It might also be argued that even though the effects of climate change on (say) polar bears are now foreseeable—and perhaps have been for twenty years—CO_2e is not being emitted *in order* to harm them. Polar bears can be the foreseeable victims of our activities, but this does not mean that we *intend* to harm them. If harms had to be directly intended in *this* extremely direct way, then no one has been harmed by climate change, including polar bears, for no one releases greenhouse gases *in order* to harm others.

This opens up a substantial debate on knowledge, intention, and responsibility that I have no hope of resolving here.[2] However, I will make some basic points relevant to thinking through the polar-bear case. It is implausible, as I maintained in chapter 6, to say that harm must be the *intended* outcome of an action before any moral responsibility for the outcome of an action exists, a view that is widely accepted. At the very least, if the setback to animals' interests can be described as predictable, foreseen, or recognized to be at high risk of occurring, then such setbacks, when they occur, should be thought of as harms (as we would think that they were in the human case). Even if, prior to 1990, it was not reasonable to think that such effects on polar bears could be the outcome of CO_2e emissions (the effect was not then widely predicted or foreseen), since 1990, these likely effects have been widely known—yet emissions have continued to rise. This is not, therefore, like Jamieson's

143

(1990) cases of accidentally knocking a boulder toward someone else when walking, something that normally one could not foresee. Once the scientific evidence for anthropogenic climate change was widely accepted and it was understood that the Arctic was at particularly high risk, negative impacts on the interests of sentient animals (and, of course, people) in Arctic areas were foreseen and predicted. Continuing with activities that intensified and enhanced these impacts, then, is rightly seen as harming sentient animals such as polar bears.

But if this is the case, perhaps it is odd to see this as an instance of special obligation to assist. After all—as I commented in the case of agricultural animals in chapter 6—surely what is needed here is that the continuing harm stops, rather than that we assume backward-looking special obligations to assist? After all, is not the problem here that the harmful processes of anthropogenic CO2e emissions, leading to a warming in the Arctic, are still ongoing?

Were the harm here of a (somewhat) more straightforward kind—such as in the case of emissions of stratospheric ozone-depleting chemicals—stopping harm would be the best way forward. But climate change presents, as is well known, one of the most intractable policy issues around—a "wicked policy problem" (Rittel and Webber 1973) without parallel—for a number of reasons. First, climate change is a collective-action problem: that is, the relatively small individual contributions made by individuals and industries collectively generate the problem; as Gardiner (2006, 399) puts it, agency is fragmented. Second, CO2 is produced by many forms of energy, in particular coal, oil, and natural gas: the engines of modern industrial and technological economies. Reducing CO2 emissions means throttling those engines back, which threatens economic growth, unless there are technological advances in energy production and conservation soon. Third, political discussion about reducing CO2e is mired in longstanding international disputes about inequality and injustice. Historically, the developed countries have produced the highest amounts of CO2e over time and still produce the greatest per capita emissions, while those nations most vulnerable to climate change are less developed, have historically produced very little CO2e, and still have low per capita emissions—and need energy in order to reach basic levels of well-being for many members of their human populations. As Gardiner (2006) and others have argued, negotiations over climate change create prisoner's dilemmas of a particularly vicious variety. And—alongside all of this—the effects of emissions are delayed (or "backloaded") so that the Earth is already committed to some degree of climate change, irrespective of what policies of CO2e emissions are now adopted (a degree that conceivably could be fatal to polar bears even if emissions dropped abruptly tomorrow).[3]

Ending harm to polar bears (or other existing sentient animals) from climate change, then, can only be a long and complicated political process. Outside this process, although there may be other reasons why individuals should reduce their own emissions, it is unlikely that some few individuals deciding to do so will have much effect—not, at least, to the extent that it would reduce or end harm to polar bears.[4] And even though the harmful anthropogenic process is still ongoing, there is nothing that is of sufficiently low risk and currently technologically feasible that can be done to reduce or halt the harm even in the medium term, given the backloading effect of CO_2e emissions.[5] The well-being of currently existing individual polar bears looks inevitably compromised, especially in Alaska.

This is a case, then, where anthropogenic harm to the well-being of individual bears cannot easily be stopped: the wrong is necessarily ongoing. On a relational approach to animal assistance, one response to an unstoppable wrong would be to offer assistance that attempts to protect against, or help in adapting to, the effects of the wrong or, if this is very difficult (as in this case), to attempt to assist in *other* ways, if possible. That is, though the anthropogenic changes in climate and ice conditions may cause the polar bears harm, there may be other ways in which they can be assisted that can, partially at least, counter the effects of the harm. It is unlikely, though, that this would be easy to do, or at least to do in ways that would not run the risk of longer-term welfare deterioration for the assisted individuals. Feeding them, for instance, is likely to habituate them to humans and encourage scavenging—and when bears and people mix, the prospects for bears are bad. Some bears' lives could be protected by reducing or eliminating hunting. But though there is certainly room for such policies, it is doubtful that the policies to reduce hunting should come at the expense of subsistence quotas for native peoples,[6] who are themselves suffering harms from the effects of climate change more acutely than almost anyone else while sharing little causal responsibility for it.[7]

It looks as though the best form of assistance, inasmuch as it is possible at all, is to protect polar bears against threats to their habitat that do not come from climate change. This might, at least in the short term, counterbalance some of the harms from climate change, making them better off with respect to some aspects of their habitat than they would otherwise be, even as climate change makes them worse off. (Admittedly, this could be read as preventing a further harm rather than as assistance, but equally one could see it as a counterfactual condition: if habitat protection is extended because of the threats of climate change, then the animals are better off than they would otherwise have been, given a very likely alternative course of events.) Oil and gas drilling in polar-bear habitat, for instance, can worsen their well-being through exposure to contaminants and disturbance (and, of course, the use of those very fossil fuels adds to the harming process). So, retreating from plans to develop polar-bear habitat for mineral extraction and withdrawing facilities that might already be contributing to harm could count as assistance (and of an appropriate kind, since the very industry that is causing a substantial part of the harm would be paying the price of assistance to the harmed, and the kind of assistance that is being given concerns bears' habitat, exactly what is being threatened—although, admittedly, no development rollback can restore lost sea ice.)[8]

Polar bears present a particularly difficult case because of the apparently intractable nature of the human-originating harm they are undergoing: a harm that is collective, flows from serious human interests, is indirect, and is backloaded. Since the harm cannot be stopped in the short term and can only be somewhat slowed in the medium term, I have suggested that we consider other forms of assistance that might, to some extent and temporarily, counterbalance the harm. The reason for the assistance is not just that the bears' well-being has been set back (as a utilitarian might maintain) but because the setback is a harm *caused by humans*. Climate change entangles at least some animals that would otherwise have much less contact with humans into the contact zone, harming them and making them increasingly vulnerable. For that reason, since stopping the harm on any reasonable timescale is near to impossible, humans have special obligations to assist existing polar bears, inasmuch as any assistance is possible.

SUFFERING IN THE WILD
Wild-elk Disease

Suppose, in a fully wild context, a painful and often fatal disease, not introduced by humans, has begun to spread in a wild population of elk. No vaccination exists (unlike in the mountain bighorn case). Killing some of the elk now—both sick ones and some that are healthy—in order to create a buffer zone could stop the disease from spreading and thus could assist many other elk to stay healthy.

This case raises another issue that I have not, so far, considered. I have maintained that there is a prima facie duty not to harm but that, although assistance may be permissible, it is not required in fully wild cases. However, I have not considered cases where to assist some may mean harming others. This is not an esoteric question, since culling some to save others (who may or may not be of the same species) is both debated and practiced in wildlife policy.

The different capacity-oriented ethical views I have considered would have distinct responses to the wild-elk case. A negative-rights view such as Regan's appears to *reject* assistance. First, on this view, there are no positive duties to assist except to protect individuals from rights violations caused by the unjust actions of other moral agents. Wild disease is not a moral agent and cannot violate rights. In addition, assistance here comes only at the expense of taking some sentient animals' lives, which fails to respect the inherent value of those animals killed, thus infringing on their basic rights. So there is also a constraint against assisting; assistance that involves harm here is *impermissible*. It is worth noting, however—and I will shortly return to this—that Regan's view about rights infringement is not an absolutist one. If this were a case where acting to violate the rights of a few were the only way of preventing the violation of the rights of the many, such an action would be required (so, according to Regan's "miniride" principle, I should violate the rights of several elk if that were the only way to prevent another moral agent from violating the rights of the entire herd).[9] On a utilitarian view, in contrast, it is likely that assistance to the majority of elk at the expense of the minority of elk in this case is required (assuming that there are not some other comparably bad consequences from doing so). Killing some elk (including some healthy ones to create a "buffer zone") if this will, in the end, protect more elk, and there is no other way of protecting them, will produce the best outcome in terms of minimizing suffering.

What would emerge from the No-contact LFI about this situation? As I have laid the elk case out so far there's no positive obligation to assist. The elk are constitutively and locationally wild—a standard case for the laissez-faire intuition. There's no requirement, on this view, to bring about the best consequences by intervening to reduce suffering. But is assistance *permissible*? In this case, the answer seems to be that it is not. There is no requirement to assist, and there is a constraint on harming. It is true that I have maintained that a constraint on harming can be overridden, but superogatory assistance, as in this case, is not going to be strong enough to outweigh this constraint.

The situation is likely to be different, however, if human beings had introduced the disease—say, it had spread into wild populations from domesticated animals, in ways that were foreseeable and not adequately prevented. What's interesting here is how we understand the role of the disease in such a case. It would be possible to argue—from a negative-rights view, perhaps—that this situation is no different from wild disease because, however a disease originates, it is not a moral agent and cannot violate anyone's rights. However, we could alternatively—and I think more plausibly—see the human-originating disease as a kind of extension of human action or, at least, a failure of a "duty of care" on the part of relevant humans. In this case, elk have been made vulnerable to suffering and death by disease because of human activity; at least, in an indirect sense, humans are harming them or exposing them to a high risk of harm. Although killing some elk to save others from human-originating disease could be described as assistance, on this view, this is not the best conceptualization of the case. It is better to see anthropogenic elk disease as a case where, whatever happens, some elk are inevitably going to be harmed by people, either indirectly from human-originating disease or directly by a cull. Put this way, a version of Regan's miniride principle could be adapted to apply here as part of a relational approach. That is, if all the individual elk should be equally protected from human-originating harm (and we have no reason here to think that some are owed more protection than others) but because of events already in train we cannot protect them all, then we should protect as many as we can, even at the expense of the few. So in the case of human-originating elk disease, as outlined here, humans should act—since they are already "in the mix" causing harm and vulnerability to harm to sentient animals. In the case of wild-elk disease that is not of human origin, humans should not act (unless there are other extremely powerful reasons independent of the well-being of the animals themselves that could justify harming some animals).[10]

Squirrel

Suppose that, hiking in a wild place, you encounter an injured and suffering squirrel. (It looks as though it has been attacked by another animal.) Your options are as follows: you could do nothing and walk on by. You could (as far as possible) painlessly kill the squirrel, taking this to be a form of assistance. You could in various other ways attempt to assist the squirrel (you could abandon your hike and carry the squirrel to a wildlife-rescue center you know that is not far off).

Like *Wild-elk Disease*, this is a case of fully wild animal distress, but it contrasts with the preceding case in several ways. *Wild-elk Disease* is a case that requires a group of people, considerable research (for instance, on how the disease originated and how best to manage a cull), some kind of deliberate policymaking about elk management, and may carry long-term implications with respect to wild-elk individuals (and populations). *Squirrel*, however, is a situation of immediacy, not one of growing observation of a spreading disease over time; it is a "one-on-one" case: you directly encounter the squirrel. You are faced with an instant decision, with a suffering individual animal before you. No policy discussion is possible, nor does policy need to be made. There is only one animal involved. Though it is possible that assisting this animal might have some long-term implications (other than for the squirrel itself), these are unlikely. If you kill the squirrel, there are probably no long-term implications (since your doing so likely only hastens what will happen in a while without your assistance). Even if you rescue the squirrel, supposing it survives at the wildlife-rescue shelter and is subsequently released back into the wild, broader issues involving the squirrel, or other animals, being moved into the contact zone are extremely unlikely. In addition, let us assume that assisting would not involve you in some major sacrifice nor any other problem of "comparative moral significance," to use Singer's terms. For example, assisting the squirrel would not require you to leave your small child unaccompanied in a wild place.

This is exactly the kind of case where I have argued that assistance is not morally required. The squirrel is constitutively and locationally *ex hypothesi* fully wild and it has not been harmed by people. You could walk on by and (in contrast to, say, a utilitarian approach to this case) you would have done nothing wrong. Yet someone might ask, if told of this encounter: well, sure, there may be no duty to assist in such a case, but what sort of person would just walk on by, leaving the animal to suffer, when they could have done something about it? Even someone who, in general, accepts the LFI—for instance, that there is no duty to go out looking to relieve wild pain nor to attempt to change ecosystems or make wildlife policy to reduce it—might flinch at the implication that if one *encountered* a suffering wild animal, it is perfectly fine just to walk past and leave it lying there. Something seems different about the immediacy of the encounter that raises questions about the general principle.

But then, it is exactly this thought—that there is something problematic about not responding in conditions of immediate, encountered need—that is used by Singer to drive his drowning-child/starving-child analogy and by Unger (1996, 25) to argue that if we should assist a bleeding birdwatcher that we encounter, even though doing so will ruin our treasured sedan's expensive leather upholstery, we should certainly assist distant starving children. For the thought here might be: since the chance of encounter is surely morally irrelevant, if we are worried about encounter cases, we should be equally worried about all the otherwise similar-featured cases that we just do not happen to encounter. So, if we think we should assist the encountered squirrel, then we should generalize to other nonencountered wild animals (such as the elk). But this would overturn the LFI.

Of course, the cases of nonanthropogenic *Wild-elk Disease* and *Squirrel* are, as I have described them, different in a number of ways (not just with respect to encounter). But even if this were not so, I think we can say something about situations of encounter in the wild where the encounter itself is a distinguishing feature and has some moral relevance. There is no *duty* to assist in cases of encounter, but we can provide an explanation as to why assistance is not only permissible but also perhaps desirable, in encounter cases where there are no reasons *not* to assist.

In chapter 3, I briefly considered contributions by ethicists of care to relational approaches to animal ethics; their concern, in particular, was with the emotional commitments of the moral agent. Related concerns about character, or what particular behaviors say about us, also emerged in chapter 7, in the context of the creation of dominating relations that do not harm the animals thus created but can be understood as demonstrating arrogance or hubris on the part of human beings. The situation of an immediate encounter with suffering is another place where thinking about a moral agent's character and emotional world is morally relevant.

If—as is widely accepted—feeling compassion or sympathy for suffering is a good character trait, even where suffering is not a result of wrongful harm, then we can hope that someone who encountered a suffering wild animal would feel such emotions. As these emotions are likely to motivate assistance, we would expect such a person to want to assist a suffering wild animal. Since acting on such responses is not proscribed on the No-contact LFI, and assuming that no other morally significant issues are raised, a virtuous person is likely to assist an animal in such a situation, even though there is no obligation (on other grounds) to do so. And if someone failed to manifest such moral emotions, and to act on them, we might think that this is evidence, at least, of someone who is unsympathetic or insensitive to others' pain. So, even though no wrong would be done by walking on by, nonetheless we could, without contradiction, think that assisting an encountered suffering wild animal, if the assistance flowed from compassion or sympathy, was a sign of morally admirable character. This could provide, at least, a weak reason for approving of assistance in such a case.[11]

Of course, one response to this might be: Well, if it is revealing of a good character to feel compassion and sympathy on encounter, why would it not be revealing of a good character to feel these emotions for sufferers *without* encounter? And if this is right, then surely this would run counter to the LFI. For in every case where there is no special obligation to assist, there are surely some animals (albeit distant animals) for whom one could feel compassion. A truly compassionate person, it might be argued, would have this response just as much toward those who are distant as to those who are encountered.

This objection does not necessarily hold. Slote (2007) seems right to maintain that the vivid immediacy of confrontation with suffering does *and should* pull on our emotional responses more powerfully than just hearing about similar situations from a distance. There is no reason why we should not say that a different disposition *is* involved in responding to encountered suffering. As Sandler (2007, 74) suggests:

> although compassion towards nonhumans need not involve dispositions to actively seek out opportunities to prevent the suffering of wild animals, it may, particularly given our biological predispositions regarding the present suffering of others, involve dispositions to assist wild animals when appropriate opportunities present themselves—e.g., when dolphins become beached nearby.

In the case of *Squirrel*, there's no obligation to assist. But we might expect a virtuous person to have a compassionate disposition toward encountered suffering and therefore to assist in such circumstances unless there are other reasons that speak against doing so. And since a compassionate disposition is one that is good to have, we could at least say that the manifestation of such a disposition in cases of encountered suffering should be regarded as morally good.[12]

Squirrel 2

But consider a variation on *Squirrel*: *Squirrel 2*. Suppose you find a dazed and bleeding squirrel at the side of a busy road. Most likely the animal has been hit by a passing car, so the cause of its injury is probably a human one, although you cannot be sure. Is the situation different from the first *Squirrel* case, since the animal might be (in some unhappily literal sense) in the contact zone?

The contrast with *Squirrel*, then, is that here some human (though not you) probably caused the squirrel's state. Either the squirrel was hit by a car or it was not. If it was not, the case is the same as *Squirrel*. If it was hit by a car, this was very likely to have been an accident (that is, it is likely that the squirrel was hit by someone who did not see it or could not stop rather than by someone trying to kill squirrels or who could not be bothered to swerve). If it is an accident, then this looks like a misfortune or a hurt rather than a harm, so again this would be indistinguishable from *Squirrel*, since the injury was not the deliberate act of a moral agent.

However, perhaps this is to move a bit too swiftly; again, as with *Coyotes* and *Polar Bears*, questions about knowledge, negligence, and responsibility are raised. If we attribute the squirrel's injuries to a car, there are two possible lines of argument that might, in a weaker and more indirect way than *Coyotes*, suggest something nearer to "harm" than "misfortune" in this case. One line of argument concerns the individual driver. The driver may have been driving too fast or recklessly and thus was not in a position to dodge or stop for the squirrel. But, of course, you as squirrel encounterer cannot know this, and no doubt many people have hurt or killed wildlife while driving carefully. Second, it might be argued, as Blustein (1997, 84) maintains, that "driving is an inherently risky activity," so that what we mean by an "accident" when driving is not something that happens, as it were, just by chance: "an accident is a foreseeable risk of it [driving]." Blustein points out that "the price one must pay for permissibly engaging in risky or dangerous activities is what, in the law, is called strict liability for causing harm." The squirrel case here is obviously not a legal one, but Blustein plausibly argues that, in *human* cases like these, because the harmer has knowingly engaged in activities that risk harming others, when such harms occur, the harmer owes assistance (for instance, compensation) to the one harmed.

However, even if we extended this to *Squirrel 2*, this would not in itself give *you*, someone stumbling across the squirrel, an obligation to assist. For surely, even if we concede that some other moral agent has harmed (rather than just hurt) the squirrel, this would not give it a backward-looking moral claim on *you*. This is where another argument—one analogous to some of those that I considered in chapter 6—might be introduced. If we take a step back from the actual situation of this encounter, we can locate it in a back story about the development of roads and motor transport. Many of the benefits (as well as some of the costs) of living in modern, industrialized societies stem from the networks of road transport mapped onto the land. Road transportation allows for much better access to more and various goods and for the maintenance of a much wider range of social and personal relations than could otherwise be available. So, in what is admittedly a very indirect way, you (as

151

someone encountering the injured squirrel) have almost certainly accepted many benefits from road transportation; injuries and deaths of humans and animals on the roads are prices paid for those benefits, and these are prices that you certainly know about. As I argued in chapter 6, entanglements such as this can provide weak reasons to assist; the squirrel's suffering is a product of an important institution in human society—road transportation—from which most of society's members, including you, benefit.

The question about causal uncertainty still remains. But since, on the No-contact LFI, there's no duty *not* to assist in cases such as *Squirrel* and *Squirrel 2*, if there is likely to be a reason based on human entanglement for the animal's suffering, and where there are not other morally significant reasons for refraining from assistance, there are weak moral reasons in favor of assisting. Coupled with the character concerns raised in *Squirrel*, we could conclude that in *Squirrel 2*, it is morally better not to walk on by—even if the only assistance possible is to kill the suffering animal.

152

LAYERED PREDATION IN THE CONTACT ZONE: BLUE TITS

A suburban blue tit nests under the eaves of the roof of a suburban house. The nest is attacked by a European magpie. The householder is in a position to chase the magpie off to protect the nest. Assume he does not. The European magpie kills and eats all but one of the blue-tit chicks. The last chick falls to the ground and, unable to fly, hops frantically around the garden of the neighbor's house. The agitated blue-tit parent flies above the distressed chick. The neighbor's cat, sunning herself in the garden, advances on the chick. The cat's owner is in a position to assist the chick by restraining the cat: should she?[13]

This real-life, garden-variety case is rather complicated. What would the capacity-oriented views we have considered have to say here? It's likely that utilitarian and capabilities approaches would recommend intervention to chase off the magpie and (if this failed) almost certainly to protect the chick from the cat. The magpie looks to be inflicting pain and death on a number of chicks; even if the magpie were to starve without this meal, the loss to the magpie looks less than the gain from the protected lives of the blue tits (measured in any utilitarian way). And on a capabilities view, the chicks are *all* prevented from fulfilling their most basic capabilities, so again, this looks like a vote against the magpie and in favor of intervention. As for the second part of this case, if we assume that there's a way of getting the chick back in the nest, the argument for the neighbor, as cat owner, to intervene to restrain the cat is even stronger. From a utilitarian point of view, the cat's interest in the matter must be much less than the chick's; suffering is averted by acting, and the cat is deprived of only a momentary (and largely substitutable) pleasure. For a capabilities approach, that the chick lives to fulfill its capabilities is of much more basic importance than that the cat preys on the chick: catching the chick might express one of the cat's important capabilities, but a toy on a string would express that capability too, without suppressing some *other* creature's capabilities. So, again, intervention would be warranted.

A rights view of the kind advocated by Regan, however, contrasts quite radically here: for no moral agent is directly acting to cause harm in these interspecies encounters. Since neither the magpie nor the cat is a moral agent, neither can infringe on any rights, whatever they do (though I will raise below a possible query about this). And since rights are not being infringed, there are no duties to assist. In addition, it is precisely cases of predation that Regan argues most strongly to be no business of humans; here animals are members of "other nations" that should be left to sort things out on their own.

But there's more going on here than these approaches take into account. These animals are all—in different ways—in the contact zone; there are back stories in each case that locate them in significant relations with human beings, relations that have some bearing, I will argue, on whether human assistance is permitted or required. For although there is one sense in which this case is a series of nonhuman, interspecies interactions, there is another sense in which humans—though some humans more than others—are deeply immersed in it.

I will begin with the blue tits. Many blue tits do not live alongside humans, so the specific relations I will talk about here do not generalize to all members of the species. But these particular blue tits—living under the eaves of a house—are clearly at least human commensals. They have come to live alongside humans and take advantage of the human physical constructions and food available in suburban settings. But the relationship is likely to be closer than this. Blue tits are birds that householders encourage to live alongside them by providing them with food—bags of nuts or fat balls—and nest boxes. We might think of this relationship as one of mutualism: a win/win relationship, from which both humans and birds gain, although the human gain is not, unlike the birds', a material one. The householder may well be happy to have the nest, may have been feeding the birds, may have enjoyed watching the chicks grow, and may feel some attachment to the birds in that particular nest. (This might, though, not apply in this case: perhaps the householder knew nothing about the nest before this incident.)

Likewise, European magpies—or some of them—have become human commensals. They too live alongside humans, scavenging food and nest-building material from human settlements. But they are much less welcome than blue tits. Some people regard them as contramensals (benefiting from living alongside humans at human expense), since they are noisy, messy, aggressive, and (as in this case) prey on other birds toward whom people generally have more positive attachments.

The relations of both blue tits and European magpies to humans, however, contrast with the cat, for the cat has been bred by human beings for human beings. Although blue tits and magpies may have adapted their behaviors to live well alongside people and may have undergone some minor evolutionary physiological changes, they have not been domesticated, in the sense that humans have not controlled their breeding.[14] The cat, though, is in some degree a human product (indeed, if the cat is a pedigree, her entire body is a mapping of human preference in shape, color, fur length, form, and, at least partially, temperament). Not only the way she looks but that she exists as an individual at all and that she exists in the household she does is also on account of deliberate human actions. She is thus located quite differently with respect to the humans around her than are the magpie and the blue tits. Her relationship with her owner[15] is almost certainly mutualist—once a domesticated cat has been born, the best life for it is likely to be a household where its needs are met. And given that this cat is living in this household, we can reasonably assume that she was chosen and wanted and that her owner benefits (albeit not materially) from having her in the house.

On a relational approach, what kinds of ethical relations might there be to the magpie, blue tits, and cat? I have suggested throughout this book that all moral agents have a prima facie (though overrideable) duty not to harm sentient animals, but in this case that is not what immediately looks to be at stake; we are more obviously interested in obligations and permissions to assist. On the account I have given, humans do not have obligations to assist all the animals here. This is clearest in the case of the European magpie, with its uneasy relationship to the humans among whom it resides. Magpies—in general—have flourished alongside humans. We are not dealing here with (for instance) a struggling population that has been dislodged by humans from its habitat, as with *Coyotes*. Nor are we dealing with a population that humans have introduced or deliberately encouraged. Of course, there may be some particular magpies that have a special relationship with some human individuals where a morally relevant back story could be told. But I will assume that this is not one of those cases. Humans should prima facie not harm the magpie, but there is no special obligation in this case to assist it, either.

The situation of the blue tits is likely to be slightly more complicated. Suppose the blue tits had become at least partially dependent on the food provided by the householder. Once a relationship of dependence is created, then withdrawing the food may be detrimental to the well-being of the birds concerned (especially were they tied to this particular location for the time being by their nest). So, it is at least possible that some kind of responsibility to provide food might have come into being in this case, owing to the deliberate creation of a dependency and hence a vulnerability. If this were so, the blue tits would be much more closely entangled in the contact zone than the magpie. However, the obligation to assist, in such a case, seems to be a relatively constrained one. It surely does not mean that the householder as-sumes a much wider range of duties to assist the birds, duties unrelated to feeding them. He has not taken on a responsibility of overall care for the birds. Should some nonanthropogenic bird disease begin to sweep the area, the householder is not (for instance) obliged to catch the blue tits and take them to a veterinary surgeon for vaccination. So if there is any human-animal obligation involved in this relation, it specifically concerns continuing with provision, given that there is a specific created dependence on that provision.

The cat's owner, on the other hand, has fairly comprehensive special obligations toward the cat. In taking her into the household, as Burgess-Jackson (2003) argues, the owner has closed off other options for support: the cat is now dependent on her, and the owner does have a responsibility of overall care. The owner should provide for the cat's well-being in a variety of ways: food, water, medical treatment, assis-tance if she is hurt or trapped in some way, and protection from threats. Like ev-eryone else, the cat's owner has a duty not to harm her—and the owner has special opportunities to harm her in ways that others do not. So, for instance, the owner could frustrate her basic desires by confining her in small spaces, distress her in a variety of ways, and perform painful operations on her that do not benefit her (such as declawing).

155

We can assume, though, from the facts of this case, that this cat is given free-dom to roam outdoors and is still in full possession of all her claws.[16] Which brings us to the question of assistance in this case. Should the householder under whose eaves the blue tits have nested assist the blue tits against the magpie? Should the cat's owner assist the chick by protecting it from the cat? Do either of these human individuals have an obligation to assist in either case? (I'll assume that assistance at either point could be successful: that the magpie could be driven off the blue tits' nest and that the nestling could be reinstated in the nest.)[17]

Assistance against magpie: Should the householder assist the blue tits by chas-ing off the threatening magpie? Given what I have already said, there is no obligation to do so; even if the householder has established a relation of dependent provision with the blue tits under the eaves, there is still no obligation to assist when the birds come under attack from another bird.

However, we might think that this case is like *Squirrel*. That is, faced with a par-ticular encounter with suffering, a virtuous person would feel compassion for the blue tits and so want to assist—even more so when there is almost a feeling of "per-sonal relation" after weeks of feeding the bird family. And this may make sense (as I will suggest shortly) with respect to the potential attack by the *cat*. However, the situation with respect to the magpie is somewhat different. For it is possible that act-ing to assist the blue tits would harm the magpie; the magpie needs to eat and to take food back to its own nest. And while I have suggested that the householder has no duty to assist the blue tits with respect to predators, he does have a prima facie duty not to harm sentient birds. If the magpie is at risk of harm by being deprived of the nestlings, then this would be a case of harming in order to assist. And though there could be occasions in which one might harm to assist, this case is similar to nonanthropogenic *Wild-elk Disease* in not being one of them. Since there is no obligation to assist but there is a duty not to harm, even though a virtuous person might feel compassion in this case (and perhaps, a sense of frustration and sorrow at the ending of the nest), if intervention could cause harm, this is a reason against it. It might be possible to attempt to compensate for the harm by intervening to save the nestlings and also feeding the magpie. However, there is *no obligation* for the householder to do anything in this case, and since there is a risk that assistance may harm, there is also a presumption against doing so.

Assistance against the cat: Should the cat's owner assist the nestling by protecting it from the cat (assuming, as I have been doing, and as is plausible, that intervention could bring about a positive outcome for the nestling)? This raises the further question of whether there are factors that distinguish the cat's situation from the magpie's situation—and that there are seems obvious: the cat's relation to humans in general, and the owner in particular, is different from that of the magpie, *and* the cat is unlikely to be harmed by being prevented from hunting the nestling.

More specifically: in anthropogenic *Wild-elk Disease*, I suggested that since this disease had been introduced by humans, it could be seen as an indirect extension of human action; that is, the animals with the disease were being harmed by it and were not merely unfortunate to catch it. Could something like this be said of the cat's actions? Were the cat to attack the nestling, would this be, in an indirect sense, a harm committed by the cat's owner? This moves us from thinking about the special responsibility of the owner to the cat to thinking about the responsibility of the owner to the sentient beings encountered by the cat.

Plainly, there are cases where the action of a pet would be seen as the moral responsibility of the owner (and indeed, this might be, as I hinted above, a rare exception where, even on Regan's terms, an animal *could* violate someone's rights). Suppose I train my dog to attack people on command when I shout "Attack!" When you next approach me, I shout "Attack!" and, sure enough, my dog attacks you. Although in a literal sense it is the dog that attacks you, I am morally responsible for the dog's action, and in any morally relevant sense it is me that has harmed you, using my dog as an extension of my will, as the tool for carrying out my purpose. Indeed, in most parts of the world, I would be *legally* responsible were I to do this: in the United States, if a dog is commanded to attack, and it kills its victim, the person who commanded the dog can be convicted of first-degree murder.[18] Less clear cases are those where dogs are kept but trained very poorly or not at all; where owners give dogs confusing and conflicting signals, so that the dog's behavior is erratic, and the dog attacks someone; or where dogs are neglected or ill treated, and this leads to dog attacks. Such cases are legally complicated[19] but in a moral sense seem more straightforward. The owner is morally responsible for the dog's behavior when the dog's behavior substantially flows from the owner's failure to care for the dog in the ways that keeping a dog requires. Care involves at least some level of training, adequate provision, and noninfliction of harm. And unlike in the case of children (where the same requirements apply) dogs will never become moral agents, able to make their own judgments about the moral appropriateness of their behavior.[20] So, in a situation where an inadequately trained, neglected, or ill-treated dog attacks a sentient animal, it seems right for the owner to intervene (if that is possible); however, this intervention is best portrayed as preventing oneself from indirectly causing harm to another.

The case of the cat and the nestling here differs somewhat. No amount of training will stop a cat from hunting a bird. Well-fed, well-cared-for cats will attack birds not much less frequently than neglected, hungry ones.[21] The attack on the nestling cannot be seen as a consequence of the owner's lack of care (that is, as a direct harm to the cat that produces another, indirect harm to the bird),[22] nor as a lack of training. So it is difficult to make a direct case that the cat's actions in hunting the chick are the causal responsibility of the owner; the cat hunts independently both of breeding and of training. Nonetheless, that the cat exists in the place she does and she is free to roam in the garden is a consequence of the owner's actions. Additionally—as was discussed in earlier chapters—the cat is located within a broader set of social structures and practices of pet ownership. So even though the cat's action in hunting is not the direct causal responsibility of the owner, there is nonetheless a back story both of human entanglement and of the more specific, close involvement of this specific owner (who brought the cat to this place and let the cat out, when it was foreseeable that the cat might attack a bird) that lies behinds the cat's advance on the struggling nestling.

If one were to take the view that this was a *harming* case—where the cat acts as an extension of the human, so the cat harms the chick—then there would be an duty to stop the harm. But although there is probably room for debate here, I think that the independence of the cat in this case is too strong and the relation of the owner to the cat's behavior too weak to successfully construct it as a harming case. The owner is not harming the chick through the cat; if the owner acts to protect the chick, this would be a case of assistance, not of stopping harm. Should the owner, then, assist the nestling? First, to do so is very unlikely to harm the cat in any meaningful way (in comparison to the magpie). The loss to the cat is momentary; this nestling is not her sole source of dinner for the day. So this is not a case of harming to assist. Second, although the cat's hunting behavior is independent of humans and not the result of a lack of duty of care (as in anthropogenic *Wild-elk Disease*), her opportunity to express such behavior on this occasion is dependent on a number of human choices. Without the owner, the cat would not be there. So there is a *loose* sense in which the owner has some kind of causal responsibility for the cat being available to hunt. Additionally, the owner benefits from the presence of the cat, yet, indirectly, gaining that benefit will, without intervention, lead to the suffering of the bird. These relational reasons are, I think, sufficient to suggest that, in the absence of reasons not to assist, the cat's owner should help the chick. Additionally, as in *Squirrel*, this is a situation of encounter; the cat owner (and, indeed, anyone passing by) may feel compassion and sympathy for the struggling nestling and the distressed parent bird, and this may motivate the desire to restore the bird to the nest. Since there is no reason not to manifest and to act on this caring disposition, this provides some further reason to assist the nestling here. So, to conclude this case: most generally, where assistance flowing from some past harm or created vulnerability is not required and where assisting will cause or risk harm, then there is a constraint against assistance (as in the magpie case). Where assistance will not cause harm and there is some human causal entanglement in animal suffering, then humans should assist (as in the cat case).

In this final full chapter, I have worked through cases where assistance (or stopping harm) might be morally required, morally permitted, both permitted and desirable though not morally required, or not permitted. In exploring these cases, I have tried to show some of the considerations that should be taken into account by anyone adopting a relational approach of the kind I have been advocating. One obvious outcome of these cases is that the analysis involved is going to be complex and fairly specific to particular contexts and situations. Questions about how individual humans and animals got to be in the places and situations in which they end up, the kinds of relations they have or have not established, and the broader back stories of human activities, past harms, and created vulnerabilities and dependencies all loom large in decisions about whether, when, and what assistance is owed to animals. And there may be yet other relevant relational considerations that I have not considered here. For all these reasons, the consideration of cases here is inevitably truncated. Nonetheless, I hope that they illustrate something about both how unreformed capacity-oriented and relational approaches may come apart in practice as well as in principle and provide at least an outline of how different problems about harm and assistance might be tackled from a relational perspective.

Conclusion

I began this book by outlining two contrasting cases: the mass drowning of migrating wild wildebeest in the Mara River and the Amersham horses whose owners allowed them to suffer and die of starvation and disease. Looking at these cases—and the public responses to them—together, I suggested, raised some puzzling questions. In both cases, there was considerable animal suffering. In both cases, people could have acted to reduce the suffering. But only in the case of the Amersham horses were there accusations of neglect and of cruelly allowing suffering that could have been relieved. What lay behind the difference in response to these cases, and could such differing responses be morally justified?

This book has argued that, indeed, what we owe to fully wild animals—animals that live in wild places and that have not been domesticated—differs from what we owe to the domesticated animals that we breed and with whom we live. I provided arguments to support one form of what I called the laissez-faire intuition: while, prima facie, we should not harm wild animals, we have no duties under normal circumstances to assist them either. So, while there would need to be strong justifications for *hunting* migrating wildebeest, we have no duties to pull them from the crocodile's jaws nor to try to help them up the steep banks of the Mara River, even if we could easily do so. The case of domesticated animals, though, is somewhat different. Since they are sentient and have a well-being, a prima facie duty not to harm them applies. But, in addition, domesticated animals have been created in particular ways to be dependent and vulnerable; I have argued that this gives us—or some of us—special obligations to care for them and to provide for them. The Amersham horses had been bred by human beings for human use. They ended up on the farm where they were found because of the actions of particular humans (those who bought and sold them) and, more generally, as a consequence of deeply embedded human institutions of domestication, horse trading, and the transport of horses to slaughter.

The Grays, who owned and kept the horses, had special moral obligations to care for them. Having been domesticated and habituated to human society, the horses were unlikely to be able to flourish in the wild, but in any case, all alternative options had been closed down by external constraints (for example, fencing) on their ability to access other sources of food and care. They were completely dependent on and vulnerable to the Grays. And the Grays failed to provide for them. The Grays were morally responsible in ways that tourists and photographers watching the drowning wildebeest were not.

Of course, explained so briefly, the "moral" of these stories is oversimplified. Much of the book has been spent exploring the complexities of who has which moral responsibilities to do what, for which animals, in what circumstances—and why. Most basically, I have tried to argue that our relations with animals—the way we create them, the situations we put them in—are relevant to our duties toward them, in particular with respect to when we should act to relieve their suffering or assist them in some other way. In attempting to make this case in a reasonably concise way, I realize that there are a number of important issues a reader might justly feel I have neglected or avoided. I want to conclude by briefly considering three of these.

HARMING ANIMALS

My primary concern in this book has been on questions about *assistance* rather than directly on *harms*. This may raise a worry that the discussion of harms here is rather insubstantial and inconclusive. Of course, harm *is* very important to this book: I define harm, discuss distinctions between harming and failing to assist, consider questions as to whether domestication or painless killing should be thought of as harms, argue that earlier harms can later provide reasons for assistance, and think about the possibility that humans can inflict indirect harms, through for example climate change or the hunting activities of companion animals. But I do not tackle, head on, questions of industrial farming or animal experimentation.

One reason for not focusing directly on animal harms here, as noted in the introduction, is that there are already persuasively argued accounts of animal harm in the philosophical animal-liberation tradition. If an animal is sentient and can undergo other pleasant and aversive experiences, it has a well-being. If one accepts that having a well-being is sufficient grounds for moral considerability—as I do—then many of the workaday harms inflicted on animals are going to be very difficult to justify morally—especially where the human interests at stake are relatively insubstantial. It does not take a very radical view about animals to find the industrial farming or international transportation of closely confined sentient animals to be morally unacceptable. As I have noted already, Zamir (2007) argues plausibly that even most forms of speciesism (for instance, those forms maintaining that human interests are generally more important than animal interests, or those taking the view that where interests of similar significance conflict, human interests should always trump animal interests) do not provide support for the position that relatively minor human interests should trump animals' most basic interests. Some forms of meat production, in which animals have good lives and are killed relatively painlessly, allow for more plausible moral arguments—especially if one takes the view I rejected in chapter 7, that painlessly killing a sentient animal does not harm it. But it is likely that less than 1 percent of current meat production in the United States fits this "more humane" category (Jamieson 2008, 185).[1] And there are few plausible ethical arguments to justify the other 99 percent of U.S. meat production from the perspective of almost any ethical theory (as has been noted many times before).

Animal experimentation poses complicated and difficult questions, for in at least some cases (and it may be difficult to determine in advance which these are) the benefits to human and (occasionally) animal welfare that may result from the inflictions of harms on other sentient animals are very substantial. And although the relational approach I have been advocating is not consequentialist, this does not mean that it refuses to take consequences into account at all; rather, it maintains that the consequences are not all that matters. Given the very complexity of the issues at stake here, it is unlikely that there is any single "answer" to the ethical questions raised by animal experimentation. We would (for instance) need to think about the nature of the experiment; the history, context, relations, and capacities of the animals to be used in it; the pain or aversive experience resulting from the experiment; what the experiment is supposed to achieve; how likely this is to happen; whether there are other ways of acquiring the information; whether the animals would be "sacrificed" at the end of the experiment; and so on. One problem I hope to explore further (elsewhere) is the creation of radically dependent and vulnerable research animals in order to make use of this very vulnerability in ways that cause suffering. A particularly thought-provoking case here is the oncomouse, bred with a high susceptibility to develop painful cancers. Standard accounts of harming do not deal well with this case, since the tendency to develop cancer is built into the mouse's constitution, and that *particular* mouse could not exist in any other way; it is difficult therefore to argue that the development of cancer in such a mouse harms it or that (for instance) its rights have been infringed. Yet—as noted in chapter 5—in the human case, such radical vulnerability and dependence would normally entitle a being to special protection, not special exploitation. A framework that focuses on relations such as created vulnerability might be able to consider the ethical issues raised here more effectively than one centering on (for instance) rights (see Satz 2009). However, even to get some part of the way to thinking in detail about animal experimentation from a relational approach would take a complete book—one that (among other things) looked at different kinds of animal experimentation for different purposes and worked through a number of cases. This was not intended to be *that* book but rather to be a different book, one that worked through some relatively untrodden ground on ethics and animal assistance.

ENVIRONMENTAL ETHICS

I have also not developed many arguments here about environmental ethics, although I envisage this work as grubbing away in one corner of that field. I have not said much about how the view I have been advocating would interface with other concerns in environmental ethics, in particular with respect to the moral considerability of, and more generally the protection of, nonsentient living beings, ecosystems, and species. This book has been neutral on many of these questions. I have maintained that sentience is *sufficient* for moral considerability; I have not claimed that it is *necessary*—although I am not yet persuaded by arguments for the moral considerability of plants and other nonsentient living organisms, nor of ecosystems and species in themselves. (This is not to deny that individual nonsentient organisms, at least, have "goods," but rather to say that it is not clear why those goods are ones we should recognize as being of moral relevance.)

The relational view of animal assistance, for which I have argued here, is *more compatible* with many positions in environmental ethics than those emerging from utilitarian and capabilities approaches. One of the central issues at stake in the animal-liberation/environmental-ethics debate has always been that animal liberation appears to require action in the wild for animal welfare and, ultimately, the transformation of the wild in ways that mean it contains less suffering (see, for instance, Sagoff 1984). But I have been defending a laissez-faire approach to the wild: what happens beyond any human contact does not require any human response, at least on behalf of animals' well-being. And this does seem to accommodate a good deal of what "holistic" environmental ethicists such as Callicott and Rolston want; at least, it is compatible with their views. Some holistic environmental ethicists may want to defend the *constraint* on wild assistance that forms part of the Strong LFI, with an argument that wild value would be lost in even *permitting* assistance to wild animals. (After all, some defenders of such a view argue that even distressed *humans* in wildernesses should not be assisted.) I do not think that this is, in principle, incompatible with a relational approach, but it requires an additional argument about the value of wildness that—as I have said in earlier chapters—I did not want to defend here.

However, such a "holistic" environmental ethicist might reject even the Strong LFI not on the grounds of its position on *assistance* but on the grounds of its position on *harm*. So, we might say, a *Hunter's LFI* could take the form that, while assistance in the wild is not permitted, (human-inflicted) harm to individual animals in the wild *is* permitted, provided that those harms do not cause undue disturbance to ecosystems, endanger species, or lead to a loss of "wildness." This view, though, may itself have many forms; we would need to ask questions about the grounds of the harm (and the view taken here would also depend on whether painless killing is to be counted as a harm: an accurate shot might kill virtually painlessly). If the claim here is that the suffering of sentient animals is just not of any moral significance, so that it would be morally fine to wander through the forest taking potshots at the feet of wild animals (though not so many as to disturb ecosystems), thus causing them to die lingering and painful deaths, then this would be completely incompatible with the view for which I have been arguing, in which animal suffering and aversive experience is of moral importance. But such a view of animal suffering is not very widely held (and is unlikely to be easy to defend). Other views on hunting may maintain that the various goods that flow from some forms of hunting outweigh any prima facie duty not to harm. I indicated in chapters 7 and 8 that subsistence hunting by native peoples is likely to fall into this category. So the question here would be: what kinds of goods are sufficiently important to outweigh the harms to animals caused by hunting (assuming that the hunting harms them)? This would involve looking more carefully at different forms of hunting, and particular cases. What Varner (1995) calls "therapeutic hunting" in cases of animal overpopulation may be permissible on a relational view, for instance (although, equally, it is worth noting, a relational approach will ask why such animal populations have overshot in the first place and what role humans had in creating the situation that now requires the "therapy"—and who will benefit from the therapy). Hunting, like animal experimentation, is not a singular phenomenon; it is a cluster of widely varying practices in very many contexts. A relational approach is likely to be able to accommodate some harm to animals by hunting in some contexts but to find it impermissible in others; again, another book would be required to untangle all the issues and relations at stake here. The approach I have been proposing takes causing harm to individual animals much more seriously than is usual in holistic environmental ethics. Nonetheless, as I have not argued that there is an absolute moral prohibition on ever committing basic harms, since few environmental ethicists would find harming sentient animals completely irrelevant to moral concern, and since my view does not mandate assistance in the wild, the differences here are of degree and are unlikely to constitute incompatibility. So although this has not been a book about broader questions in environmental ethics, I hope that it can at least accommodate a range of answers to such questions. I will say a little more about this in my final comments.

INTERFACE WITH ALTERNATIVE APPROACHES

Although I have pointed out difficulties with existing approaches to animal ethics, I have also suggested that this relational approach to animal assistance could work alongside some other accounts of animal ethics that focus on harm. Most obviously, as I have maintained, aspects of this view could supplement a rights view such as Regan's. Understandably, Regan's main goal was to argue against serious harms to animals, not to make a case about when and whether animals should be assisted. But arguments about reparation-like special obligations are obviously compatible with a rights view, and other aspects of this case are not incompatible with it. However, a thoroughgoing rights advocate would maintain that my account (such as it is) of the possibility of outweighing harms to animals is too weak. Nonetheless a tweaked version of this relational view (with respect to assistance) could easily be merged with a negative rights view (with respect to harm).

It seems much less likely—as became clear in chapter 4—that the relational approach for which I have been arguing could be reconciled with utilitarian or capabilities views. Utilitarians might be able to support what I called a "contingent LFI" where, since one might generally anticipate that the consequences of assistance in the wild would be worse than failing to assist, "no wild assistance!" would be the default setting, a kind of rule of thumb. This might frequently create similar outcomes to the approach I have been proposing, though the underlying reasoning—and, more importantly perhaps, what one concluded in a "cool hour"—might be rather different. Given Nussbaum's views on moving from nature to justice, it seems unlikely that her version of a capabilities approach, at least, would find what I have been suggesting to be a path worth treading. And neither standard utilitarian nor capabilities approaches straightforwardly incorporate backward-looking concerns and special relations, both of which I have argued to be important.

Finally: how could this view relate to other relational approaches? As I made clear in chapter 3, I have drawn extensively on ideas from other relational approaches. I maintained (especially in chapter 8) that moral emotions such as sympathy and compassion should have a place in animal ethics, although this only forms part of the case for which I've argued. And although I rejected the device of the domesticated animal contract, I accepted one of its motivating ideas—that special relations between humans and animals, in particular domestication, do generate special obligations. So I hope that adherents to other relational approaches may find something useful here, even if they reject some aspects of the arguments I adopt. Indeed, a more general hope for the book is that even those who take quite different theoretical approaches will find parts of the argument here useful (whether to develop or refute) and thus that it will contribute to complicating some existing debates in animal ethics.

SOME FINAL COMMENTS

This has been a longstanding and difficult project to pursue. In part, my difficulties have flowed from continuing to see the attractions both of wholly capacity-oriented approaches and of the consequentialist view that there *is* no real distinction between harming and failing to assist, when one could have assisted without causing a harm of equal or greater moral significance. So I am, therefore, sympathetic to readers who remain unpersuaded by central arguments in this book. Nonetheless, I conclude that the relational approach to animal assistance I have been defending does have significant advantages and is at least theoretically plausible (even if I have not done its plausibility best justice). And, as I began to suggest above, one of the advantages it presents concerns the rift—never well healed—between advocates of philosophical animal liberation, with their focus on the lives and well-being of sentient animals, and advocates of "holistic" environmental ethics, who focus on ecological "wholes" such as ecosystems and species. While my reading of history may be tendentious and somewhat oversimplified, here is one way of thinking about the development of these two traditions. The philosophical animal-liberation tradition developed primarily as a response to concerns about the pain and other aversive experiences caused to domesticated animals, particularly in the contexts of the meat industry and animal research. But in developing a case intended to protect *these* animals, many animal-liberation advocates put forward arguments that applied to all animals who shared relevant capacities—including constitutively and locationally wild animals— even though wild animals were not their original targets of concern. On the other hand, one major strand of environmental ethics (in the United States at least) might be thought of as having grown out of the wilderness-preservation movement, with (correspondingly) an intense concern for place and context. But the place and context on which this concern focused was the wild. Other less wild environments were thought to be of less interest and often of less value, and the animals that inhabited them, especially the domesticated ones, were regarded either as being of little ethical concern or as being artifactual and inferior to wild animals. But neither of these views led to a coherent animal ethic across *all* contexts: on (most) animal-liberation views, we seem to be overcommitted to wild animals, while on most holistic environmental ethics views, we seem to be undercommitted to domesticated ones.

The relational approach for which I have been arguing here steers a course between these two problems. It provides considerable protection for most domesticated animals, not only in terms of harm but also by giving reasons for assistance— the creation of special obligations on account of the creation of vulnerability and dependence. And it does this without generating what has always been a thorn in the side for philosophical animal liberation—requirements to assist animals in the wild, beyond human "contact." The absence of such requirements should also make this position more appealing to holists in environmental ethics. So one advantage of this view might be that both a holist in environmental ethics and an advocate of philosophical animal liberation could find it acceptable.

A second, related advantage is that this relational approach intentionally undermines any clear idea of a wild/domestic opposition (however those terms are interpreted) and highlights the importance of a wide range of human relations with animals, where place, breeding, history, causal relation, encounter, and context all play some part. Although I have probably talked more about the "fully wild" situation than any other, this was primarily to facilitate the development of the argument by looking at an "end of spectrum" case rather than to suggest that there is something especially important about this (absence of) relationship in the wild. Indeed, quite the contrary; I hope that this kind of relational approach will open up more discussion of animals in the contact zone: animals in our homes and gardens, animals displaced by urban sprawl, and animals scavenging around our settlements. These animals have been neglected in both animal and environmental ethics: they are insufficiently wild to interest most environmental ethicists, they are often uncharismatic, and they are outside the zone of systematic harm that is associated with the meat industry and animal research, thus falling below the radar of most work in philosophical animal liberation. Finding a place to think about feral and commensal relations, for instance, alongside the fully wild and domesticated, seems to me to be another advantage of the relational approach.

To conclude, then: This book has begun to develop a new, relational approach, in which I have argued that while we have prima facie duties not to harm sentient animals, our obligations to assist them vary according to relation and context. I maintain that we have no duties to assist fully wild animals, but we may have extensive special obligations to assist those sentient animals that *we* have made vulnerable and dependent by (for instance) destroying their habitats, breeding them, or confining them. I hope that such a relational approach may be able to bring holistic environmental ethics and philosophical animal liberation closer together, diminish some powerful objections to philosophical animal liberation, and provide tools that can contribute to the development of a more complex and context-sensitive form of animal ethics.

166

NOTES

1. "10,000 Wildebeest Drown in Migration 'Pileup,'" *National Geographic News* (October 1, 2007), http://news.nationalgeographic.com/news/2007/10/071001-wildebeest.html.

2. "'Worst Ever' Animal Neglect Case," *BBC News* (May 9, 2009), http://news.bbc.co.uk/1/hi/uk/8038249.stm.

3. The British Horse Society's verdict on the trial: http://amershamhorses.com/category/bhs/.

4. See the Vegetarian Society UK's campaign at http://www.butcherscat.com/.

5. See also Derrida (2002, 416), who comments: "The confusion of all non-human living creatures within the general and common category of the animal is not simply a sin against rigorous thinking, vigilance, lucidity, or empirical authority; it is also a crime. Not a crime against animality precisely, but a crime of the first order against the animals, against animals."

6. The relevant areas of Kenya and Tanzania are not uninhabited by people, but they are not densely developed, and the animals' movements are not significantly constrained by humans; this is all that "fairly wild" should be taken to mean here.

1. ANIMALS' CAPACITIES AND MORAL STATUS

1. Warren, however, conflates moral considerability and moral significance in her later discussion.

2. Many discussions of indirect moral concern for animals already exist, for example, Regan (1984, 150–194), DeGrazia (1996, 41–43), and Nozick (1974, 35–42).

3. Regan's arguments about animal rights (see chapter 2) seem to conflate rights with moral considerability. But Regan is not absolutely committed to this view; see Regan (1981).

4. "Capacity" and "capability" may be distinguished, taking the former as more passive and the latter as more active. I am not implying this distinction but rather using "capacity" to avoid confusion with current "capabilities" approaches to animal ethics. See Nussbaum (2004, 2006), Irvin (2004), and chapter 2.

5. This is not to imply a "bright line" between mammals and birds and other kinds of beings. If evidence strengthens, they should be included; best policy might, anyway, be precautionary. See Varner (1998) and Allen (2004).

6. Not "necessary and sufficient," as I do not want to rule out other grounds for moral status. Carruthers (1999) suggests that it may be possible to argue for moral standing on the basis of *unconscious* frustrated preferences; Frey (1980, 145) points out that there are humans who cannot feel pain, and many environmental ethicists argue that nonsentient individuals and ecological collectives have moral status.

7. I am grateful to Alice Crary for this example.

8. See Lee et al. (2005).

9. Allen (2004) suggests that our commonsense responses toward animals who manifest what we see as pain-displaying behavior prejudices us against reptiles, fish, and other creatures who are not able so obviously to display such behaviors, even if they do feel pain.

10. For much more detailed discussion of animal pain, see, among others: Bateson (1991), Dawkins (1980), DeGrazia and Rowan (1991), DeGrazia (1996), Allen (2004), and Smith and Boyd (1991).

11. See DeGrazia (1996, 110ff.)

12. See Varner (1998) for a much fuller discussion.

13. What "conscious" means here is also controversial. "Phenomenally conscious" might be the best term to use, but this also has a variety of interpretations.

14. It may not even be necessary, of course, since (if one took a functional view of pain) it is at least conceivable that some other non-nociceptive physiological system could function in such a way that it generated painlike experiences, even though we do not know of any such system.

15. It is possible that pain is a "spandrel," but given its usefulness, as Dawkins suggests, this is implausible.

16. One exception is Peter Harrison (1991, 45–60), who considers these arguments separately and maintains that none is convincing. See Bernstein (1998, 137–145) for a critical discussion of Harrison.

17. There are, of course, occasions when humans (from martyrs to marathon runners) choose to enter pain situations they could avoid, when desire for some other end outweighs the aversion to pain. There may be correlates of this behavior in animals.

18. On some theories, sentience and desire cannot be conceptually separated; obviously, this is a complicated area. Carruthers (1992, 54), for instance, maintains that "the idea of pain seems conceptually tied to desire for its avoidance." I am not working with this view

here. See Bernstein (1998, 69) for discussion of this view.

19. There is some philosophical discussion as to whether pain is an intentional state. I have treated pain separately from intentional states; this does not imply a commitment to the view that pain is not an intentional state.

20. DeGrazia (2009, 205) makes this distinction: animals can at least have protodesires and protobeliefs that, although not conceptual, have content.

21. See Dretske (1999) and Ingold (1988, 84–97).

22. Although, again, stress hormones can be released by fetuses before they are thought, on the basis of other physiological developments, to be able to be aware of discomfort.

23. There are difficulties with animal-choice tests as pioneered by Dawkins (see Aiken n.d.), but the problems do not focus on whether animals may have pleasurable and aversive feelings (not directly of pain).

24. DeGrazia (1996, 120ff.) distinguishes between fear and anxiety and argues that mammals at least (and perhaps other vertebrates) feel both. Although I prefer not to use the term "emotions," it is much less problematic if it is clear that these emotions are of the noncognitive variety (i.e., not emotions such as shame). See Doris (2002, 159) for a distinction between basic and cognitive emotions and see Roberts (2009) for a discussion of animal emotions.

25. Regan seems to move too quickly from claims that animals have memory and short-term expectations about the future to insufficiently justified claims about their self-awareness/self-consciousness. Research does suggest, however, that a *bodily* sense of self-awareness can be attributed to cetaceans and primates (see Herman et al. 2001).

26. Standard objections to experientialist accounts of human well-being do not transfer easily to animals (see chapter 7).

27. This account of interests is close to Feinberg's (1974, 41). I am not claiming that *it does not make sense* to talk about a living but nonsentient organism as having nonexperiential interests. The question is how these interests are morally relevant.

28. Some objectivist accounts of well-being deny that pain is intrinsically bad, asserting that the badness in pain lies in its interference with function (e.g., Kraut 1994, 47). However, these accounts still maintain that pain is bad for animals, even though the badness is indirect.

29. Kant is usually thought to have taken this view, but modern Kantians have mostly revised Kant's work to include animals (Korsgaard 2004; Wood 1998). My concern here is with moral contractarianism rather than social-contract theory. These may be closely related, but *social* contractarians need not be *moral* contractarians.

30. Though this does not seem to be *necessarily* the case.

31. Scanlon (1998) suggests the idea of animal trustees in the moral contract, although he prefers the view that the moral contract does not cover the whole sphere of morality, while Bernstein (1998, 162–165) proposes what he calls "altruistic contractualism," which includes animals directly.

32. See Dombrowski (1997).

33. Gauthier's (1986) egoistic contractarianism presents moral constraints as "constraints on unimpeded utility-maximizing that it is rational to agree to in order to increase one's own utility." In such an account, "beings that have little or no capacity to make credible significant threats and offers will receive little or no consideration" (Arneson 1999, 107). This presumably includes some humans.

34. A more complex case could be developed here, drawing on Don Marquis' (1989) "Future Like Ours" argument.

35. Of course, unless modified, they also imply that (however early) fetuses have the same moral status as moral agents, which is likely to be problematic for other reasons.

36. This is one of a battery of arguments Nobis (2004) makes against Cohen's position.

37. So, for instance, Franklin (2005, 71): "The fact that sentient beings cannot be taken as mere things proves fatal to any moral theory founded on some universal agreement among rational beings."

38. This contrasts with an alternative parsing (such as by Regan 1983, 96) where harms come in two kinds: those that wrong (those carried out by moral agents) and those that do not. Although I use the terminology differently, I think the distinction remains the same.

39. This formulation should avoid some of the difficulties arising from counterfactual conditions generated by cases of overdetermination of harm, but I will pass over these here. See Feinberg (1992b, 9–11) for a fuller discussion.

40. But not necessarily. Euthanasia, of course (among other things), terminates unpleasant experience by terminating all experience. However, perhaps if one takes an animal's experiential well-being over time, a shorter life without a negative end-of-life experience is better than a longer life incorporating that experience.

2. CAPACITY-ORIENTED ACCOUNTS OF ANIMAL ETHICS

1. Many other variations exist, for instance, total, average, or prior-existence utilitarianism; or subjective or objective utilitarianism.

2. There are (nonmaximizing) satisficing forms of consequentialism, but I will put these aside here.

3. Some important consequentialist discussions of animals I do not discuss in detail here include Bentham (1789), Frey (1983, 1987, 2007), VandeVeer (2003), and Norcross (2004).

4. In *Practical Ethics*, Singer suggests that this emphasis on furthering interests differentiates this view from classical hedonistic utilitarianism.

5. Singer insists it is the happening of that which satisfies the preferences that counts, rather than the bare feeling of preference satisfaction (which may or may not correspond with what has happened in the world).

6. See Frey (1983, 1987, 2007) and VandeVeer (2003).

7. Singer (1999, 297) adopts a form of "two-level" utilitarianism, with a critical, reflective level where we decide what traits and principles will generally bring about best consequences and a practical, everyday level where we develop and practice those traits and principles.

8. Williams, of course, is a hostile commentator on utilitarianism, but I do not think that a utilitarian would deny this claim.

9. Therapeutic hunting refers to kinds of culling where, it is argued, overall suffering (usually due to overpopulation in the absence of predators) can be reduced by killing some animals (preferably painlessly). See Varner (1998).

10. See Bergman (2005) for a discussion of tracking animals by radio in this context.

11. Usually spillover arguments take the form that if humans hurt animals, they may develop characters with tendencies to hurt people. Regan's version is that if humans hurt some animals (non-subjects-of-a-life), they may develop characters that will lead them to hurt subjects-of-a-life. While the possibility of mistakes and borderline uncertainty seems more plausible in Regan's case, the reasons for rejecting such spillover arguments (see Nozick 1974, 35) are strong. However, Regan (1984, 319) is clear that being subject-of-a-life is sufficient, not necessary, for having rights.

12. Although Regan does think it wrong to harm, here he is not using the term "harmed" to imply wronged.

13. This understanding of what a right is is, of course, controversial; see, for instance, Griffin (1986, 31).

14. This move is strongly criticized by Taylor (1987), who rejects the view that rights emerge out of duties (such as those encapsulated in the principle of respect); rather, he maintains, rights have priority over duties and, in fact, generate them.

15. See, for instance, Sunstein (2005) on Francione.

16. This distinction between positive and negative rights is problematic but adequate here.

17. Regan's use of the expression "other nations" here is derived from Beston (1971, 25). It is an idea expressed by Wenz (1988) and Nussbaum (2006), among others, and one on which I will draw later.

18. One way of reading Regan's position, as noted above, is that duties (or at least principles) generate rights, which then generate further duties. I am not clear how this would feed into this objection, however.

19. Interestingly, Francione draws on Shue's account of rights, arguing that Shue is correct to claim that there are some basic rights on which all other rights depend. However, Francione does not discuss the positive duties that Shue insists follow from rights claims, and his account here , like Regan's, emphasizes only negative duties.

20. See Frey (1983, 152) for a discussion of this.

21. This need not necessarily commit one to interference with predation, for preventing predation would eventually result in the loss of the inherent value of the predator.

22. This is obviously relevant to my account of experiential well-being in chapter 1, where I maintained that a commitment to experiential well-being in the case of animals did not commit me to understanding well-being purely experientially in the case of humans. Of course, similar questions might be raised in the animal case (for instance, where humans shape animal preferences). I will consider this later.

23. The account (Nussbaum 2006, 362) is slightly more complex than this in theory, but sentience is the practical border that Nussbaum adopts for moral considerability.

24. There are some similarities here, I think, to Rollin's (1998) idea that animals should be permitted to fulfill their species-specific *telos*.

3. CAPACITIES, CONTEXTS, AND RELATIONS

1. Indeed, views of this kind are widely held in animal ethics, even outside the standard utilitarian/rights literature; Gary Varner (1998) and David DeGrazia (1996), for instance, both opt for versions of this class-based approach (though early on DeGrazia does suggest that context will be important).

2. Although recent studies on knockout mice indicate the possibility of breeding genetically modified animals such that the affective dimension of pain is reduced or eliminated while the sensory dimension of pain continues. See Shriver (2009).

3. Marvin (2006) suggests that this understanding of relationship as including the non-affective is a "sociological" one. Certainly, this idea of "relation as effect" is close to some of Foucault's interpretations of a power relation (see Palmer 2002). The expression "states of affairs" is problematic (see Foot 1985), but I do not intend it to carry a consequentialist sense here.

4. Gruen (1999), for example, identifies many different interpretations: the golden rule, Kantian ethics, appealing to an ideal observer, and the veil of ignorance, all incorporating a (somewhat different) understanding of universalizability.

5. Those who advocate various forms of moral particularism, for instance; see Dancy (2004).

6. Burgess-Jackson (1998) makes an argument of this kind with respect to pet ownership.

7. Care may not be interpreted in an emotional sense at all but rather as a practice—this is not intended to be a comprehensive account of care ethics.

8. This is not necessarily the case, I suppose, as Fisher (1992) hints, but the more developed emotion-oriented views of animal ethics all seem to take this position.

9. Slote (2007) is one of the most interesting and systematic accounts of care ethics; unfortunately he does not in this book consider empathetic caring relations to animals (see Slote 2007, 19).

10. This need not be understood in a *conceptual* way but rather read off behavioral cues. See the final section of Palmer (2003). Gaita (2002) provides some interesting examples of something like this.

172

11. I want to leave open the possibility of developing a view based on the moral emotions, but I will not develop it further here. Difficulties of doing so are well discussed elsewhere (see just one account in Regan 2001, 58–62). This worry is not intended to extend to sub-jectivist *metaethical* theories of value where sentiment is important, such as in Hume. See Lo (2001b).

12. Although I will not be developing this criticism here, it is worth noting that Ignatieff (1984, 82) is plausibly skeptical of the idea that we can love the human race.

13. That Callicott's view really can be traced back to Hume in anything other than its broadly sentimentalist form has been a subject of debate. See, for instance, Partridge (2002) and Lo (2001b).

14. See Blum's (2008) review of Slote for a brief discussion of this.

15. This is not to say that some argument where "being of the same species" is relevant could not exist. I suggest a possible argument of this form in Palmer (2009).

16. I discuss this in much more detail in Palmer (2006).

17. This is discussed by Singer (1988, 224). See also Elliott (1984), Fuchs (1981), Manning (1981), Prichard and Robinson (1981), and VanDeVeer (1979). It is partly summarized in a discussion in Thero (1995) as well as, most recently, Smith (2008).

18. See Salt's *Animals' Rights*, chapter 2. His reservations are similar to mine.

19. Morris suggests that there might be multiple contracts; Telfer (2000, 221) considers the possibility of different "bargains" for companion animals and food animals.

20. Shepard (1998) argues that hunting and gathering societies are better than societies with domestication and agriculture.

21. See, for instance, Cohen (1997), Clutton-Brock (1994), Bökönyi (1989), and Hayden (1992).

22. See Bulliet (2005) for an extended discussion of this.

23. I am grateful to Michael Hammond for pointing out parallels between the animal con-tract and Pateman's work on the sexual contract.

4. WILDNESS, DOMESTICATION, AND THE LAISSEZ-FAIRE INTUITION

1. See Cassidy (2007, 1–26). I am indebted to Cassidy's overview of debates about domesti-cation here.

2. A number of arguments maintain that wildernesses are (in different ways) human con-structs (most famously Cronon 1996 and Birch 1990). As I will explain in chapter 8, this is not fatal to the argument here.

3. A former student, Craig Aubuchon, brought cases of this kind to my attention; they are also discussed in Fuentes (2007, 128).

4. Kareiva et al. in *Science* (June 2007) argue that as of 1995, 17 percent of Earth can be thought of as "without direct influence" from humans, where influence is measured as "human population density greater than one person/km2; agricultural land use; towns or

cities; access within 15 km of a road, river, or coastline; or nighttime light detectable by satellite."

5. This is a shrinking group, however, as human intervention in animal breeding in zoos, animal parks, etc. is increasing, in particular in the case of endangered species.

6. It has been argued that *humans* also changed physiologically, as a result of animal domestication—for instance, human teeth also became smaller. There may be some sense in which humans can be thought of as domesticated. However, I do not think this has any particular implications for the arguments in this book.

7. I prefer the expression "contact zone" to Donna Haraway's (2003) "naturecultures," but there is an overlap in meaning between these expressions.

8. See Burt (2006, 56).

9. For a useful discussion of the distinction, see Singer (1965).

10. Arguments about harm have been well developed in other books. See, most recently, Zamir (2007), whose work I mention elsewhere.

174   11. This refers to a remark of Scanlon's recorded by Scheffler (1994, 109).

12. Indeed, of course, the best outcome may be brought about by harming, in order to prevent more harms or other comparable bad things occurring. However, since I have only talked about not harming as a prima facie duty, I do not think I am here committed to the view that some harms should never be carried out, even if they would bring about a better state of affairs, seen from an impersonal perspective.

13. Satisficing forms of consequentialism do not require the production of best states of affairs, but there is no form of satisficing that would map onto the kind of distinction being made here.

14. I take my use of this term from Nagel (1980).

15. Importantly, Regan's miniride principle, which I will discuss in chapter 8, is an exception to this; Regan maintains that the miniride principle is not consequentialist.

16. Although Scheffler does not say much about special obligations, where he mentions them, he thinks of them as a grounding for an agent-centered prerogative: individuals' special obligations are central to their ground projects. However, on my account, special obligations to animals need not be central to any individual's ground projects; indeed, they might be demanding and disruptive to such projects.

17. Scheffler (1994, 174) argues that it is normally much more trouble to actively harm than to just fail to assist, so, for instance, $10,000 from murder comes at a much higher cost to the murderer than $10,000 saved from failing to prevent someone from dying.

18. That this applies in the animal case is accepted by Zamir (2007), but he leaves this unexplained.

19. This is not to rule out cases where assistance is *mutually* beneficial.

20. If the person were in need of assistance *because of our actions*, however, this situation would be quite different; here the needy person's situation is assumed to be *entirely independent* of us.

21. Nagel's discussion of agent-relative values in *The View from Nowhere* (1986), for instance, defends a view like this. This kind of argument fails, though, in cases where the agent must harm to avert more cases of similar harms—that is, where all the harms would be carried out by agents.

22. A case for a Very Weak LFI, perhaps, might be argued on this basis—I just have not done so.

5. DEVELOPING A NEW, RELATIONAL APPROACH

1. It is possible that some kind of rule consequentialism could be developed here that would make nonassistance a rule, even if in some particular cases assistance would bring about better consequences.

2. Regan mentions Everett's article approvingly in the new introduction to the 2004 edition of *The Case for Animal Rights*.

3. There seems to be some uncertainty, however, about the effectiveness of this vaccine. See Kraabel et al. (1998) for the case that the vaccine does, at least, improve animals' immunity.

4. In a personal communication, Norton confirmed that this interpretation is correct.

5. Here I will just consider the paradigmatic cases of wild and domesticated animals, but some of what applies to domesticated animals will work more broadly in the "contact zone," as I will suggest.

6. Kamm (2007, 345) has an interesting discussion of the "standard-distance" problem.

7. For a discussion of boundaries in this sense, see Chatterjee (2003).

8. Nussbaum and Regan are happy to use the term "justice" of animals, and I do not have any objection to this, but as nothing specifically rides on the use of the term here, I do not think I need to develop an argument for it.

9. Again, this raises questions about native peoples and about climate change—I will consider these further in later chapters.

10. On some capacity-oriented views—for example, that of Frey (2007)—quite the reverse view is adopted. Sometimes vulnerability is due to diminished psychological capacities, and for Frey, this can mean lesser moral significance. It is preferable to experiment on beings of less moral significance, whatever species they are; so human vulnerability is not grounds for special protection. However, this is a minority view.

11. Blustein (1997), fairly plausibly, argues that voluntary consent is *sufficient* but not *necessary* to generate special obligations in the context of parenthood: causality is enough, without consent. Although I do not use his account here, as I will suggest in chapter 6, I think he is correct to maintain that not all special obligations are voluntarily assumed.

12. This claim is not intended to imply any particular conclusion with respect to accidental conception (it does not follow that if one does not intend to procreate one has no obligations to one's offspring). Nor has it any implications for abortion. Goodin (1985) appears

to reject this claim about parental responsibility.

6. PAST HARMS AND SPECIAL OBLIGATIONS

1. Of course, it is worth noting that traditionally in cases of reparation after war, nations that lost wars were required to pay reparations even if they were not the aggressor. However, these are not the kinds of cases I am considering here.

2. This is, obviously, a version of Parfit's nonidentity argument.

3. So, it might be argued that the *group* would have been better off without the past harm, even if none of the currently living individuals would have existed without it. However, this argument (made by Thomson 2002) relies on contentious arguments about the nature of groups and about group harms. Meyer (2006) suggests that harm can be perceived as passing on through several generations because each new generation suffers harm on account of the failure to compensate their parents.

4. Relatedly, Waldron (1992) argues that land-ownership claims are circumstantially sensitive and that the claims of those separated from land diminish over time, since land becomes less central to their autonomous projects, while the claims of those currently using the land strengthen, since over time the reverse process occurs: the land has become *more* important to their autonomous concerns.

5. See the argument for trustees made by Goodin, Pateman, and Pateman (1997) in the context of simian land sovereignty.

6. I am indebted to Harry Silverstein, in comments on an earlier paper on this subject, for clarification here.

7. Silverstein takes an even stronger view than I do on this, maintaining (in unpublished comments): "assuming that we can defend some sort of requirement to make reparations to animals at all, I think we can defend it for cases where the perpetrator . . . the housing developer . . . not only intended no harm, but took all reasonable care (including acquiring the requisite knowledge) to avoid it." See Silverstein (2005) for support for this view.

8. In chapter 8, I will consider a case where the harm cannot easily be stopped. There may be other domesticated-animal cases where the language of reparation fits better. For instance, we might understand animal-rescue centers—at least, no-kill shelters—as some kind of reparation.

9. I have selected coyotes because they are fairly widespread; similar stories may be told in some areas of the United States about the effects of suburbanization on mountain lions. See, for instance, Gullo, Lassiter, and Wolch (1998).

10. Thus they meet four of the five conditions outlined by Brooks (2003, 107) for cases of reparation, if one is willing to call the original action an "injustice." The missing condition is documentation. I have tried to deal with that condition by not looking further back than one generation.

11. The creation of counterfactuals is intrinsically less complex in animal cases (since, for instance, if the land-grab had not happened, animals could not have sold the land to another settler for a fair price, etc.). But receding-victim problems are especially pernicious in animal cases, both because animals do not create documentation (Fudge 2002) and because where humans create documents about animals, they rarely provide the kind of evidence that would be useful. This is not to say that there could not be cases where relevant documentary evidence could be gathered.

12. A possible argument here, I suppose, is that since humans have property rights to land, they can reasonably exclude animals from their land. To make this argument, one would need to think that property rights hold against those who are not moral agents and take precedence over the most basic morally significant interests of animals.

13. Most coyote territory is already occupied, and coyotes do not do well when relocated.

14. Michelfelder (2003) rightly argues that urban wildlife should generally be treated as part of an interspecies community of neighbors. The coyote case provides an *additional* and more pressing reason to think this: because this interspecies community has been created by moving into land that was already occupied by wildlife

177

15. If we had reason to think that the parent rat had been deliberately killed by a human, then the situation would be somewhat less clear cut; if I had killed the parent rat myself, then this definitely would generate some responsibility for me, probably to kill the offspring painlessly. This raises questions both about knowledge and painless killing; see chapter 7.

16. Scheffler (2001, 105) makes a similar and more detailed argument. See also Goodin (1985), who opposes voluntarism with respect to special obligations.

17. There is some dispute about the use of the term "pet" and a growing preference for "companion animals" instead. See, for instance, Burgess-Jackson (1998). Although I use the term "companion animals" most of the time, "pet ownership" seems a better way of describing the *institution*.

18. Some aspects of this finding have been questioned, but the on-balance view still seems to be that pet owners do gain health benefits from their pets. See Parslow and Jorm (2003), who dispute the evidence about cardiovascular risk (while not denying other possible health benefits from pet ownership).

19. 2007–2008 National Pet Owners Survey, quoted by the American Pet Products Manufacturers Association, at http://www.appma.org/press_industrytrends.asp. I have excluded reptiles and fish here—if these are included, the numbers are substantially higher.

20. See Headey et al. (2005).

21. My thinking here has been influenced by May (1987, 1991).

7. SOME PROBLEMS AND QUESTIONS

1. Ingold (2000, 58) considers this view to be worryingly common.

2. Although she *does* argue that there is a problem about restricting moral considerability to sentient animals rather than extending it to include all living things.

3. As I have noted, Zamir's (2007) argument that even most speciesists cannot morally defend the industrial-scale farming of animals for food is persuasive here, I think.

4. Another relational argument that could be used to draw a similar conclusion via the route of an ethics of care is Engster (2006).

5. It is unclear what the implications of Francis and Norman's view might be for nonassociated humans (such as Venusians) or for future generations. It seems to me that, as their position stands, Venusians and future generations (probably) possess morally relevant capacities but lack the community membership that applies to present humans on Earth. If one accepted a communitarian intergenerational view, such as De-Shalit's (1995), near-future generations would be in our community as well. This suggests that there would at least be negative duties toward these human groups and perhaps weak positive duties toward near-future generations. This position is consistent with the relational view that I have been developing.

6. I will not here develop an account of "group harm," although I think that this claim can (on occasion) make sense in an animal context (see Palmer 2009). I will briefly consider later how a nonexperientialist account of individual harm might be relevant.

7. Obviously, this is a version of a Parfitian nonidentity problem.

8. Another objection focuses on the artifactual nature of domesticated animals. This objection has several forms; for examples, see Shepard and Shepard (1998, 84) and Callicott (1980).

9. A point also well made by Alistair MacIntyre in *Dependent Rational Animals* (2001).

10. Provided that one accepts that domination can be an objective description of a state of affairs rather than having to be subjectively experienced by the dominated. Of course, animals would subjectively experience the effects of the domination, but they could not have a conceptual grasp of the idea that they are being dominated. But most scholars of domination (including Lovett) do not require this subjective condition.

11. Cooper (1998) puts forward an alternatively developed kind of virtue-theory objection to animal biotechnology, focusing on the lack of humility, in the sense of a "selfless respect for reality" involved.

12. I am grateful both to an anonymous reader of this manuscript and to Harry Silverstein in his comments on another paper for successfully undermining any confidence I had in this position!

13. Jamieson captures this well in his discussion of why empathy provides no good reason for objecting to painless killing. See Jamieson (1983, 137).

14. This claim is actually spoken by a character in Cavalieri's dialogue, but (unlike in the case of Elizabeth Costello in Coetzee's novels) there seems little question that this actually is Cavalieri's view.

15. Singer's arguments in *Practical Ethics* are problematic on this point, however: he tends

to interpret evidence that only supports a lower level of mental ability as evidence of a higher level of ability.

16. See Singer's *Practical Ethics* (2nd ed.) and Michael Lockwood's (1979) paper on Singer.

17. I accept that this may not be a good reason for not pursuing a view: its unpalatability does not in itself make it mistaken.

18. McMahan's (2002) account is considerably more complex than this, but this is an adequate approximation for my purposes here.

19. For details about problematic issues this view might seem to raise (e.g., with regard to those with severe mental disabilities, the apparent variable wrongness of killing, etc.), see McMahan (2002, chap. 3).

8. PUZZLING THROUGH SOME CASES

1. Widely reported in September 2007, based on work carried out by scientists at the National Snow and Ice Center, University of Boulder, Colorado. See http://www.colorado.edu/news/releases/2007/362.html.

2. The debate on knowledge, negligence, and moral responsibility is a substantial and complex one. See, for instance, Zimmerman (1986, 1988, 1997) and Raz (2009).

3. The USGS (2007) predicted that by 2050, polar bears in Alaska would be locally extinct and that other populations in the Canadian Arctic and Greenland would be struggling.

4. Whether individuals reducing their emissions outside a political process will have any effect on climate change and whether, if it will not, individuals should reduce their own emissions anyway has recently been a subject of debate. See for example Sinnott-Armstrong (2006), Johnson (2003), and Hourdequin (2008).

5. Of course, this process harms people, too, but this is further evidence that the problem is virtually intractable. For if something that harms people is so difficult to control, it is even less likely that it will be controlled for the sake of the members of another species.

6. The continuing bear hunting in Chukotka, Russia, is illegal, so it would be possible to police this. For more details, see http://alaska.fws.gov/fisheries/mmm/polarbear/issues.htm.

7. Although where the community-subsistence benefits from quotas are indirect, derived from the income from selling hunting tags to trophy hunters, there are good arguments for pursuing alternative ways of providing the relevant subsistence.

8. However, the USFWS, in its "Interim Final Rule on the Polar Bear" (as part of its recent listing as a threatened species), insists that the oil and gas industries have had "minimal impact" on the well-being of individual polar bears. If this is really correct, there may be little to be done for polar bears except for that which can emerge from international climate-change policy.

9. Regan discusses a trapped-miner case in which one must either kill one to rescue fifty or kill fifty to rescue one. But it is not clear, based on negative rights alone, that there are

any duties to rescue any of them, since this seems to be a case of assistance, not of rights violation. Note the contrast here to the deontological position I outlined in chapter 4.

10. There may be cases where the origin of a disease is unclear or where causes are mixed—for instance, a fire is started by a human, but in a place where a buildup of flammable material has happened independently. In these cases, decisions have to be made based on the best information there is.

11. One difficulty that might flow from sympathy-inspired assistance, however, is that while killing is likely to be the best form of assistance in some cases, sympathy-inspired motivation for assistance can undermine the possibility of actually rendering it.

12. I am not sure how a situationist critique such as that of Doris (2002) would pan out in this case.

13. I am grateful to Peter Jones for his description of this incident in suburban London.

14. There may have been some selective physical adaptations that allowed blue tits to benefit from living alongside humans: some argue that the digestive system of the blue tit adapted when they (legendarily) began to drink cream from doorstep milk bottles in the 1920s. However, there are (as far as I know) no substantial physiological changes distinguishing locationally wild from suburban populations of blue tits.

15. Even if, like Francione, one agrees that it is objectionable to see sentient animals as property, this term reflects the current legal situation.

16. This is a British example, and cat declawing is, any case, illegal in Britain.

17. Apparently birds do not reject their offspring if returned to nests; they have an undeveloped sense of smell.

18. See a 1992 case in Cleveland, Ohio, where Jeffrey David Mann was convicted of first-degree murder for setting a pit bull on the woman he lived with, who subsequently died.

19. For some of these legal complications, see this examination of dog-bite law in the United States: http://www.dogbitelaw.com/PAGES/legal_ri.htm.

20. But see Hearne (1986), who comes close to suggesting that a trained dog does have some kind of moral sense with respect to behaviors it has been trained not to do (such as biting people).

21. This may also be true of some breeds of dog that have been bred to chase, for instance; not all uncommanded dog attacks on sentient animals are the result of neglect, ill treatment, or poor training.

22. Unless letting the cat out at all is seen as irresponsible.

CONCLUSION

1. Some scholars, however, are very skeptical of the "humane-meat" movement, arguing that it fails to address legal and moral inconsistencies with respect to the treatment of animals and encourages the growth of only slightly more humane practices, for example, using soft rather than hard tubes to force-feed geese for foie gras. See, for example, Satz

WORKS CITED

Aiken, Gill. n.d. Choice tests: Are they as good as they sound? Unpublished.

Allen, Colin. 2004. Animal pain. *Nous* 38: 617–643.

Anderson, W., C. Reid, and G. Jennings. 1992. Pet ownership and risk factors for cardiovascular disease. *Medical Journal Australia* 157: 298–301.

Arneson, Richard. 1999. What renders all humans morally equal. In *Singer and his critics*, ed. Dale Jamieson, 103–127. Oxford: Wiley Blackwell.

Baier, Kurt. 1991 [1972]. Guilt and responsibility. In *Collective responsibility: Five decades of debate in theoretical and applied ethics*, ed. Larry May and Stacey Hoffman, 197–218. London: Rowman & Littlefield.

Barkdull, John. 2002. How green is the theory of moral sentiments? In *Land, value, community: Callicott and environmental philosophy*, ed. Wayne Ouderkirk and Jim Hill, 37–58. Albany: State University of New York Press.

Barker, Sandra, and Aaron Wolen. 2008. The benefits of human-companion animal interaction: A review. *Journal of Veterinary Medical Education* 35, no. 4: 487–495.

Bateson, P. 1991. Assessment of pain in animals. *Animal Behavior* 42: 827–839.

Bekoff, Marc. 2003. *Minding animals*. Oxford: Oxford University Press.

Bekoff, Marc, and Dale Jamieson, eds. 1995. *Readings in animal cognition*. Cambridge, Mass.: The MIT Press.

Belmont Report. 1979. Regulations and ethical guidelines, National Institute for Health. http://ohsr.od.nih.gov/guidelines/belmont.html#ethical.

Benn, Stanley. 1973. Abortion, infanticide, and respect for persons. In *The problem of abortion*, ed. Joel Feinberg, 135–144. Belmont, Calif.: Wadsworth Press.

Bentham, Jeremy. 1843. On the cultivation of benevolence. In *Principles of penal law*. Edinburgh: William Tait. http://oll.libertyfund.org/?option=com_staticxt&staticfile=show.php p%3Ftitle=2009&chapter=140139&layout=html&Itemid=27.

——. 1987 [1789]. Principles of morals and legislation. In *Utilitarianism and other essays*, ed.

Alan Ryan. London: Penguin.

Bergman, Charles. 2005. Inventing a beast with no body: Radio-telemetry, the marginalization of animals, and the stimulation of ecology. *Worldviews: Environment, Culture, Religion* 9, no. 2: 255-270.

Bermond, B. 1997. The myth of animal suffering. In *Animal consciousness and animal ethics: Perspectives from the Netherlands*, ed. Marcel Dol et al., 125-144. Assen: Van Gorcum.

Bermúdez, José Luis. 2003. *Thinking without words*. Oxford: Oxford University Press.

——. 2007. Thinking without words: An overview for animal ethics. *Journal of Ethics* 11: 319-335.

——. 2009. Mindreading in the animal kingdom. In *The philosophy of animal minds*, ed. Robert W. Lurz, 145-164. Cambridge: Cambridge University Press.

Bernstein, Mark. 1998. *On moral considerability*. Oxford: Oxford University Press.

Beston, Henry. 1971 [1928]. *The outermost house: A year of life on the great beach of Cape Cod*. New York: Ballantine.

Birch, Tom. 1990. The incarceration of wildness: Wilderness areas as prisons. *Environmental Ethics* 12, no. 1: 3-26.

Blum, Lawrence. 2008. The ethics of care and empathy: Review of Slote. *Notre Dame Philosophical Reviews*. http://ndpr.nd.edu/review.cfm?id=12524.

Blustein, Jeffrey. 1997. Procreation and parental responsibility. *Journal of Social Philosophy* 28: 79-86.

Bokonyi, Sandor. 1989. Definitions of animal domestication. In *The walking larder: Patterns of domestication, pastoralism, and predation*, ed. Juliet Clutton-Brock, 22-27. London: Unwin Hyman.

Brandt, Richard. 1964. The concepts of obligation and duty. *Mind* 73: 374-393.

Brooks, Roy L. 2003. Reflections on reparations. In *Politics and the past*, ed. John Torpey, 103-116. Oxford: Rowman & Littlefield.

Brown, M. 2000. The morality of abortion and the deprivation of futures. *Journal of Medical Ethics* 26: 103-107.

——. 2002. A future like ours revisited. *Journal of Medical Ethics* 28: 192-195.

Budiansky, Stephen. 1992. *The covenant of the wild: Why animals chose domestication*. New York: Wiedenfeld and Nicholson.

Bulliet, Richard. 2005. *Hunters, herders, and hamburgers: The past and future of human-animal relationships*. New York: Columbia University Press.

Burgess-Jackson, Keith 1998. Doing right by our animal companions. *Journal of Ethics* 2: 159-185.

Burt, Jonathan. 2006. *Rat*. London: Reaktion Books.

Callicott, J. Baird. 1980. Animal liberation: A triangular affair. *Environmental Ethics* 2: 311-338.

——. 1992 [1988]. Animal liberation and environmental ethics: Back together again. In *The animal liberation/environmental ethics debate: The environmental perspective*, ed. Eugene Hargrove, 249-262. Albany: State University of New York Press.

Caney, Simon. 2006. Environmental injustices and reparations. *Journal of Social Philosophy* 37, no. 3: 264–482.

Card, Robert. 2006. Two puzzles for Marquis' conservative view on abortion. *Bioethics* 20, no. 5: 264–277.

Carruthers, Peter. 1992. *The animals issue.* Cambridge: Cambridge University Press.

——. 1999. Sympathy and subjectivity. *Australian Journal of Philosophy* 77, no. 4: 465–482.

——. 2004. Suffering without subjectivity. *Philosophical Studies* 121: 99–125.

Carruthers, Peter, and P. Smith, eds. 1996. *Theories of theories of mind.* Cambridge: Cambridge University Press.

Cassidy, Rebecca. 2007. Introduction to *Where the wild things are now: Domestication reconsidered,* ed. Rebecca Cassidy and Molly Mullen, 1–26. Oxford: Berg.

Cassidy, Rebecca, and Molly Mullen, eds. 2007. *Where the wild things are now: Domestication reconsidered.* Oxford: Berg.

Cavalieri, Paula. 2009. *The death of the animal: A dialogue.* New York: Columbia University Press.

Chatterjee, Deen. 2003. Moral distance: Introduction. *Monist* 86, no. 3: 327–332.

——, ed. 2004. *The ethics of assistance: Morality and the distant needy.* Cambridge: Cambridge University Press.

Clark, Stephen. 1977. *The moral status of animals.* Oxford: Oxford University Press.

Clutton-Brock, Juliet. 1989. *The walking larder: Patterns of domestication, pastoralism, and predation.* London: Unwin Hyman.

——. 1994. The unnatural world. In *Human and animal society,* ed. A. Manning and J. Serpell, 23–35. London: Routledge.

Coetzee, John. 2001. *The lives of animals,* ed. Amy Gutman. Princeton, N.J.: Princeton University Press.

Cohen, Carl. 1986. The case for the use of animals in biomedical research. *New England Journal of Medicine* 315, no. 14: 865–870.

Cohen, M. 1997. *The food crisis in prehistory: Overpopulation and the origins of agriculture.* New Haven, Conn.: Yale University Press.

Colpaert, C., et al. 2001. Opiate self-administration as a measure of chronic nociceptive pain in arthritic rats. *Pain* 91, no. 1–2: 33–45.

Cooper, David. Intervention, humility, and animal integrity. In *Animal biotechnology and ethics,* ed. Alan Holland and Andrew Johnson, 145–155. London: Chapman and Hall.

Cronon, William. 1996. The trouble with wilderness, or, getting back to the wrong nature. *Environmental History* 1, no. 1: 7–55.

Cudd, Ann. 2002. Contractarianism. *Stanford Encyclopedia of Philosophy.* http://plato.stanford.edu/entries/contractarianism/.

Curtin, Deane. 1996. Toward an ecological ethic of care. In *Beyond animal rights,* ed. Josephine Donovan and Carol Adams, 60–76. New York: Continuum.

Dancy, Jonathan. 2004. *Ethics without principles.* Oxford: Clarendon Press.

Dawkins, Marian. 1980. *Animal suffering: The science of animal welfare*. Dordrecht: Kluwer.

———. 1995. *Unraveling animal behavior*. 2nd ed. Harlow: Longman Scientific and Technical.

Dawkins, Marian, et al. 2003. What makes broiler chickens range? In situ measurement of habitat preference. *Animal Behavior* 66: 151–160.

DeGrazia, David. 1996. *Taking animals seriously*. Cambridge: Cambridge University Press.

———. 2002. *Animal rights: A very short introduction*. Oxford: Oxford University Press.

———. 2009. Self awareness in animals. In *The philosophy of animal minds*, ed. Robert W. Lurz, 201–217. Cambridge: Cambridge University Press.

DeGrazia, David, and Andrew Rowan. 1991. Pain, suffering, and anxiety in animals and humans. *Theoretical Medicine* 12: 193–211.

Derrida, Jacques. 2002. The animal that therefore I am (more to follow). Trans. David Wills. *Critical Inquiry* 28, no. 2: 369–418.

Derocher, A., N. Lunn, and I. Stirling. 2004. Polar bears in a warming climate. *Integrative and Comparative Biology* 44: 163–176.

De-Shalit, Avner. 1995. *Why posterity matters: Environmental policies and future generations*. London: Routledge.

Desjardins, Joseph. 2003. *Environmental ethics*. 3rd ed. Belmont: Wadsworth.

DeWeaver, Eric. 2007. *Uncertainty in climate model projections of Arctic sea ice decline: An evaluation relevant to polar bears*. Reston: Va.: U.S. Geological Survey.

Diamond, Cora. 2008. The difficulty of reality and the difficulty of philosophy. In *Philosophy and animal life*, by Stanley Cavell et al., 43–89. New York: Columbia University Press.

Dombrowski, Daniel. 1997. *Babes and beasts: The argument from marginal cases*. Champaign-Urbana: University of Illinois Press.

Donovan, Josephine, and Carol Adams, eds. 1996. *A feminist caring ethic for the treatment of animals*. New York: Continuum.

Doris, John. 2002. *Lack of character*. Cambridge: Cambridge University Press.

Dreckmann, Frank. 1999. Animal beliefs and their contents. *Erkenntnis* 51: 93–111.

Dretske, Fred. 1999. Machines, plants, and agency. *Erkenntnis* 51: 19–31.

Elliot, Robert. 1984. Rawlsian justice and nonhuman animals. *Journal of Applied Philosophy* 1: 95–106.

———. 1997. *Faking nature*. London: Routledge.

Engster, Daniel. 2006. Care ethics and animal welfare. *Journal of Social Philosophy* 37, no. 4: 521–536.

Everett, Jennifer. 2001. Environmental ethics, animal welfarism, and the problem of predation. *Ethics and the Environment* 6, no. 1: 42–67.

Feinberg, Joel. 1974. The rights of animals and unborn generations. In *Philosophy and environmental crisis*, ed. William T. Blackstone, 43–68. Athens: University of Georgia Press.

———. 1978. Human duties and animal rights. In *On the fifth day: Animal rights and human ethics*, ed. Richard Knowles Morris and Michael Fox, 45–59. Washington: Acropolis.

———, ed. 1992. *Freedom and fulfillment*. Princeton, N.J.: Princeton University Press.

Fineman, Martha. 2008. The vulnerable subject: Anchoring equality in the human condition. *Yale Journal of Law and Feminism* 20, no. 1: 1–20.

Fisher, John. 1992 [1987]. Taking sympathy seriously: A defense of our moral psychology toward animals. In *The animal rights/environmental ethics debate: The environmental perspective*, ed. Eugene Hargrove, 227–248. Albany: State University of New York Press.

Foot, Philippa. 1985. Utilitarianism and the virtues. *Mind* 94: 196–209.

Francione, G. 2000. *Animal rights: Your child or the dog*. Philadelphia: Temple University Press.

——. 2006. Equal consideration and the interest of animals in continuing existence: A response to professor Sunstein. *University of Chicago Legal Forum* 231: 239–240.

——. 2008. *Animals as persons*. New York: Columbia University Press.

——. n.d. Pets: The inherent problems with domestication. http://www.opposingviews.com/arguments/pets-the-inherent-problems-with-domestication.

Francis, Leslie Pickering, and Richard Norman. 1978. Some animals are more equal than others. *Philosophy* 53: 507–527.

Franklin, Julian. 2005. *Animal rights and moral philosophy*. New York: Columbia University Press.

Frey, R. G. 1977. Animal rights. *Analysis* 37, no. 4: 186–189.

——. 1983. *Rights, killing, and suffering*. Oxford: Blackwell.

——. 1987. The significance of agency and marginal cases. *Philosophica* 39, no. 1: 39–46.

——. 2007 [1988]. Moral standing, the values of lives, and speciesism. In *Ethics in practice*, ed. Hugh Lafollette, 192–204. Oxford: Blackwell.

Friedmann, E. and H. Son. 2009. The human-companion animal bond: How humans benefit. *Veterinary Clinics of North America Small Animal Practice: Veterinary Public Health* 39, no. 5: 291–332.

Fuchs, A. 1981. Duties to animals: Rawls' alleged dilemma. *Ethics and Animals* 2: 83–87.

Fudge, Erica. 2002. A left-handed blow: Writing the history of animals. In *Representing animals*, ed. Nigel Rothfels, 3–18. Bloomington: Indiana University Press.

Fuentes, Agastin. 2007. Monkey and human interconnections: The wild, the captive, and the in-between. In *Where the wild things are now: Domestication reconsidered*, ed. Rebecca Cassidy and Molly Mullen, 123–146. Oxford: Berg.

Gaita, Raimond. 2002. *The philosopher's dog*. New York: Random House.

Gardiner, Stephen. 2006. A perfect moral storm: Climate change, intergenerational ethics, and the problem of moral corruption. *Environmental Values* 15: 397–413.

Garvey, James. 2008. *The ethics of climate change*. London: Continuum.

Gauthier, David. 1986. *Morals by agreement*. Oxford: Oxford University Press.

Gewirth, Alan. 1978. *Reason and morality*. Chicago: University of Chicago Press.

Goodin, Robert E. 1985. *Protecting the vulnerable*. Chicago: University of Chicago Press.

Goodin, Robert E., Carole Pateman, and Roy Pateman. 1997. Simian sovereignty. *Political Theory* 25, no. 6: 821–849.

Goodpaster, Kenneth E. 1978. On being morally considerable. *Journal of Philosophy* 22: 308–325.

Gould, J. L. 1982. *Ethology: The mechanisms and evolution of behavior*. New York: W. W. Norton.

Griffin, James. 1986. *Wellbeing*. Oxford: Oxford University Press.

Gruen, Lori. 1999. Must utilitarians be impartial? In *Singer and his critics*, ed. Dale Jamieson, 129–149. Oxford: Blackwell.

Gullo, Lassiter, and Jennifer Wolch. 1998. The cougar's tale. In *Animal geographies: Place, politics, and identity in the nature-culture borderlands*, ed. Jennifer Wolch and Jody Emel, 139–161. London: Verso.

Hadley, John. 2005. Nonhuman animal property: Reconciling environmentalism and animal rights. *Journal of Social Philosophy* 36, no. 3: 305–315.

Haraway, Donna. 2003. *The companion species manifesto: Dogs, people, and significant otherness*. Chicago: Prickly Paradigm Press.

Hare, Richard. 1981. *Moral thinking*. Oxford: Oxford University Press.

——. 1982. Ethical theory and utilitarianism. In *Utilitarianism and beyond*, ed. Amartya Sen and Bernard Williams, 23–38. Cambridge: Cambridge University Press.

Hargrove, Eugene, ed. 1992. *The animal rights/environmental ethics debate: The environmental perspective*. Albany: State University of New York Press.

Harris, D. R. 1989. An evolutionary continuum of people-plant interaction. In *Foraging and farming: The evolution of plant exploitation*, ed. D. R. Harris and G. Hillman, 11–24. London: Unwin Hyman.

Harrison, Peter. 1991. Do animals feel pain? *Philosophy* 66: 25–40.

Hayden, B. 1992. Models of domestication. In *Transitions to agriculture in prehistory*, ed. Anne B. Gebauer and T. D. Price, 11–19. Madison, Wis.: Prehistory Press.

Headey, Bruce, and Warwick Anderson. 2005. *Health cost savings: The impact of pets on the Australian health budget*. Petcare Information and Advisory Service.

Hearne, Vicki. 1986. *Adam's task: Calling animals by name*. Knopf: New York.

Held, Virginia. 2002. Group responsibility for ethnic conflict. *Journal of Ethics* 6, no. 2: 157–178.

Herman, Louis M., et al. 2001. The bottlenosed dolphin's (*Tursiops truncatus*) understanding of gestures as symbolic representations of its body parts. *Animal Learning and Behavior* 29, no. 3: 250–264.

Hettinger, Ned, and Bill Throop. 1999. Refocusing ecocentrism. *Environmental Ethics* 21, no. 1: 3–21.

Hill, Thomas. 2007 [1983]. Ideals of human excellence and preserving natural environments. In *Ethics in practice*, 3rd ed., ed. Hugh Lafollette, 654–663. Oxford: Blackwell.

Hobbes, Thomas. 1962 [1660]. *Leviathan*. London: Collins.

Holland, Alan, and Andrew Johnson, eds. 1998. *Animal biotechnology and ethics*. London: Chapman and Hall.

Hourdequin, Marion. 2008. Climate, collective action, and individual responsibility. Unpublished conference paper.

Hurley, Susan. 2003. Animal action in the space of reasons. *Mind and Language* 18, no. 3: 231–256.

Ignatieff, Michael. 1984. *The needs of strangers*. London: Hogarth.

Ingold, Tim. 1994 [1988]. The animal in the study of humanity. In *What is an animal?*, ed. Tim Ingold, 84–97. London: Routledge.

——. 2000. *The perception of the environment: Essays in livelihood, dwelling, and skill*. London: Routledge.

Irvin, Sherri. 2004. Capacities, context, and the moral status of animals. *Journal of Applied Philosophy* 21, no. 1: 61–77.

Jamieson, Dale. 1983. Killing persons and other beings. In *Ethics and animals*, ed. Harlan Miller and William Williams, 135–146. Clifton, N.J.: Humana Press.

——.1990. Rights, justice, and duties to provide assistance: A critique of Regan's theory of rights. *Ethics* 100, no. 1: 349–362.

——, ed. 1999. *Singer and his critics*. Oxford: Blackwell.

——. 2002. Science, knowledge, and animal minds. In *Morality's Progress*, ed. Dale Jamieson, 52–70. Oxford: Oxford University Press.

——. 2008. The rights of animals and the demands of nature. *Environmental Values* 17, no. 2: 181–200.

Johansen, J. P., and H. L. Fields. 2004. Glutamaturgic activation of anterior cingulated cortex produces an aversive teaching signal. *Nature Neuroscience* 7, no. 4: 398–403.

Johnson, Baylor. 2003. Ethical obligations in a tragedy of the commons. *Environmental Values* 12: 271–287.

Kagan, Shelly. 1992. The structure of normative ethics. *Philosophical Perspectives* 6 (*Ethics*): 223–242.

Kamm, Frances. 2007. *Intricate ethics*. Oxford: Oxford University Press.

Kareiva, Peter, et al. 2007. Domesticated nature: Shaping landscapes and ecosystems for human welfare. *Science* 316, no. 5833: 1866–1869.

Korsgaard, Christine. 2004. Fellow creatures: Kantian ethics and our duties to animals. The Tanner Lectures on Human Values, University of Michigan. http://www.tannerlectures. utah.edu/lectures/documents/volume25/korsgaard_2005.pdf.

Kraabel, B. J., et al. 1998. Evaluation of a multivalent *Pasteurella haemolytica* vaccine in bighorn sheep: Protection from experimental challenge. *Journal of Wildlife Diseases* 34, no. 2: 325–333.

Kraut, Richard. 1994. Desire and the human good. *Proceedings and Addresses of the American Philosophical Association* 68, no. 2: 39–54.

LaGraize, S., et al. 2004. Differential effect of anterior cingulate cortex lesion on mechanical hypersensitivity and escape/avoidance behavior in an animal model of neuropathic pain. *Experimental Neurology* 188: 139–148.

Larrère, Catherine, and Raphael Larrère. 2000. Animal rearing as a contract? *Journal of Agricultural and Environmental Ethics* 12, no. 1: 51–58.

Leach, Helen M. 2007. Selection and the unforeseen consequences of domestication. In *Where the wild things are now: Domestication reconsidered*, ed. Rebecca Cassidy and Molly Mullen, 71–100. Oxford: Berg.

Lo, Y. S. 2001a. The land ethic and Callicott's ethical system (1980–2001): An overview and critique. *Inquiry* 44: 331–358.

———. 2001b. A Humean argument for the land ethic? *Environmental Values* 10: 523–539.

Lockwood, Michael. 1979. Killing and the preference for life. *Inquiry* 22: 157–190.

Lovett, Francis. 2001. Domination: A preliminary analysis. *Monist* 84, no. 1: 98–113.

MacIntyre, Alasdair. 2001. *Dependent rational animals*. Chicago: Open Court.

Mamdani, Mahmood. 2001. A diminished truth. In *After the TRC*, ed. James Wilmot and Linda Van de Vijver, 58–61. Athens: Ohio University Press.

Manning, Russ. 1981. Environmental ethics and Rawls' theory of justice. *Environmental Ethics* 3: 155–166.

Marquis, Don. 1989. Why abortion is immoral. *Journal of Philosophy* 86: 183–202.

———. 2001. Deprivations, futures, and the wrongness of killing. *Journal of Medical Ethics* 27: 363–369.

———. 2007. An argument that abortion is wrong. In *Ethics in practice*, 3rd ed., ed. Hugh Lafollette, 137–147. Oxford: Blackwell.

Marvin, Garry. 2006. Wild killing: Contesting the animal in hunting. In *Killing Animals*, ed. The Animal Studies Group, 10–29. Champaign-Urbana: University of Illinois Press.

May, Larry. 1987. *The morality of groups*. Notre Dame, Ind.: University of Notre Dame Press.

———. 1991. Metaphysical guilt and moral taint. In *Collective responsibility*, ed. Larry May and Stacey Hoffman, 239–254. Baltimore, Md.: Rowman & Littlefield.

McCloskey, H. J. 1979. Moral rights and animals. *Inquiry* 22, no. 1–2: 23–54.

McKibben, Bill. 1989. *The end of nature*. New York: Anchor Books.

McMahan, Jeff. 2002. *The ethics of killing*. Oxford: Oxford University Press.

McPhail, E. M. 1998. *The evolution of consciousness*. Oxford: Oxford University Press.

Meyer, Lukas H. 2006. Reparation and symbolic restitution. *Journal of Social Philosophy* 13, no. 3: 406–422.

Michelfelder, Diane. 2003. Valuing wildlife populations in urban environments. *Journal of Social Philosophy* 31, no. 1: 79–90.

Midgley, Mary. 1983. *Animals and why they matter*. Athens: University of Georgia Press.

———. 1992. The significance of species. In *The animal rights/environmental ethics debate: The environmental perspective*, ed. Eugene Hargrove, 121–136. Albany: State University of New York Press.

Mills, Charles. 1997. *The racial contract*. Ithaca, N.Y.: Cornell University Press.

Morris, Desmond. 1990. *The animal contract*. London: Morris Books.

Murphy, Jeffrie G. 1980. Blackmail: A preliminary inquiry. *Monist* 63, no. 2: 156–171.

Nagel, Thomas. 1980. The limits of objectivity. In *The Tanner lectures on human values*, ed. Sterling M. McMurrin, 75–139. Salt Lake City: University of Utah Press.

——. 1986. *The view from nowhere.* Oxford: Oxford University Press.

Narveson, Jan. 1983. Animal rights revisited. In *Ethics and animals*, ed. Harlan Miller and William Williams, 45–59. Clifton, N.J.: Humana Press.

——. 1987. On a case for animal rights. *Monist* 70, no. 1: 30–49.

——. 2002. Collective responsibility. *Journal of Ethics* 6: 179–198.

——. 2003. We don't owe them a thing! *Monist* 86, no. 3: 454–468.

Nelkin, Norton. 1986. Pains and pain sensations. *Journal of Philosophy* 83, no. 2: 129–148.

Nobis, Nathan. 2004. Carl Cohen's "kind" arguments for animal rights and against animal rights. *Journal of Applied Philosophy* 21, no. 1: 43–59.

Noddings, Nel. 1984. *Caring.* Berkeley: University of California Press.

Norcross, Alistair. 2004. Puppies, pigs, and people: Eating meat and marginal cases. *Philosophical Perspectives* 18: 229–245.

——. 2007. Animal experimentation. In *Oxford Handbook of Bioethics*, ed. Bonnie Steinbeck, 648–670. Oxford: Oxford University Press.

Norton, Bryan. 1987. *Why preserve natural variety?* Princeton, N.J.: Princeton University Press.

——, ed. 1995. *Ethics on the ark: Zoos, animal welfare, and wildlife conservation.* Washington D.C.: Smithsonian Institute.

Nozick, Robert. 1974. *Anarchy, state, and utopia.* New York: Basic Books.

Nussbaum, Martha. 2004. Beyond "compassion and humanity": Justice for nonhuman animals. In *Animal rights*, ed. Cass Sunstein and Martha Nussbaum, 299–320. Oxford: Oxford University Press.

——. 2006. *Frontiers of justice.* Cambridge, Mass.: Harvard University Press.

O'Neill, John. 1993. *Ecology, policy, politics.* London: Routledge.

O'Neill, Onora, and William Ruddick, eds. 1979. *Having children: Philosophical and legal reflections on parenthood.* Oxford: Oxford University Press.

Palmer, Clare. 1997. The idea of the domesticated-animal contract. *Environmental Values* 6, no. 4: 411–425.

——. 2002. Taming the wild profusion of existing things? A study of Foucault, power, and animals. *Environmental Ethics* 23, no. 4: 339–358.

——. 2003. Placing animals in urban environmental ethics. *Journal of Social Philosophy* 34, no. 1: 64–78.

——. 2006. Rethinking animal ethics in appropriate context: How Rolston's work can help. In *Nature, value, duty: Life on Earth with Holmes Rolston III*, ed. Christopher J. Preston and Wayne Ouderkirk, 183–200. New York: Springer-Verlag.

——. 2009. Harm to species? Species, ethics, and climate change: The case of the polar bear. *Notre Dame Journal of Law, Ethics, and Public Policy* 23, no. 2: 587–603.

——. Forthcoming [2010]. Le contrat domestique. In *Philosophie animale. Différence, éthique et communauté*, ed. Hicham-Stéphane Afeissa and Jean-Baptsite Jeangène Vilmer, trans. Hicham-Stéphane Afeissa. Paris: Vrin.

Parfit, Derek. 1984. *Reasons and persons*. Oxford: Oxford University Press.

Parslow, Ruth, and Anthony Jorm. 2003. Pet ownership and risk factors for cardiovascular disease: Another look. *Medical Journal of Australia* 179, no. 9: 466–468.

Partridge, Ernest. 2002 [1996]. Ecological morality and nonmoral sentiments. In *Land, value, community*, ed. Wayne Ouderkirk and Jim Hill, 21–35. Albany: State University of New York Press.

Pateman, Carole. 1988. *The sexual contract*. Cambridge: Polity Press.

——. 1996. The sexual contract and the animals. *Journal of Social Philosophy* 27, no. 1: 65–80.

Plumwood, Val. 2000. Integrating ethical frameworks for animals, humans, and nature: A critical feminist ecosocialist analysis. *Ethics and the Environment* 5, no. 2: 285–332.

Pogge, Thomas. 2002. *World poverty and human rights*. London: Polity Press.

——. 2007 [1997]. Eradicating systematic poverty. In *Ethics in Practice*, 3rd ed., ed. Hugh LaFollette, 633–646. Oxford: Blackwell.

Povinelli, Daniel. 1996. Chimpanzee theory of mind? The long road to strong inference. In *Theories of Theories of Mind*, ed. Peter Carruthers and Peter K. Smith, 293–329. Cambridge: Cambridge University Press.

Prichard, Michael, and Wade Robinson. 1981. Justice and the treatment of animals: A critique of Rawls. *Environmental Ethics* 3, no. 1: 95–106.

Price, D. D. 2000. Psychological and neural mechanisms of the affective dimension of pain. *Science* 288: 1769–1772.

Price, Edward O. 1999. Behavioral development in animals undergoing domestication. *Applied Animal Behavior Science* 65, no. 3: 245–271.

Rachels, James. 2007. Punishment and desert. In *Ethics in Practice*, 3rd ed., ed. Hugh Lafollette, 510–517. Oxford: Blackwell.

Rawls, John. 1971. *A theory of justice*. Oxford: Oxford University Press.

Raz, Joseph. 2009. Responsibility and the negligence standard. http://papers.ssrn.com/sol3/papers.cfm?abstract_id=1436022.

Regan, Tom. 1981. The nature and possibility of an environmental ethic. *Environmental Ethics* 3, no. 1: 19–34.

——. 1982. *The case for animal rights*. Berkeley: California University Press.

——. 2001. *Defending animal rights*. Champaign-Urbana: University of Illinois Press.

——. 2004. *The Case for Animal Rights*. 2nd ed. Berkeley: University of California Press.

Ristau, Carolyn. 1995 [1991]. Aspects of the cognitive ethology of an injury-feigning bird, the piping plover. In *Readings in animal cognition*, ed. Marc Bekoff and Dale Jamieson, 78–89. Cambridge, Mass: The MIT Press.

Rittel, Horst, and Melvin Webber. 1973. Dilemmas in a general theory of planning. *Policy Sciences* 4: 155–169.

Roberts, Robert C. 2009. The sophistication of non-human emotion. In *The philosophy of animal minds*, ed. Robert W. Lurz, 218–236. Cambridge: Cambridge University Press.

Rollin, Bernard. 1998. On *telos* and genetic engineering. In *Animal biotechnology and ethics*, ed. Alan Holland and Andrew Johnson, 156–171. New York: Springer.

Rolston, Holmes. 1988. *Environmental ethics: Duties to and values in the natural world.* Philadelphia: Temple University Press.

——. 1994. *Conserving natural value.* New York: Columbia University Press.

——. 2003. Life and the nature of life—in parks. In *The full value of parks: From the economic to the intangible,* ed. David Harmon and Allen Putney, 103–113. Lanham, Md.: Rowman & Littlefield.

Rosenberg, Alexander. 1995. "Is there an evolutionary biology of play?" In *Readings in animal cognition,* ed. Marc Bekoff and Dale Jamieson, 217–228. Cambridge, Mass: The MIT Press.

Rowan, Andrew, Franklin Loew, and Joan Weer. 1994. *The animal research controversy.* North Grafton, Mass.: Tufts Center for Animals and Public Policy.

Russell, Nerissa. 2007. The domestication of anthropology. In *Where the wild things are now: Domestication reconsidered,* ed. Rebecca Cassidy and Molly Mullin, 1–26. Oxford: Berg.

Sagoff, Mark. 1984. Animal liberation and environmental ethics: Bad marriage, quick divorce. *Osgood Hall Law Review* 22, no. 2: 297–307.

Salt, Henry. 1980 [1892]. *Animals' rights: Considered in relation to social progress.* London: Centaur Press.

Sandler, Ron. 2007. *Character and environment.* New York: Columbia University Press.

Satz, Ani B. 2009. Animals as vulnerable subjects: Beyond interest convergence, hierarchy, and property. http://papers.ssrn.com/sol3/papers.cfm?abstract_id=1397026.

Scanlon, Thomas. 1998. *What we owe to each other.* Cambridge, Mass.: Harvard University Press.

Scheffler, Samuel. 1994 [1982]. *The rejection of consequentialism.* Rev. ed. Oxford: Oxford University Press.

——. 1997. Relationships and responsibilities. *Philosophy and Public Affairs* 26: 189–209.

——. 2001. *Boundaries and allegiances.* Oxford: Oxford University Press.

Schmidtz, David. 2008. *Person, polis, planet: Essays in applied philosophy.* Oxford: Oxford University Press.

Searle, John. 1998. Animal minds. *Etica and Animali* 9: 37–50.

Sen, Amartya, and Bernard Williams, eds. 1977. *Utilitarianism and beyond.* Cambridge: Cambridge University Press.

——. 1998. *The tender carnivore and the sacred game.* Athens: University of Georgia Press.

Shepard, Paul, and Florence R. Shepard. 1998. *Coming home to the Pleistocene.* London: Icon.

Sher, George. 2001. Other voices, other rooms? Women's psychology and moral theory. In *Vice and virtue in everyday life,* ed. Christina Sommers and Fred Sommers, 634–649. Orlando, Fla.: Harcourt College Publishers.

Shrader-Frechette, Kristin. 2002. Biocentrism, biological science, and ethical theory. In *Land, value, community,* ed. Wayne Ouderkirk and Jim Hill, 85–96. Albany: State University of New York Press.

Shriver, Adam. 2006. Minding mammals. *Philosophical Psychology* 19, no. 4: 433–442.

———. 2009. Knocking out pain in livestock: Can technology succeed where morality has stalled? *Neuroethics* 2: 115–124.

Shue, Henry. 1996 [1980]. *Basic rights: Subsistence, affluence, and U.S. foreign policy.* Princeton, N.J.: Princeton University Press.

Silverstein, Harry. 2005. Justice and strict liability. In *Law and social justice*, ed. J. Campbell, M. O'Rourke, and D. Shier, 163–178. Cambridge, Mass.: The MIT Press.

Simmonds, M., et al. 2003. *Oceans of noise.* Bath: Whale and Dolphin Conservation Society.

Simmons, John. 1979. *Moral principles and political obligations.* Princeton, N.J.: Princeton University Press.

Singer, Brent. 1988. An extension of Rawls' theory of justice to environmental ethics. *Environmental Ethics* 10: 217–231.

Singer, Marcus. 1965. Negative and positive duties. *The Philosophical Quarterly* 15, no. 59: 97–103.

Singer, Peter. 1972. Famine, affluence, and morality. *Philosophy and Public Affairs* 1, no. 3: 229–243.

———. 1973. Food for thought. *New York Review of Books* 20, no. 10. http://www.nybooks.com/articles/9822.

———. 1983 [1975]. *Animal liberation.* Wellingborough: Thorsons.

———. 1993. *Practical Ethics.* 2nd ed. Cambridge: Cambridge University Press.

———. 1999. A response. In *Singer and his critics*, ed. Dale Jamieson, 269–332. Oxford: Blackwell.

Sinnott-Armstrong, Walter. 2005. It's not *my* fault: Global warming and individual moral obligations. In *Perspectives on climate change*, ed. Walter Sinnott-Armstrong and Richard Howarth, 285–307. Amsterdam: Elsevier.

Slicer, Deborah. 1991. Your daughter or your dog? A feminist assessment of the animal-research issue. *Hypatia* 6, no. 1: 108–124.

Slote, Michael. 2007. *The ethics of care and empathy.* London: Routledge.

Smith, J. A., and K. M. Boyd. 1991. *Lives in the balance: The ethics of using animals in biomedical research.* Report of a Working Party of the Institute of Medical Ethics. Oxford: Oxford University Press.

Smith, Kimberly. 2008. Animals and the social contract. *Environmental Ethics* 30: 195–207.

Steiner, Gary. 2008. *Animals and the moral community: Mental life, moral status, and kinship.* New York: Columbia University Press.

Sumner, Wayne. 1992. Two theories of the good. In *The good life and the human good*, ed. Ellen Frankel Paul, Fred Miller, and Jeffrey Paul, 1–14. Cambridge: Cambridge University Press.

Sunstein, Cass, and Martha Nussbaum, eds. 2005. *Animal rights.* Oxford: Oxford University Press.

Taylor, Paul. 1986. *Respect for nature.* Princeton, N.J.: Princeton University Press.

———. 1987. Inherent value and moral rights. *Monist* 70, no. 1: 15–30.

Telfer, Elizabeth. 2000. Using and benefitting animals. In *The moral status of persons: Perspectives on bioethics*, ed. Gerhold K. Becker, 219–232. Amsterdam: Rodopi.

Thero, D. P. 1995. Rawls and environmental ethics: A critical examination of the literature. *Environmental Ethics* 17, no. 1: 93–107.

Thompson, Janna. 2002. *Taking responsibility for the past*. London: John Wiley.

Tooley, Michael. 1972. Abortion and infanticide. *Philosophy and Public Affairs* 2, no. 1: 37–65.

———. 1983. *Abortion and infanticide*. Oxford: Clarendon Press.

Unger, Peter. 1996. *Living high and letting die: Our illusion of innocence*. Oxford: Oxford University Press.

United States Animal Welfare Act. 1966. http://www.animallaw.info/statutes/stusawa.htm.

VandeVeer, Donald. 2003 [1979]. Interspecific justice. In *The environmental ethics and policy book*, ed. Donald Van deVeer and Christine Pierce, 150–163. Belmont: Wadsworth.

Varner, Gary. 1995. Can animal-rights activists be environmentalists? In *Environmental ethics and environmental activism*, ed. Donald Marietta and Lester Embree, 169–201. Lanham, Md.: Rowman & Littlefield.

———. 1998. *In nature's interests?* Oxford: Oxford University Press.

Waldron, Jeremy. 1992. Superseding historical injustice. *Ethics* 103, no. 1: 4–28.

———. 1994. John Locke: Social contract versus political anthropology. In *The social contract from Hobbes to Rawls*, ed. David Boucher and Paul Kelly, 51–72. London, Routledge.

———. 2003. Who is my neighbor? Humanity and proximity. *Monist* 86, no. 3: 333–354.

Warburton, Harriet, and Georgia Mason. 2003. Is out of sight out of mind? The effects of resource cues on motivation in mink. *Animal Behavior* 65: 755–762.

Warren, Mary Anne. 2000. *Moral status*. Oxford: Oxford University Press.

Welchman, Jennifer. 2009. Hume, Callicott, and the land ethic: Problems and prospects. *Journal of Value Inquiry* 43, no. 2:201–220.

Wenz, Peter. 1988. *Environmental justice*. Albany: State University of New York Press.

Williams, Bernard, with J. C. C. Smart. 1973. *Utilitarianism: For and against*. Cambridge: Cambridge University Press.

Wood, Allen. 1998. Kant on duties regarding nonrational nature. *Proceedings of the Aristotelian Society Supplement* 72: 189–210.

Zamir, Tzachi. 2007. *Ethics and the beast*. Princeton, N.J.: Princeton University Press.

Zeuner, F. E. 1963. *A history of domesticated animals*. London: Hutchinson.

Zimmerman, Michael. 1986. Negligence and moral responsibility. *Nous* 20: 199–218.

———. 1988. *An essay on moral responsibility*. Totowa, N.J.: Rowman & Littlefield.

———. 1997. Moral responsibility and ignorance. *Ethics* 107, no. 3: 410–426.

INDEX

dependence, 5; asymmetry of power and, 53, 92–93, 125, 127; of children, 94; of domesticated animals, 53, 60, 90–95, 125; external, 92; by feeding, 154; forms of, 91–92; Goodin on, 92–93; internal, 92

Derrida, Jacques, 167n5

desire frustration, 15, 17, 18, 155; McMahan on, 132, 136

desires, 15–17, 79–80, 131–37

desire satisfaction, 19, 131–33; Cavalieri on, 132; experience of, 133; Francione on, 132; future-oriented, 131–32; killing and, 131–33; role in well-being, 133; value of, 131

Desjardins, Joseph, 116

Diamond, Cora, 129–30

dignity, 39

disease, wild, 146–48

displacement, 67, 99

distance, moral significance of, 85, 119–20; emotional, 85; wildness in terms of, 85, 86. See also emotional closeness

dogs, 120–21, 156–57; bite law, 180n19; trained, 180n20

Dolly the Sheep, 60

domestication, 7–8, 65–67, 159–60; assistance and, 84, 86, 120; benefits of, 60; Budiansky on, 57–60; Clutton-Brock on, 60, 65, 66; contract, 57–62; dependence and, 91–95; Francione on, 126; as harm, 124–28; Harris on, 60; human gain from, 58; humans changed from, 174n6; internal changes with, 58, 60, 66, 91–95; irreversibility of, 60; as loss of options, 58; nonidentity problem, 61; responsibility for, 56, 91, 95, 120; Rolston on, 56; Russell on, 65; unintended effects of, 66; voluntary, 57–58; vulnerability and, 91–94; Zeuner on, 60

domination, 89, 126–28, 178n10; absence of

rules, 127; conditions of, 127; contract and, 61; dependency, 127; imbalance-of-power, 127; Lovett on, 127

Donovan, Josephine, 52–53

duty: acquired (Regan), 38; of care, 101, 147; general, 123; negative, 67–68; not to harm, 68, 118; obligations and, distinguishing between, 108–9; positive, 67–68; Scheffler on, 123

ecological alienation, 117

ecosystem: animals and, 10, 117, 138, 163; assistance and, 78; consequences of changing, 29–30; management of, 30–31, 36, 42–43; moral status of, 78, 162, 168n6. See also nature

egoistic contractarianism, 170n33

elk, 146–49

emotional closeness, 52, 85

emotions: moral, 51, 173n11; noncognitive, 169n24. See also specific emotions

empathy, 51–52

encounter cases, 106–14, 139, 148–52

endogenous opioids, 13

environmental ethics, 104, 127–28, 162–63, 165; holistic, 162–63; native peoples and, 117–19

Ethics of Killing, The (McMahan), 135–37

euthanasia, voluntary, 135

Everett, Jennifer, 79–81

evolutionary theory, 14

excessive knowledge problem, 138–40

experience machine, 133

experimentation, 127, 161–62; on humans (Belmont report), 93

fear, 15, 18; anxiety and, distinguishing between, 169n24; behavioral/physiological evidence of, 17

Feinberg, Joel, 20, 23, 122